Methods for
Experimental
Social Innovation

Methods for Experimental Social Innovation

George W. Fairweather

Research Social Scientist
V.A. Hospital, Palo Alto, California

Associate Consulting Professor
Stanford University, Stanford, California

John Wiley & Sons, Inc.　　New York · London · Sydney

FIRST CORRECTED PRINTING, MAY, 1968

Preface

The current status of the social scientist is a comfortable, middle-class position with role requirements stressing verbal behavior. This role, with its emphasis upon discussions, writings, meetings, and so on, has left the arena of social change through action to others. The traditional, verbally-oriented role, however, is no longer meeting the needs of society if, indeed, it ever did. This book is offered as a beginning effort to bring the experimental methods of the social scientist to bear upon the pressing social problems of our time. It tries to build a path from the laboratories, meeting halls, and lecture platforms to the stage where social change occurs. The philosophical position presented here is that the social scientist *does have the responsibility* to aid his society in solving its problems in their real-life settings.

Students of mine, few in number but talented and dedicated to humanitarian values, have repeatedly reminded me of the continuing value-free emphasis of the scientists in the universities today. The inculcation processes are so forceful that to resist them is to be labeled "soft-headed." They have been told, and many believe, that there are only two alternative roles for those interested in social problems—the value-free "hard-headed" scientist's role or the "soft-headed" humanitarian value-oriented position of the service person. This book takes the position that there is yet another course. It is here maintained that scientific methods can be applied to social problems so that changes can occur in a society in a systematic, planned, and orderly manner which is compatible with, indeed is essential to, humanitarian values. Experimental methods for social innovation are thus a combination of scientific and humanitarian thought. They take features from all the social sciences combining them into a *multidisciplinary* approach aimed at solving social problems.

The title of this book is meant to express its main purpose, which is to provide a possible answer to each of two questions. The first

v

question is, "How can society effect needed changes in ongoing social processes with a minimum of disruption?" I propose that the answer to this question is to create a new social subsystem whose methods include innovating models as alternative solutions to social problems, experimentally evaluating them, and disseminating the information to those who can make the appropriate changes. This is experimental social innovation.

The second question is, "How can this be done?" The answer to this question is by the methods presented in this book. The ideas for these methods came from many sources. They came from 13 years of experimental work aimed at solving the problems of several marginal groups (chronic mental and tubercular patients, criminals, and so on). During that time the two questions just posed have recurred time and again. This book presents those answers which experience has provided me. They, of course, do not represent the views of the Veterans Administration. To the extent that one individual's experiences can serve to generate needed methods, this book may accomplish its purpose. To the extent that one is limited by his own perceptual field, it may not.

Some of the experiences represented in these pages, however, are not mine alone but, rather, those of my students and associates. Although there is not space here to name them all, to all of them I express my deepest appreciation. But special indebtedness is due David H. Sanders, David L. Cressler, and Roger D. Jennings, who aided in innumerable ways in the preparation of this manuscript. Particular gratitude is expressed to Hugo Maynard, who continuously insisted that this book be written and made many helpful comments during its preparation. Although I had felt the need for a book of this kind for some time, it was my hope that someone else would write it. He convinced me that no one else would. Constantly helpful in its preparation has been the untiring assistance of Mrs. Helen Pearson, Mrs. Betty Fairweather, and Mrs. Dorothy Bleck. Finally, to Robert C. Tryon, John H. Vitale, John L. Holland, C. Scott Moss, and Marvin Hersko goes my appreciation for their excellent comments, many of which have been incorporated in the following pages. I am also indebted to several publishers for their permission to reprint material first published by them. They are: The American Psychological Association, the American Sociological Association, *The Nation*, The Iowa State University Press, Harper & Row, Inc., and John Wiley & Sons, Inc.

Throughout the book there are continuous references and examples from two social innovative experiments that illustrate the experimen-

tal methods presented here.   One was reported in a book called
*Social Psychology in Treating Mental Illness: An Experimental Ap-
proach.*   The other is an NIMH-sponsored community experiment [1]
with the mentally ill, soon to appear in book form, tentatively titled
*Treating Mental Illness in the Community: An Experiment in Social
Innovation.*   Both are used because they are operational examples of
social innovative experiments for which I had principal responsibility.   Consequently, I am so familiar with all the experimental
procedures and data analyses contained in them that they are frequently used as illustrations.

This book gives general experimental procedures from the inception
of the ideas to publication and the planning of subsequent researches.
In the course of presenting material, the logic of concepts associated
with measurement, such as validity, reliability, and scaling techniques
are discussed.   In addition, various comparative and associative statistical techniques useful to the social innovative experimenter are described.   While every attempt is made to present the reader with an
understanding of the basic concepts of scientific methodology, it is
not the purpose of this book to present these methods in great detail.
Rather, the aim is to demonstrate how they can be utilized in dealing
with contemporary social problems.   For this reason, in those chapters
dealing with scaling and statistical techniques, no actual computational examples are presented.   Instead, the reader is referred to the
many excellently written statistical methods and measurement technique textbooks currently available.   The references have been carefully selected to present the reader with readily understandable computational examples.   For those who are more theoretically inclined,
the method-oriented reference books themselves refer to the theoretical
mathematical aspects of the measurement techniques and the statistics
presented here.

It is my belief that the social innovative experimental methods presented in this book have general applicability to the entire spectrum
of current social problems.   They should be especially useful in helping to attain a more meaningful participation in society for persons
who are marginal to it.   It is my hope that these methods will be
widely and wisely used in enhancing the quality of our democratic
society.

George W. Fairweather

November 1966

[1] This investigation was supported by Public Health Service Research Grant No.
Rll MH01259, from the National Institute of Mental Health.

Contents

Section III
An Institution for Social Innovation

Methods for
Experimental
Social Innovation

Section I
Social Experiments and
Orderly Social Change

Chapter 1

The Need for Experimental
Social Innovation

Introduction

"We need people to build bridges from research to community programs. The bridges must lead from scientific symposia to the halls of Congress, to Federal office buildings, state legislatures, city halls, school boards, chambers of commerce, trade unions, service clubs, PTA's, churches and temples, neighborhoods, street corners, and every other arena of opinion and action." (Humphrey, 1963.)

Man is easily distinguishable from all other animals not only by his well-developed cerebral cortex but also by his highly complex societies. His culture, which is the product of his own genius, has become both his savior and his tormentor. While the continuity of a society is maintained by the consistency of its social system, this same consistency frequently slows or prevents essential social innovation. Thus certain reciprocal statuses and their associated role behaviors, such as father-child, employer-employee, and doctor-patient, are maintained from one generation to the next and serve the function of establishing expected behaviors for each individual. To the extent that such behavioral expectancies are adaptive, a society benefits from its culture. To the extent that time has changed the need for these traditional reciprocities, a society is the victim of its culture.

Twentieth century America is daily experiencing this dilemma. The forces of cultural lag oppose those of social change and, in this society, a continuing and increasing need for social innovation has been brought about by population growth, accumulation of technical knowledge, and changing social roles, particularly those of women and minority group members. Furthermore, it appears that the need for social change increases in quantity and rapidity as a society becomes more complex. For example, mass education and improved communications are changes that have themselves increased the need for other social changes by making dissatisfied members aware of their political power in a democratic society. Consequently, those desiring change are now cognizant that social pressure can be utilized to bring about necessary changes in their statuses through political organization and action.

There is an urgent need for society to create procedures that will bring about social change in a systematic, orderly, and rational manner. To accomplish this, however, information concerning the outcomes of possible alternative solutions to any given social problem must be obtained and disseminated to legislators and other decision-makers *before* a particular solution is adopted. This is necessary because once a solution is adopted and codified through legislation, the possibility of change in the solution is much more difficult. Ideally, procedures for social change should be organized to create in a society the readiness to meet new conditions; they should also specify how to test alternative solutions to social problems. Alternative solutions to current social problems *can* be evaluated *if* a small and well-controlled model for each possible solution is implanted in the community and rigorously investigated. But these model social subsystems cannot be established and, in turn, compared, unless a research methodology is created for this precise purpose. Such experimental procedures have certain unique characteristics that differentiate them from other research procedures used in naturalistic social action studies, laboratory experiments, surveys, and social action service programs. Specific differences are discussed in detail later, but for the moment it is important to set forth some of the distinguishing characteristics of these social innovative procedures.

First, these experiments *create new social subsystems* which clearly define the statuses and roles of the participating members.[1] Second, the new subsystems, designed as alternative solutions to significant social problems, are *systematically varied, controlled, and compared.* Third, they must be *imbedded in selected social institutions* so that they are an integral part of that society and are established so that *society need only passively accept them* and need not, economically or physically, endorse or support them. Finally, *social innovative experimenters must assume responsibility for the members* participating in the subsystems. This methodology thus brings together selected

---

[1] A definition of the term "social subsystem" may be found on p. 25 as well as in Chapters 3 and 6.

features of naturalistic social action research, classical design and statistical procedures, laboratory-like controls, social action service, and survey methods. Social innovative experimental methods are a specialized marriage of service procedures and research techniques. A more detailed discussion of the definition of social innovative experiments with comparative examples appears in Chapter 2; methods for their implementation are presented in Chapters 3 through 13.

The urgent need for methods of experimental social innovation is recognized clearly in the words of the Vice President of the United States with which this chapter opened. This need stems from two primary sources. First, our society needs to create a mechanism for evaluating possible solutions to the critical social problems it is facing today; and, second, there is a growing conviction among many social scientists that a research methodology is needed to compare the effects of these proffered solutions *prior* to their adoption and implementation by our society's members.

Marginal Status in America as a Source of Critical Social Problems

The need for methods of conducting experiments in social innovation stems initially from certain changes in contemporary American society. The recent antipoverty programs placed the Federal government in direct need of experimental evidence to evaluate the programs established by legislation. These laws are the codification of a society's consensus that programs can and must be developed to change the status of those who only marginally participate in the rights and duties required by their citizenship status. Social innovative experiments to compare programs designed to improve the lot of men who are marginal to their society are, therefore, urgently needed. But experiments to explore programs that offer alternative solutions to their plight cannot be realistically established until the attributes of their social position are fully defined.

Every complex society has an almost infinite number of statuses occupied by its members, and each status has certain reciprocal rights and duties that are normative for that society. There are statuses for childhood, adolescence, old age, sex, occupation, etc. Each individual, during every phase of his life, holds one status which is considered his "key" status. Hiller (1947, pp. 339–343) describes "key" status in the following manner.

"Among a person's various paired relations, there is usually one that is considered to be most distinctive, that is, one by which he or she is classified, and with reference to which his or her conduct is most widely judged. This is the *characteristic* or *key* status."

This concept of key status is intimately linked to the problem of social change. In our society, with the disappearance of the frontier, technological advances, urbanization, and persistent prejudices, a status occupied by individuals who are marginal to their society has developed. Most of the individuals who occupy this status of marginal man are participants in one of the many current social problems of American society.[2] An incomplete list of these problems includes violations of civil rights, unemployment, aging, mental illness, alcoholism, drug addiction, criminality, inadequate schooling, delinquency, mental retardation, physical incapacity, social underprivilege, and technologically induced difficulty in the use of leisure time. Most people experiencing any of these problems have or will have a marginal status in this society. A marginal status for those who occupy it may become the *key* status for that individual.

As with all other statuses, marginal status can be either assumed, ascribed, or achieved (Hiller, 1947, pp. 335–337). Marginal status can be ascribed to an individual without his permission by other members of society simply because he has identifiable characteristics of age, race, physical deformity, and the like, or because of low socioeconomic status. On the other hand, marginal status can be assumed by an individual because of his maladaptive behavior. The mentally ill, criminals, school drop-outs, and delinquents are included here. In occupying the marginal status, a person's rights and duties are abridged; the society usually assumes major jurisdiction over his behavior. The reciprocal roles are usually defined as superordinate-subordinate. Finally, it is important to note that for men in a marginal status, achieving a higher status is extremely difficult. This is fully discussed in Myrdal's (1944) monumental work on the social position of the American Negro.

However, a description of the status of the marginal person does

---

[2] The term marginal man is used here as a sociological status defined by Hiller (1947, pp. 331–648). The term has been used by others to indicate marginal membership in a society as a result of social forces or personality characteristics. For a comprehensive discussion of these different points of view, the reader is referred to Sherif and Sherif (1956, pp. 635–637), Park (1928), Tyhurst (1957), Merton (1949, p. 215), Thomas (1909, p. 18), Mannheim (1936, pp. 247–248), Cumming (1963), and Stonequist (1937). Discussions of contemporary American social problems have been presented by Merton and Nisbet (1961), Bredemeier and Toby (1960), Rabb and Selznick (1964), Elliott and Merrill (1961), and Landis (1959).

not adequately reflect the feelings or perceptions of those who occupy this position. Perhaps the perception of his position and the feelings involved are most eloquently captured by Hiller (1947, p. 509) in the following quotation.

"A lowly status leaves its mark on persons as truly as the more applauded position does. An old aphorism states that responsibility makes the person. Although this is an important half-truth, the converse is equally true; for occupational subordination and lack of a voice in reciprocities tend to produce either resignation and a feeling of inferiority or a high sensitivity to the implied inequity. Insofar as a culture emphasizes equalitarianism there is an imputed adverse comparison in all subordinate positions. . . ."

Many of the social problems extant in our society today are intertwined with the marginal status. An excellent current example of this is the problem of violations of civil rights, often exemplified by the status occupied by Negroes. The Negro is usually ascribed a lower status by this society. Although it is possible for the Negro or, for that matter, anyone who has been ascribed a marginal status, to be upwardly mobile socially, it is exceedingly difficult. The probability of remaining in a marginal status, once it has been ascribed, is relatively high. Witness here too the lowly social position often ascribed to the paroled prisoner and the discharged mental patient (State of California, 1963, 1965; Wohl, 1964, pp. 163–165). There are also people who have other characteristics which almost immediately define their status as marginal. For example, the blind and those having physical deformities are usually ascribed a lowly status by others. Once attained, it is very difficult for such individuals to assume a more responsible social position.

Men in a marginal status often react to their social situation with one or two types of behavior. On the one hand, they may display hostile aggressiveness and attempt to solve their problems through revolutionary tactics. Currently, some civil rights activities are clear examples of this behavior. On the other hand, they may attempt to solve their problem of marginality by becoming apathetic and assuming no responsibility at all. Here, the attitude toward society is, "Since you put me here, I will do nothing." This is frequently the attitude of the chronically mentally ill, certain people on welfare, some individuals in the ghettos, and other groups. In either case, the problem for our society involves changing both attitudes and behaviors inextricably associated with a marginal status, for marginal man is the product of his society. He exists as such because his social status and role are clearly defined at the fringes of social organization. This status effectively isolates him from meaningful social participation. He therefore has little commitment to or identity with the generic goals of his society. The permanent social problem of marginal groups therefore is their need for new social statuses and roles which will bring about their integration into the social life of the community accompanied by some personal feelings of achievement.

Since ours is an open society and, theoretically, each individual can aspire to and achieve a change in status, the likelihood of any individual who occupies the status of marginal man remaining in that status can be stated in probabilistic terms. In the field of mental illness, for example, leaving the hospital or remaining out of it is associated with fewer weeks of hospitalization during one's lifetime (Fairweather, 1964, p. 275). Thus the longer a patient is hospitalized, the less likely he is to be discharged from the hospital or to remain out of the hospital even if discharged. This example suggests the likelihood that the longer a mental patient has been a marginal member of his society, the longer he will remain a marginal member.

It is possible that this same relationship between time and marginal status exists for other people occupying marginal membership in contemporary American society. For example, marginal persons with a high probability of remaining in that status are most likely to be found in what are today termed ghettos. It may be that the longer a person lives in the ghetto, the higher the probability he will remain in a marginal and peripheral relationship to the society of which he is a member. If the society should consider the existence of such ghettos undesirable, it may be necessary to create entire new subsystems in order to define new statuses for the ghetto dweller. In this case, primary emphasis is placed upon the social conditions under which the individual lives.

The high or low probability of a marginal individual remaining in his status depends, however, not only upon the social context in which he lives, but also upon his personal characteristics. For example, an educable individual who has become a school drop-out, who has left school for personal reasons, who is white, and who has high native ability but little scholastic achievement may be able, under the appropriate external circumstances, to perfect his study habits and increase his individual motivation so that he eventually achieves an education which serves to remove him from his marginal status. On the other hand, an individual may be a school drop-out because of brain damage. Here the individual is only capable of performing routine and simple tasks for which there is little need in the community at large. In the former case, the individual may have a low probability of remaining in marginal status provided appropriate external circumstances exist, whereas in the latter case, because of personal limitations, his probability of remaining marginal is high regardless of external circumstances.

These probabilities point out the need for the development of different social subsystems for marginal man. In the case of the school drop-out with high achievement potential, a program similar to that currently available in the Job Corps might provide an adequate system to prepare him for returning to community living. On the other hand, the brain-damaged individual will probably need a continuing and supportive situation in the community, requiring the establishment of a living and working situation. In either case, social subsystems for both of these groups would have to be experimentally tested by comparing them with as many alternative programs as can logically be contrived to meet the aforementioned specific social problems.

There are thus two main problems for marginal man requiring immediate attention and solution. The first is to provide the opportunity for the low probability group to reach a more responsible status. It is this group that is most capable of upward social mobility. A first step in providing such opportunities has been taken by legislative passage of an antipoverty program, part of which has been advanced with upward mobility as its paramount objective. The Job Training Corps, as an example, provides marginal people with the opportunity to advance their status through improved educational opportunities and training. The second problem is to provide a meaningful community role for those individuals who reside in marginal status because they are unable to achieve a higher status. In this high probability group there are certain marginal employables, chronic mentally ill, mentally retarded, physically handicapped, chronic drug addicts, and others. A social innovative experiment currently being carried out with chronic mental patients in a community setting represents an attempt to solve the second problem (Fairweather, Sanders, Maynard, and Cressler, 1966). A living and working situation in the community, with a person's occupational and daily living statuses clearly defined for each individual, has been established. These former mental patients operate their own business under consultation from several different professional groups. Compared with a matched control group, a significantly greater proportion of the individuals in the working-living situation have been able to remain out of the hospital and have assumed employment. Thus, more responsible social statuses have been created for a high probability group in society. Their contributions to that society have increased and their feelings of achievement are pronounced.

The relationship between the status of marginal man and social problems demonstrates the urgent need to establish entire social subsystems that will define new and meaningful statuses for marginal individuals so that they can become an integral part of the society. Their assimilation would reduce social conflicts that exist as a result of their social isolation and would lead instead to identification with their society and its general values. But these proposed social subsystems do not exist in society today. Accordingly, new subsystems must be *created* and *evaluated* in order to ascertain their effectiveness in meeting the problems of such marginal persons. And it is just such comparative evaluations that social innovative experiments can be designed to perform.

The pressing social need and the changes occurring as this need is more clearly perceived generate an immediate necessity for the establishment of institutes for the conduct of such experiments and the training of scientists in the associated methods. The goal of these centers thus would be to evaluate alternative solutions to critical social problems and to train a new generation of researchers in the appropriate experimental methods. The locus of action for such centers would be in the community where small samples of people representative of the social problem under consideration, particularly those of marginal groups, would live and work within the framework of a proposed social subsystem. These research centers for social innovation would be responsible to the legislators and other agents of society for the health and well-being of the individuals participating in their programs. Thus a center would systematically compare alternative solutions to significant social problems and disseminate the information to responsible social agents. It is in this way that the historical advances in the social sciences can be used by society at large to meet its needs. Furthermore, such an experimental and training concentration upon social problems might make it possible to anticipate them and discover solutions before they become crises. The newly created statuses for the participants would have to emphasize humanistic values so that no individual could validly criticize such programs as being automated, regulative, or inhuman.

Much more will be said of such a prospective research and training center in Chapter 14.

Social progress, in the long run, can be made in an orderly, rational fashion only through the use of such evaluative research systems. Comparative empirical evidence is urgently needed. Society's needs are so great that it can no longer allow its social scientists to give anything less than their utmost to the solution of its critical problems. It seems inevitable that the alternative to planned social change based upon empirical research findings in a humanistic setting is a continuation of inadequate and temporary problem solutions forced upon the leaders of society through social upheaval. What could be more inhuman when social processes *can* be adequately understood so that all members of society may benefit and when they *can* be managed in a reasonable manner that will preserve the cherished individual freedoms of our society.

Changes in the Social Science Research Climate in America

Social innovative research procedures require a change in the mores and folkways of twentieth century American culture because, historically, cultural innovation and social science research have proceeded relatively independently, with neither one affecting the other to any great degree. For example, the recent antipoverty programs were introduced into society without prior experimental validation. Furthermore, no experimental evidence comparing the outcomes of alternative ways in which these working and living social subsystems could be established to best accomplish their mission was available to program administrators. This is true in spite of the voluminous amount of writing and experimentation done in the past several years by social scientists who have been interested in the plight of lower socioeconomic groups.

The physical sciences, however, seem to have accomplished quite well the development of research techniques appropriate to the solution of real-life problems. Perhaps the most dramatic current example of this is the space program. Its personnel and methodology come from many of the scientific disciplines. The researchers and service personnel alike are completely devoted to the research aspect of exploring space, for they are aware that each step into space must be tirelessly evaluated with the best research methods available and that new methods must continuously be developed. As new problems arise, new solutions are invented to cope with them and they, in turn, must be subjected to research through the use of *active and natural models* before the next step in space exploration can be taken. It is also important to note that scientists from the various disciplines lose their old occupational identity and assume new roles requiring a commitment to conquering space—physicists, engineers, and physicians have recently become astronauts. This space program can therefore be described as a research center whose purpose is to *create* working models for space exploration and to *evaluate* their effectiveness in the *natural setting*. The solution to social problems requires nothing less.

But why have the space scientists been able to establish so quickly a massive research program with real-life models which can be evaluated, even at the risk of human life, while social scientists have not? Certainly, social problems ought to be considered as important as technological ones. The space effort is a phenomenon which has historical traditions of very recent origin. Research was established as an integral part of the program at the outset and is, in fact, the key function around which the effort evolves, because each new exploration is an experiment. Thus its procedural norms require experiments to establish the validity of its programs. The opposite has been the case with social problems, for there are three historical traditions which have isolated comparative experimental studies from actual social change; and they have effectively isolated the social scientist, as a scientist, from his society.

Foremost among these has been the attempt on the part of the social scientists to emulate only selected aspects of the physical sciences. About this state of affairs, Sanford, a psychologist, has recently said the following:

"Yet there is no denying that at the present time there exists a wide gap between research and practice. Psychology participates fully in the trend toward specialization and disciplinary professionalism that dominates in the universities today. The discipline is still much concerned to establish itself as a science, but the psychologists' naive conception of science has led them to adopt the more superficial characteristics of the physical sciences. This has made it difficult for them to study genuine human problems, since quantification, precision of measurement, elegance of experimental design, and general laws are so much more difficult to achieve once one goes beyond simple part processes." (Sanford, 1965.)

It is important to note here *what* the social scientists have adopted from the physical sciences. Sanford's statement suggests that the social scientist has principally attempted to emulate the *superficial* characteristics of the physical scientists, such as making precise measuring devices, and complex experimental designs. Although measurement and meaningful designs are important, two aspects most important in the physical sciences have *not* been emulated by social scientists. From the time of Galileo to the present, physical scientists have emphasized the need for careful observation in controlled experimental field situations where important variables and their interactions can be observed over a period of time. The social scientist has not adopted this procedure from the physical scientist, despite the fact that meaningful experimental methodologies in his field may have as their foundation the same premises about observation and controlled conditions that are inherent in those of the physical sciences.

A second tradition which has prevented social innovative experiments from emerging has been the *lack* of alternative mechanisms for social change in our society. Change usually occurs as the direct result of social, economic, or political crises. A thoughtful review of the past several years gives many examples of these crises. An increasing interest in the educational system became crystallized *after* the launching of a Russian satellite. Violations of civil rights became a pressing social problem *after* the sit-ins and particularly *after* the "March on Montgomery." The efficacy of the rehabilitation programs in our prisons and mental hospitals is being questioned *after* pressure from mental health workers because of their concern over lack of space in these overcrowed institutions and *after* the economic pressure arising from limited state budgets. The McCone Commission was convened *after* the Watts riots in Los Angeles.

All of these are perceived as current problems, principally because they have created crises through political and economic pressures. Social change is instituted quickly when these pressures are at their height and scientists are cast in the role of experts in their field without, necessarily, ever having carried out research in the area. They are frequently required to tell investigating committees of the Congress and other interested administrators their opinions about possible courses for social change. Once these statements have been made, they are accorded the status of experimental findings. The scientist has thus perpetuated the myth of his complete knowledge. He may feel it is his responsibility in a citizen's role to inform inquiring legislators of his opinions even though he ordinarily would not accept such information as definitive in the scientific domain. Because of the immediate need for action in crises, a complex modern society demands an *expert* who will give his opinion even though his knowledge is inadequate. This process frees a society to act in an attempt to remedy crises.

A third important historical tradition has also contributed to the failure of social scientists to become involved in social innovative experiments. This is the isolation of the academic institution from industrial, political, and other social institutions of our society. Isolation of the social scientist from efforts to solve significant social problems has, of course, been periodically reinforced by the actions of other agents in the society. Certainly, the postwar years made the scientists' isolation all the more attractive, for this decade was a time of extreme stress for academicians (Lazarsfeld and Thielens, 1958, p. 71). During this time, an interest in social problems sometimes resulted in cruel punishment by demagogues.

Regardless of these political conditions, such isolation has a prior existence since it has been perpetuated through the mores and folkways of the academic institution. One important folkway is that many academic scientists have defined their role as seekers of "truth" who have no interest in the social significance of their findings. They are merely interested in discovering the laws of nature as unencumbered explorers. Because of the divorce of many academic persons from the fields of social action, research in day-to-day community social problems has been avoided. Even when the social scientists do venture forth into the community, they usually study old, established social systems by the survey method (p. 22). They appear to have a reluctance to create new social subsystems that can then be studied. By their failure to innovate new solutions to social problems, they avoid interaction with politicians and legislators who might be concerned about the utility of their findings for society as a whole. The academic belief system often emphasizes "pure" rather than "applied" research; hence "pure" research is defined as "basic" and is therefore assumed to have far more importance than applied. In the field of psychology, Tryon (1963) has recently described this tradition in the following manner:

"By academic psychology I mean a concern with theory and method without regard to applicability. Academic writing is oriented to students and other academicians. Academic research is designed to pare out critical problems and to investigate them in the laboratory or in the field, without any concern as to whether the results will be socially useful."

But the academic institution has also established another custom which has prevented concentration upon significant social problems. This has been the emphasis upon each discipline as a separate subject matter. The humanities, social sciences, and physical sciences are perceived as discrete entities with little or no overlap. Therefore it is most difficult for students in separate disciplines to obtain perceptions integrating these discrete subject matters into a meaningful whole.

Yet a third folkway of the academic institution has been its emphasis upon quantity rather than quality of research, as delineated in *The Academic Market Place* (Caplow and McGee, 1958). This tradition grants to academic scientists with many publications a higher status than those with few publications. The academic researcher is therefore rewarded for short-term studies that do not yield information upon which social change can be validly based. He is systematically encouraged to make cross-sectional studies of static processes and hence discouraged from experimenting with real-life social problems that usually involve long-term, dynamic situations.

The academic institution has isolated itself from the community by defining its research as "pure," by treating its subject matter as separate rather than integrated and as irrelevant to social need, and by establishing academic status on the basis of number of publications. It has become a relatively independent organization with its own social system which functions in a detached manner from society at large. Since students' attitudes and behaviors are usually shaped by institutional standards, it is not surprising that little interest has been displayed in developing experimental methods aimed at systematically introducing and studying social innovations to solve critical social problems. Nevertheless, as Znaniecki (1940) has pointed out, the scientist's status in his society is largely determined by his value to that society. So, recently, the social value of these three historical traditions—social scientists' naive attempts to emulate the physical scientists, the lack of alternative mechanisms for rational social change, and the isolation of the academic from industrial, political, and other institutions of the society—has been seriously questioned by social scientists and community leaders alike. As a result of this inquiry, change in these traditions is occurring.

First, social scientists are expressing dissatisfaction with a preoccupation about the preciseness of methods when it results in the exclusion of social problems. Instead, there has been an increasing desire to contribute to the solution of social problems and to develop methods appropriate for this. A vivid statement illustrating one sociologist's concern about the effect upon the social scientists of this exclusive concentration upon method was made by Bierstedt (1960).

"Our preoccupation with method has still other consequences, not yet mentioned. It frequently dominates our inquiries and determines the kinds of questions we address to society; that is, the method becomes the independent variable, the problem the dependent one. Instead of setting for ourselves tasks of large dimensions and then devising methods appropriate to their solution, we are apt to ask only those questions that are answerable in terms of methods presently available. We have even been invited to forego those larger problems of human society that occupied our ancestors in the history of social thought and to seek instead what T. H. Marshall called, in his inaugural lecture at the University of London, 'stepping stones in the middle distance,' and other sociologists since, 'theories of the middle range.' But what an anemic ambition this is! Shall we strive for half a victory?"

A society's need for social change also brings into question the established practice of devising immediate solutions to problems following crises through the medium of expert opinion. Representatives of society are becoming more and more aware that the complexity, severity, and speed with which social problems emerge do not allow for the luxury of crisis as an antecedent to problem solution. Furthermore, as scientists continue to speak out as experts on social problems, it becomes evident that they often offer divergent points of view because of their lack of knowledge. A recent study by Blum and Funkhouser (1965), who interviewed California state legislators, revealed

". . . the dramatically low standing which psychologists—and their colleagues in sociology, psychiatry, and university medical schools—appear to have in the capital pecking order. Legislators specifically complain that we are vague and disagree with one another . . . are . . . impractical . . . are afraid of religious or ethical issues . . . ."

What the legislators fail to understand is that the social scientist usually does not have direct empirical evidence relating to the solution of a specific social problem, and the scientist, without such definitive research information concerning a particular problem, is no more of an expert than any other lay person. For he, the scientist, is an expert only in the experimental findings of his own field and in his knowledge of scientific methodology. As an "expert," he often violates his own premises of reliance upon observation and controlled experimentation which he would expect from any other scientist. Although the scientist most certainly has a right and even a duty to speak up as a citizen upon important social matters, it is equally true that he has the duty of informing the public that he has left his role of scientist and is now speaking purely on the basis of conjecture. But rarely does the "expert" say, "I don't know," or recommend the establishment of a research organization to investigate the social problems at issue in the community setting which could provide empirical information of a substantive nature to be used by those in the position of making decisions. It is this increasing awareness by the scientist himself that the experimental investigation of social problems can serve as information for cultural change that is further questioning the method of "crises-expert" solutions to social problems which is often used nowadays.

Academic traditions are also changing. The scientists' role as an uninvolved seeker of truth was first openly questioned by his own actions. This occurred with the first nuclear explosion in Alamogordo, New Mexico, in 1945. Dr. Robert Oppenheimer, in his testimony before the U.S. Atomic Energy Commission (*Personnel Security Board Hearing*, 1954, p. 33) revealed his recollection of the emergence of social concern brought about by the creation of the bomb when he said, "There was, however, at Los Alamos a change in the feel of people . . . . This was partly a war measure, but it was also something that was here to stay. There was a great sense of uncertainty and anxiety about what should be done about it."

This represented, of course, a change in attitude from that of the nonparticipant observer to a concern for the effect of a physical scientist's acts upon the lives of his fellow man. Social scientists are showing a similar concern. Rose (1953) has described his concern for "The Social Responsibility of the Social Scientist." More recently, Gouldner (1962) maintained that educating young sociologists in the belief that their science is value-free merely leads to avoidance of social responsibility for their work. The verbalization of concern is only one manifestation of such a change in attitude by the social scientist. In a more subtle, but nonetheless similar manner, the activities of the social scientist are also redefining his role as a more active, value-oriented participant in critical social change. Criminologists, economists, sociologists, and psychologists are working in mental and criminal institutions and are daily making decisions that affect the lives of members of these institutions and the greater society as well. The psychologist is also helping to determine, through his tests, who will be allowed to undertake university training and, in certain cases, who will receive employment or an advancement in job status. This has not gone unnoticed by the public or the social scientist. The public's concern resulted in hearings in both the United States Senate and the House of Representatives (*American Psychological Association*, 1965). The scientists' concern was shown in another issue of the *American Psychologist* that was mainly devoted to a discussion of the public responsibility of psychologists using tests. In it, Stalnaker (1965) said the following:

"A testing program of any scale, much as we might like to view it as a purely technical device, is a social force as well. Its social functions may be conscious or unwitting, noble or mean, broad or narrow; but its involvement in society cannot be escaped."

And in a recent article Tryon (1963) has pointed out that even the laboratory psychologists' techniques and results are being utilized increasingly by industry and the military establishment. It is thus clear that the scientist, whether physical or social, has become involved in the problems of his society, and it would appear that changes in his job expectancies are occurring with this involvement.

There is also a growing change in that folkway of the academic institution concerning the separateness of subject matters. As the scientist becomes more involved in the problems of his community, he becomes increasingly aware that economic, sociological, political, psychological, biological, and other variables are continuously interacting and are not, in the real-life situation, separate subject matters as presented in the academic institution. About the divorce of subject matters, Bierstedt (1960) has recently said:

". . . I wish to contend . . . that whether or not sociology is or ought to be a science it owns a rightful place in the domain of humane letters and belongs, with literature, history, and philosophy, among the arts that liberate the human mind."

There is an equal concern that the training of young social scientists should include much broader aspects of human experience than the traditional, rigidly defined subject matters can offer. An indication of a desire for change in this direction is contained in the statements of two outstanding psychologists. Sanford (1965) has stated, "The psychologists who are filling up the journals today just do not have sensitivity to human experience, and the fault lies in their training—which is an expression of what *academic* psychology has become."

Koch (1961), another psychologist, has also expressed dismay about the narrowness of the subject matter of his discipline.

"I am going to engage a problem . . . concerning the relations between science and the humanities . . . . Little that my field has done during its brief history as an independent science could equip me for work on the present question. Moreover, the climate of my field has not been such as to develop any sensibility in humanistic domains. Indeed, if there ever was such sensitivity, its suppression, starvation, and eventual atrophy seems to have been a necessary condition for Guild membership."

Further rebellion is under way against the evasion of social responsibility which resides in the notion of "pure" research and its pre-eminence over "applied." This has blocked work on significant social problems and fortified the ivory tower. Scientists concerned about this matter are speaking out. Schenck (1963) recently attacked this folkway in this outspoken manner.

". . . Yet he (the scientist) is both victim and staunch defender of the most pernicious of all science myths. This is the belief in the primary importance of "pure" rather than "applied" science . . . . I believe this myth is almost wholly without verification by the history of science and technology . . . . Now why does this particular myth form a core of the scientist's belief structure? Because it is the primary myth that relieves science of responsibility . . . ."

Chapter 2

Experimental Social Innovation Defined

The history of science reveals that experimental methodology proceeds from crude observations and measurement toward more precise observations and accurate measuring instruments. Each science gradually develops its own theory and methods as scientists become more knowledgeable about its subject matter and the particular problems which differentiate it from other sciences. Because experimental methods for social innovation are evolving step-by-step from successive attempts at problem solution, they are comprised of some old and some new methods. The general attributes of social innovative experiments were described in Chapter 1. They may now be more explicitly stated as follows.

1. Definition—defining a significant social problem.
2. Naturalism—making naturalistic field observations to describe the social parameters of the problem in its actual community setting.
3. Innovation—creating different solutions in the form of innovated social subsystems.
4. Comparison—designing an experiment to compare the efficacy of the different subsystems in solving the social problem.
5. Context—implanting the innovated subsystems in the appropriate social settings so that they can be evaluated in their natural habitat.
6. Evaluation—continuing the operation of the subsystems for several months or even years to allow adequate outcome and process evaluations to be made.
7. Responsibility—assumption of responsibility by the researchers for the lives and welfare of participants in the subsystems.
8. Cross-disciplinary—using a multidisciplinary approach with the social problem determining the subject matter—economic, political, sociological, and the like.

Research methods for investigating social problems are, of course, not new to the social sciences. These methods have been developed by the pioneering efforts of individuals interested in the social issues of their society. Collectively, their work contains some, but not all, of the methods for social innovative experiments. It is therefore necessary to review some common research methods so that the similarities and differences between them and experimental methods for social innovation can be clarified. Because the contributions are so numerous, it is also useful for clarity to categorize approaches to the investigation of social problems into six commonly used methodologies. A summary of these six categories of methodology is presented in Table 2.1.

First, there are the *descriptive-theoretical* discussions of important social problems. These publications serve as the basis for the formulation of hypotheses and they generate interest which can result in social innovative experiments. These are to be distinguished from more general theoretical works such as those presented in the recently published *Social Change* (Etzioni and Etzioni, 1964) which approaches such problems mainly from the perspective of sociological theory and is not necessarily restricted to specific social problems or by

Table 2.1. Characteristics of Methods for Social Problem Solution

Methods	Characteristics							
	Significant social problem	Naturalistic observations	Innovates subsystems	Designs experiment	Implants subsystem	Longitudinal	Responsible for participants	Multi-disciplinary
Descriptive-theoretical	X							X
Survey	X	(X)		(X)				X
Laboratory	X			X		(X)		(X)
Participant-observer	X	X		(X)		X	(X)	X
Service	X	X	X		X	X	X	X
Experimental	X	X	X	X	X	X	X	X

X Present
(X) Sometimes present

empirically-gathered data. Descriptive-theoretical treatises, in contrast, summarize empirical facts to illustrate theoretical positions about selected problems. Often problem solutions are proposed. No new empirical evidence is presented. Their impact upon the subsequent course of social change is frequently great since quite often these summaries and deductions from them arouse interest in the selected social problems. Most often the writings define and describe social problems by synthesizing current knowledge. Myrdal's (1944) provocative work about the social and economic position of the American Negro, as presented in *An American Dilemma,* is one example of such a descriptive theoretical discourse. Another contemporary social problem, the effects upon people of mental hospitals and other total institutions, is summarized and discussed by the sociologist Goffman (1962) in his book, *Asylums.* Galbraith (1958), an economist, identifies and discusses the social problems that accrue to a society possessing extraordinary wealth in his work, *The Affluent Society.* And Harrington (1962) presents the problems created by poverty in such a society. These four selected works illustrate descriptive-theoretical writings that are concerned with particular social problems. They analyze and describe specific social problems. Descriptive-theoretical formulations have two of the eight attributes of experimental methods for social innovation. They define a significant social problem and use a multidisciplinary approach. They do not require naturalistic field observations, designing experiments, creating new social subsystems, implanting them in their natural social setting, or assuming responsibility for the lives and welfare of the participants.

A second category of methods used in exploring social problems is the *survey.* Surveys are most frequently utilized to define clearly the variables operative in social problems. Demographic studies such as the census, public opinion polls, and attitude questionnaires about consumer products are all examples. In the arena of social problems, *The Academic Market Place* (Caplow and McGee, 1958) presents a survey concerning the mores and folkways of the academic institution. Other outstanding illustrations of the survey technique as applied to the social problems of mental illness and of drug addiction are Hollingshead and Redlich's (1958) *Social Class and Mental Illness* and Chein's (1963) *The Road to H.* The survey gives information which makes the parameters of the social problem more definitive. The survey method, like the descriptive-theoretical method, has two of the eight attributes of experimental methods for social innovation—problem definition and a multidisciplinary approach. The survey does not require naturalistic observations, longitudinal study, designing experiments, creating new social subsystems, implanting them in society, or assuming responsibility for the lives and welfare of the participants.

A third category of research methods for social problems are those used in *laboratory* settings. Here, important social problems are explored by artificially creating various conditions for learning or performing. Studies with biracial work groups (Katz and Benjamin, 1960) and teams (Katz and Cohen, 1962), under artificially created and controlled conditions, are excellent examples of this method. Experiments with democratic, laissez-faire, and authoritarian social climates are classic examples of this method (Lewin, Lippit, and White, 1939; Lippit, 1939). Laboratory research has two of the eight experimental social change attributes. The laboratory method defines a significant social problem and designs experiments to explore selected aspects of it. It does not require observations in the real-life setting, innovating new social subsystems, implanting them in appropriate social institutions, nor are they, necessarily, longitudinal in time or multidisciplinary in subject matter.

A fourth category of methods utilizes the *participant-observer*. An example can be found in the research done by Stanton and Schwartz (1954) as presented in *The Mental Hospital* and Caudill (1958) in *The Psychiatric Hospital as a Small Society*. Such researchers gather data by the formal methods of interviews, testing, and questionnaires as well as the informal methods of taking notes in situations such as lunch hours, spontaneous or arranged meetings, and so forth. Other examples of such research are to be found in the Sherif and Sherif (1964) publication, *Reference Groups*, and in Whyte's (1955) book, *Street Corner Society. The Social Structure of an Italian Slum*. The participant-observer method allows for direct experience and observation while the processes are in action. This is its chief characteristic. Studies using participant observation usually have four of the eight characteristics of experimental methods for social innovations. They define a significant social problem, make naturalistic observations, use a multidisciplinary approach, and are longitudinal in time. They do not create new social subsystems, implant them in appropriate social settings, or experimentally compare them; nor do the researchers, necessarily, take the responsibility for the lives and welfare of those members participating in the observed social situations.

A fifth method establishes new social subsystems by providing *services* for its members. The Synanon House for drug addicts, as described by Yablonsky (1964), is an example of one service program. Alcoholics Anonymous (1955) and sheltered workshops (Olshansky, 1960) are examples of others. In the field of treating mental illness,

Maxwell Jones' (1953) *The Therapeutic Community* is a classic representative work. It describes the establishment of a new social subsystem in a mental hospital. The Job Corps of the antipoverty program is another. It establishes new learning and living subsystems for the socially deprived. Demonstration projects providing services that create one innovated solution to a social problem but do not compare it to existing practice or alternative solutions are here also classified as service programs. The limitations placed upon inferences that can logically be made from exploratory projects lacking control or comparative conditions are presented in Chapter 13. This method meets seven of the eight requirements for experimental social innovation. It defines a significant social problem, makes naturalistic observations, creates *one* new social subsystem and implants it in the appropriate social setting, is longitudinal in time, assumes responsibility for lives and welfare of the members participating in it, and uses a multidisciplinary approach. It does not create different subsystems as alternative solutions to the social problem and, hence, does not design experiments to compare these created solutions.

Experimental methods for social innovation combine features of these five methods as well as introducing some of their own. Some examples of experimental social innovation can be found in Madge's book *The Tools of Social Science* (1953, pp. 254–289). It can be most clearly understood in the context of a recent experimental study completed in a mental hospital. Here, the significant social problem was the effect of usual hospital treatment upon the recidivism and low discharge rate of chronic mental patients (Fairweather, 1964). This problem had been documented in previous studies (Fairweather and Simon, 1963; Fairweather et al., 1960). Naturalistic observations were made on mental hospital wards which are the natural social action units of a mental hospital. A new social organization (subsystem) for an entire ward was innovated and implanted on a selected ward while a second experimental ward in the same hospital utilized the traditional treatment subsystem (the existing social practice). An experiment was designed to compare both the outcome and processes of these two social organizations (subsystems). Evaluations were made over several months' time. The research staff was held responsible by the hospital management for the welfare of all the patients participating in both programs. The staff was multidisciplinary, representing social work, psychology, psychiatry, nursing, and sociology. All staff members participated in planning and carrying out the program. Instruments to measure administrative, social psychological, and sociological processes were created and used, as were many different measures of outcome. This study is defined as a social innovative experiment because it (1) *defined* a significant social problem, (2) carried out *naturalistic* observations, (3) *innovated* a new social subsystem, (4) designed an experiment to *compare* it with a traditional subsystem, (5) implanted the two subsystems in the appropriate *social context*, (6) was longitudinal in time so that appropriate *evaluations* could be made, (7) made the researchers *responsible* for the welfare of its participating members, and (8) was *multidisciplinary* in nature. The reader will find a detailed account of all its experimental procedures in a recent publication, *Social Psychology in Treating Mental Illness: An Experimental Approach* (Fairweather, 1964).

A social subsystem may be defined as the social organization within which an individual lives. A man may be a father, lawyer, country club member, and churchgoer. Each of these statuses prescribes his rights and obligations as well as his particular role behaviors. The interrelationships among these several statuses and roles define the subsystem within which he lives. As another example, individuals in total institutions have status relationships with all other individuals living in the institution—other inmates and staff alike—and this complex of statuses defines their social subsystem. Institutions are also often linked with the general society. An individual may be a member of the junior class in a high school, a basketball player, a member of certain clubs, and hold a part-time job. The institution—the school, in this case—is intimately linked with the general community, and all these statuses define the social organization (subsystem) within which this adolescent lives. Or a mental patient may live with his relatives and return to the mental hospital daily for treatment while at the same time working in the community. It is this set of status relationships and roles which describes the mental patient's social subsystem. All persons in a society live within a circumscribed subsystem. *A subsystem is the total social environment that is generated for any person by his statuses in the different social institutions of which he is a member.* Examples of proposed social subsystems designed to solve selected social problems are presented in Chapter 3. The definition and measurable dimensions of a social subsystem can be found in Chapter 6.

The development and comparison of *model* social subsystems that clearly define the status relationships between the subsystem and society, usually with small representative samples, is the task of the social innovative experimentalist. Such researches are controlled longitudinal studies carried out in the naturalistic social setting. Variables important in these settings are controlled either by equating the various subsystems for them or through statistical manipulation. For example, a simple comparison for exploring two different subsystems to integrate prisoners into the society could be established. To do this, the researcher might create the following two subsystems: (1) the usual subsystem of prison, parole, and seeking employment in the community, compared with (2) prison, attending designated schools in the community, and placement in employment upon completion of educational programs.

There are many unique characteristics of the methods for experimental social innovation. These distinctive features are given detailed consideration in later chapters but, for clarity, they are briefly presented here. Foremost among them is one of the design characteristics of each innovative experiment. *The control subsystem is always defined as the usual social practice for the social problem* (pp. 199–207). This is necessary because current social practice is the best social subsystem for the problem as far as society is concerned. Furthermore, it is desirable because any current social practice is imbedded in the customs, mores, folkways, and other traditions which have been developed by a society, and it is therefore possible that the current social practice is an excellent one. A society would not be willing to accept a different solution for the social problem *until* it had been clearly demonstrated to be superior to the current practice. For this reason, it would be foolhardy for the researcher to recommend changes in working social subsystems until he has sufficient empirical evidence to warrant such advice.

It also must not be overlooked that in order to be allowed the opportunity to do research in social innovation, many subgroups within a society need to approve such research. It is highly improbable that realistically-oriented lay people would be willing to set aside social traditions without a great deal of evidence indicating that the new methods are better. An attempt to change the educational system can be used as an example. Teachers, school boards, taxpayers, parents, and state and federal authorities who grant money to the educational institutions must all be shown that any changes are warranted. Therefore it is in the best interest of a society to require that experimental practices demonstrate a greater beneficial effect than current practices before social changes are made. Of course, once a new ongoing social subsystem is established as the basic comparative social practice, several other subsystems, some quite deviant, can be compared with it (pp. 44–48).

Another unique characteristic of experimental methods for social innovation is the need for agreements among affected members of society (pp. 51–62). For example, researches which involve institutions, such as prisons, schools, and industries, require commitments from the administrators of the involved institutions. They must be willing to allow the establishment of various subsystems and to support them for the duration of the research program. Furthermore, the research staff itself will initially be comprised of members of various academic disciplines. The research endeavor therefore requires clear delineation of all roles and a commitment to the research program by the members of the research team as well as the participating social institutions. All these agreements must be made prior to the onset of the research project.

Experiments involving social innovation may also be differentiated from other researches because they are primarily empirical in nature. Most theoretical models in the social sciences are specific to a given subject matter such as psychology, sociology, and economics. Since the subject matter for social problems comes from all disciplines, there are few, if any, appropriate theoretical models. Therefore it is probable that theoretical models will necessarily follow the empirical findings of such experiments. Indeed, it is possible that this sequence of events represents the historical development of theories in all the sciences.

Not only does experimental social innovation have unique characteristics concerning its social organization, but it also requires new approaches to measurement and analyses (pp. 122–179). Few instruments are available to measure dynamic social processes that involve economic, psychological, biological, and sociological variables. The investigator is often faced with the task of creating new instruments, determining their reliability, and attempting to establish their units of measure. This is exceedingly difficult when social processes are continuously changing. In addition, the longitudinal nature of the research program may require the creation of new instruments during the course of the research project. Nonetheless, measurement can be achieved and measuring devices created to meet changing conditions.

Of paramount importance, however, is the selection of an appropriate outcome criterion (pp. 81–85). The criterion must be one that is socially acceptable and meaningful for those who are acquainted with the problem. For example, in the previous prison model, where different subsystems for re-entry of the prisoner into society were mentioned (p. 26), a combined criterion of days out of prison, employment, and personal satisfaction might be an appropriate outcome criterion. This is based upon the knowledge of a high recidivism rate, unemployment, and dissatisfaction with a lowly status, particularly among those criminals who have had several incarcerations

(State of California, 1965, pp. 90–94). Of course, many other types of measurement will be necessary in order to describe fully the social processes and the perceptions of the individuals involved. The relationship of these measures to the criterion can be ascertained through the appropriate associative techniques (pp. 164–179). Nevertheless, it is essential that the basic criterion be a socially useful one. *Such a criterion should represent the consensus of members of the social institutions that have been charged by society with the responsibility for solving the problem.* Other more esoteric measures should most certainly be obtained, but their relationship to the social criterion should always be ascertainable.

It is also important to note here that the usually accepted sampling, design, and statistical procedures are frequently inappropriate for investigation and analysis of social problems. In sampling, for example, the continuous input and output of individuals participating in dynamic social processes often require a combination of random and stratified sampling techniques, the combination varying at different moments in time. The data may be "nonparametric" or "parametric," simple or complex, and therefore any one study may require the use of many different statistical techniques. Current techniques frequently need to be modified, and new ones that are appropriate for the problem must be developed. Much will be said in Chapters 6 through 13 on such issues related to measurement, sampling, design, and statistics.

Another characteristic of social innovative experiments which, although not unique to them, is exceedingly important and frequently minimized in other social science researches, is that of field observations in the naturalistic social setting (pp. 40–41). The investigator must have observed in the natural setting the phenomenon upon which he wishes to experiment. Illustratively, a great deal of research has been published on treating mental illness without the researcher having spent much time in mental institutions where the chronic psychotic lives. Such researchers frequently emphasize one aspect of chronic mental illness to the exclusion of others. The same could be said for the social problems of the ghetto, the prison, and other such social subsystems.

Finally, it is of great importance that the results of these longitudinal studies dealing with socially significant problems be published in journals or books to which the public has access. This is particularly important because each research represents a great investment in both time and money and the expense is most frequently borne by the public. It is also important that the information is available to legislative and administrative officials (pp. 207–209).

Since existing experimental methods for social innovation are in an embryonic stage, their eventual status is, of course, unknown. Although the methodology is borrowed from the humanities and the sciences, it appears that the methods for social innovation to date are following a developmental pattern most similar to that which transpired in the field of agronomy. In this regard, the chemistry laboratory provides the chemical research that creates different fertilizers and agriculture itself presents the agronomist with hybrid seeds and farming methods. The agricultural field researcher, who has a working knowledge of both agriculture and chemistry, is charged as an agronomist with the responsibility of bringing together his knowledge of chemistry and agriculture in designing and carrying out controlled experiments under field conditions which will evaluate the effect of the experimental variables—fertilizers, seeds, and the rest—upon crop yield. Usually such experiments compare several different variables. They are carried out on plots of land where soil, water, and other natural variables are equivalent. This historical development occurred because agricultural experts were aware that in order to make accurate *recommendations* to farmers about planting and fertilizing their crops, researchers must experiment with agricultural products in their natural setting.

While the agronomist's role was being established, he faced many new problems which are now being shared by experimentalists concerned with social change. He found, for example, a great difference between his responsibilities when making recommendations to farmers about crop yield compared with his conducting chemical experiments in the laboratory. Furthermore, he was held responsible by the farmers and other members of society for his recommendations. This had the effect of making him cautious about excessive experimental claims, for he received direct feedback from affected farmers when his recommendations were inaccurate. He also found resistance to change in agricultural practices. For, on many occasions, even though replicated experiments showed the advantage of particular fertilizers, farmers who had a tradition of not using them sometimes refused to accept the experimental findings. He also found resistance from affected social organizations. For example, when his research results affected the economic position of the dairy industry, as was the case when oleomargarine was discovered, the anger of the affected industry was borne by him. Thus the agricultural researcher found that society held him responsible for his findings and, in addition, that his research affected social institutions. To the extent that favored cultural traditions were threatened, he received a hostile response.

At the present time, the social innovative experimentalist is entering an era where he is experiencing many of the phenomena previously experienced by the agronomist. First, he has discovered, as the agronomist did, that social variables must be evaluated under equivalent field conditions. Second, when the results of his experiments are utilized by appropriate societal agencies, the researcher is held responsible for the participants and the results. And finally, even when the results of experiments are highly significant, the forces of cultural lag often oppose their implementation.

Although there exists this developmental analogy between experimental agriculture and social innovation, the subject matter of these fields is quite different and requires a different experimental methodology. Social subsystems have more variables and they are continuously operative; they are dynamic and not static. Agronomists design the experiment, control important variables, supervise the growth of the experimental plants, measure their yield, analyze the data, and make inferences from the experiments. At this point the process has temporarily stopped. This is not true of social phenomena. Such variables as age of the culture, population increases, differing fads, new mores, and economic conditions affect each situation and can change rapidly with time. These variables may very well have different effects at the end of the experiment than they do at the beginning. Consider, for example, the use of employment as a criterion in a longitudinal research when economic conditions are changing rapidly; or consider the meaning of hospitalization for mental illness in peace or in war. In addition to these time changes, the importance of any given variable, whether it is economic, psychological, sociological, or whatever, changes with the situation as well as with time. To take but one example, formal authoritarian status relationships are of great importance in a medical institution, but of far less importance in agricultural work camps.

Table 2.1 shows that social innovative experiments most closely resemble service programs. It is therefore important to understand clearly their differences. Psychiatrists, psychologists, social workers, criminologists, economists, and political scientists are involved daily in programs to meet the needs of society. In this capacity they are considered experts and frequently bear the label of consultant, psychotherapist, human relations specialist, to name a few. They meet human problems in their daily work as professional persons. One thinks here of the criminologist who works in a prison conducting group meetings where criminals explore their personal problems and make future plans; one thinks also of the school consultant, the industrial consultant to management, the human relations expert, the private practitioner, and others. These experts are not usually researchers and their duties involve establishing or carrying out existing programs. The generic label used to define these statuses is *service personnel* because they are giving programmed service to the public. In this regard, service and research personnel are similar.

But in spite of the similarities resulting from the public responsibility shared equally by service and research personnel in conducting such programs, there are pronounced differences in other aspects of their social statuses. Even at a time when both are involved in programs designed to promote the welfare of individuals and society, service personnel are usually utilizing the accepted practices of their particular professions which are based upon historical tradition. On the other hand, researchers are attempting to evaluate these same practices and to create new ones. For this reason service personnel, who are the bearers of the culture, and researchers, who are attempting to evaluate that culture, may be in conflict.

To clarify how these two statuses resulting from the different obligations to service and research sometimes conflict, it is useful to cite an example which occurred in treating the mentally ill. In a recent experiment (Fairweather, 1960), the researcher was attempting to evaluate the effectiveness of selected mental hospital treatment programs under field social conditions. Three of the experimental conditions for the mentally ill patients had, as part of their program, group and individual psychotherapy. To evaluate either type of psychotherapy adequately, it was necessary to establish a fourth group whose members received all aspects of the treatment programs except either type of psychotherapy. At the outset of the experiment, patients were randomly assigned to these four conditions. The experimenter came under severe criticism from practitioners (service personnel) who were advocates of either group or individual psychotherapy. From their point of view, people in the fourth group were being denied one of the best treatments. It must be noted here that the adoption of this position rests upon the assumption that the merits of the three psychotherapy conditions had already been established. As far as experimental verification was concerned, however, it was equally tenable that the no-psychotherapy fourth condition might bring about the same or even more desirable results than any of the three psychotherapy programs. The research eventually did proceed, but only with great misgivings on the part of these service personnel. The experimental results showed that at the end of 18 months' community living, patients in the no-psychotherapy fourth group were making as adequate a community adjustment as those who participated in the more expensive and time-consuming psychotherapy programs (Fairweather and Simon, 1963). Other examples and an extended discussion of the need for control groups in human experiments is presented by Madge (1953, pp. 257–261).

This example makes it apparent that researchers must entertain the hypothesis that any service program may or may not be beneficial to the problem population. The researcher adopts this position until comparative empirical evidence indicates which service programs are in fact the most beneficial. This is a simple matter of logic and need not serve as the basis for conflict between service and research personnel. The goal of each is the same. Moreover, research evaluating service programs shows what needs to be changed and should be considered an indispensable part of service. Indeed, research provides a logical basis for social change in the whole of society and may be one effective way of instituting progressive and orderly social change by establishing a procedure through which society can adjust to changing social conditions. It also highlights the responsibility of researchers interested in social problems to investigate impartially any social practice that may be helpful to the individual. Not only should he compare traditional practices but he should also propose and evaluate new programs that have, to the full extent of his knowledge, an opportunity to advance the humanitarian values of his society, for, unlike the traditional image of science, social innovative research is not value free.

In this regard, research activities that might have detrimental effects—for example, inflicting painful injuries on people merely to discover the effects of such painful injuries, or jury tampering, which might destroy the judicial process itself—are, in view of these humane principles, logically unacceptable as investigatable problems. As far as service programs are concerned, the researcher denies no one aid. Until the relative merits of different programs are experimentally established, the beneficial or deleterious effects produced by different treatments are unknown. There is no other logical way to evaluate their effects. The aim of research in service programs is to provide new and better treatment than currently exists. One can readily generalize the personnel conflict mentioned above in the field of mental health to similar situations in education, programs for the socially disadvantaged, and rehabilitation programs for prisoners, delinquents, and other marginal persons.

It is precisely because of service personnel's lack of experimentally-validated knowledge that social innovative research must be carried out. The humanitarian approach to social problems *is* a research approach since its end goal is to separate those programs which provide the highest probability of solving social problems from those that are deleterious or not helpful. Social subsystems, whether designed for rehabilitation, education, aid to the socially disadvantaged, or whatever, can and should be subject to such experimentation. But such researches require a full-time commitment to and interest in solutions for such critical social problems.

There are many situations in which such research is needed and can be carried out. For purposes of clarity, they can be arbitrarily divided into two generic research situations. One exists within institutions and the other in the community. *Institutional research* is usually carried out in institutions such as mental hospitals, prisons, schools, and rehabilitation camps. The features which distinguish institutional research from research carried out in community settings are mainly attributable to the institutions themselves. They are: (1) the size and bureaucratic structure of the organizations in which the research is done; (2) the usual geographical isolation of the institutions from the community; and (3) the fact that institutions are primarily established for service and therefore research programs are more difficult to initiate in that setting.

One usually needs to consider fewer variables when research is done in the institution rather than in the community, because some variables are eliminated from consideration by the social structure of the institution itself. For example, economic variables, as far as the residents of these institutions are concerned and quite aside from the budget needs of the administrators, are usually relatively invariant. In these institutional settings, social innovation may usually be carried out on two or more selected resident units or classrooms where important variables can be highly controlled (p. 53). The researcher evaluates new programs in these controlled settings. At the same time, the longitudinal nature of studies in social innovation allows him to observe his population over extended periods of time, an essential factor in evaluating the effects of such programs. In addition, he can also study the effect of such longitudinal programs upon institutional personnel and other residents of the institutions, as well as upon management and institutional practices.

On the other hand, *community research* is quite different from institutional research. Since the research unit has no history, it can be established by the researchers. Research conducted in the community is its primary function and the created subsystem can usually be smaller and thus not subject to the same bureaucratic and administrative pressures as those existing in larger and more unwieldy service institutions. Formal management agreements need to be made with representatives of society rather than with the administrators of such institutions.

A current research study carried out partially in the community may serve as an example to explain this point (Fairweather, Sanders, Maynard, and Cressler, 1966). One part of this research is being carried out in the community where former mental patients are living in a leased lodge and have formed a janitorial and gardening service (pp. 68–74). They have their own trucks, power equipment, and other tools. The lodge serves as a residence for them, much as a fraternity house does for college students. They advertise for business in local papers, have a business manager and organization, and get along in the community much as any other businessmen whose employees have citizenship status. This places them in the position of being subject to all of society's forces. Because the rehabilitation center is located in the community, it is necessary to establish agreements with representatives of industry, unions, law, medicine, and other social institutions. Obviously the economic variable is important here and is, in fact, one of the major criteria of the program's effectiveness. Social innovative research in the community, then, is different from institutional research because it is an integral part of and not differentiable from the community itself. The advantages in making generalizable inferences from community research and applying them to other community situations are discussed in Chapter 13.

Methods for experimental social innovation are not independent of the experimenter himself and cannot be fully understood without describing the personal characteristics needed by such a researcher. Of paramount importance is his interest in and dedication to the solution of social problems. He receives rewards from values that are different from those of either the practitioner or the academician. In contrast to the practitioner, he does not claim any "expert" knowledge except his competence as a researcher. His approach to social problems is one aimed at solving them through experimentation. Although the very act of choosing problems indicates that he is biased, as are all researchers in this manner, he is aware of this and, therefore, he makes every attempt to provide an equal opportunity for the success of every experimental program so that his results may be unbiased. He is not content with current social practices. His role is also markedly different from the academic social scientist. He must be satisfied with fewer publications since each single study may take months or even years. He is an astute observer who attempts to describe the variables important in real-life situations without regard to method or discipline. There is no place for disciplinary chauvinism in his role. He must be willing to bear the label of an "applied" contrasted with a "basic" researcher—a comparison that is a shibboleth with prestige connotations. Whereas the academician or consultant may enter and leave the field of social action without taking responsibility for the participating people, the social innovative experimenter cannot. His full-time position and commitment to experimental social innovation require that he, in common with the practitioner, be responsible for the lives and welfare of individuals participating in the subsystems being compared. Whether his research is carried out in an institution, the community, or both, his comparative evaluations have

Table 2.2.   Phases of Experimental Social Innovation

Phases	Methods
Planning	Choosing the problem Obtaining the administrative commitments Forming the research team Making the subsystems comparable Defining the population and obtaining the sample Identifying the variables of the subsystems Measuring the variables Selecting the comparative, relationship, and process methods Stating the experimental hypotheses Creating the plan for the experiment
Action	Initiating the subsystems' operations Collecting the data Keeping the experimental conditions constant Following the experimental design Scoring the research data Closing the subsystems
Evaluation	Scoring the remainder of the data Preparing the computer sheets Analyzing the data
Dissemination	Making inferences from the experimental data Preparing the publication of the experiment Providing consultants who can establish the successful research programs as service programs Planning the next experiment

a humanitarian aspect consistent with the mores of his society and he chooses for evaluation those programs which have a potential of advancing the general welfare. He is always a skeptic but never a cynic. Along with all researchers, his attitude is best described in the phrase, "I don't know, but I do know how to study the problem."

The burden of this chapter has been to present a cursory description of the field of social research and the different methods which lie within it. The principal focus in the chapter, as in this book, is to present a new method in this field—experimental social innovation. Its characteristics were outlined in Table 2.1 and subsequently discussed in greater detail. Chapter 3 begins by examining in detail the actual processes, operations, and procedures of experimental social innovation. The next eleven chapters consist of an operational definition of the methodology as it passes through the four stages or phases of planning, action, evaluation, and the dissemination of information. The last section of the book presents a prospective social institution whose purpose is to implement these methods. Table 2.2 serves as a general orientation to the chapters that follow. It presents the four phases and their associated procedures in outline form.

Section II
Methods for Experimental
Social Innovation

The Planning Phase

Chapter 3

Choosing the Problem

At any moment there exists in every society a population of significant social problems whose solution is essential to the survival of that society. The greater the number of changing conditions within the society, the greater is the number and severity of such problems. In twentieth century America there has been a recent and rapid expansion of unsolved social problems arising from continuously changing social conditions. The researcher concerned with innovative solutions to these problems must be knowledgeable about them because his role requires that he obtain agreements among the representatives of society's institutions concerning the possible contribution of a research approach in solving these problems. In order to obtain the consensus necessary to permit the needed experiments, he articulates the problems and suggests alternative courses of action. A consensus among a society's representatives can only be accomplished when the alternatives are logically admissible as possible solutions to the selected problem and when they are pragmatic enough to be implemented upon a large scale should the research reveal the superiority of one solution contrasted with others. The role of the social innovative experimentalist, therefore, requires that he be aware of current social problems, propose alternative realistic and pragmatic solutions for them, and carry out research programs to evaluate these alternatives.

Since problems that have no acknowledged social value will probably receive no social support, the researcher must select either a problem that has a known value to a society, or he must attempt to obtain support through lucidly presenting an undefined problem to members of the social institutions affected. Unfortunately, the researcher has greatest difficulty in bringing about a consensus when such problems are not yet apparent, even though they may arise in the future, and when those which society does not wish to investigate

—those placed under taboo—are recognized openly. If the researcher cannot discover sufficient social interest to establish a consensus, the problem usually will not be investigable, because establishing social subsystems as alternative solutions cannot be achieved without the cooperation of many institutions within the society. The difficulty of establishing a consensus is one of the limitations of social innovative experiments and, indeed, with the current need for social approval reflected in most research budgets, it may be a limitation upon large-scale research in our era. This situation raises the issue of how active the experimenter should be in shaping the consensus on which the research depends. A discussion of this will be reserved for the last chapter, which describes the form and function of a possible social institution that would be devoted to social innovative experimentation and training.

From among those social problems that are both important to society and not circumscribed by taboos, the researcher selects the one which interests him most and which at the same time appears amenable to experimental test. The knowledge and interest of the researcher are therefore of paramount importance in selecting a problem for investigation, for it is the researcher's knowledge of his society which results in the selection of meaningful problems and permits appropriate inferences from research results. His knowledge of social problems stems primarily from four sources. They are: (1) observations and experiences with problems in the social context in which they occur; (2) historical development of the problem as revealed in the technical literature; (3) exposure to the direct experiences and ideas of others usually shared in verbal discussions; and (4) the researcher's own experiments.

Observation of social processes in natural social settings where one experiences their effect is probably the single most important factor in accumulating the information that is essential for problem selection. It is also the one source of information most frequently lacking in the experimenter's formal training. Little time in the researcher's education is usually devoted to observing social processes as they occur in the natural setting. Youthful experimenters typically come to the social innovative research setting with an extensive background in the theoretical propositions of their major discipline, knowledge of experimental design, and common statistical methods. They usually have little, if any, day-to-day living experience with a social phenomenon that might be under consideration. Experience is an especially important ingredient in selecting problems for experiments in social innovation because such problems are multidisciplinary and therefore no single discipline can adequately provide its students with a thorough understanding of them. For this reason, there are no well-developed theoretical models. Consequently, at this early stage of development, experiments are mainly empirical in nature.

Furthermore, the embryonic state of the field makes it exceedingly important to accumulate a body of knowledge through accurate observations and descriptions of the relevant social phenomena. For example, researchers who wish to become involved in the educational problems of delinquent children should spend a good deal of time observing the behavior of such children in their homes, at school, and at play; and they should become acquainted with these children, their parents, their siblings, their goals, their socioeconomic status, their health problems, the area in which they reside, the role society has prescribed for them, and other related information. It is necessary to understand and have some insight into these children's perceptions of themselves, others, and their environment before meaningful hypotheses which will result in practical changes for improving their general education can be formulated.

As another example, researchers concerned about the problems of the Negro should spend as much time living in their situation as they do in formulating theories about them. Life in the Negro ghettos is frequently unknown through daily experience to many of those who propose programs to alleviate the conditions of the individuals residing in these segregated residential areas. Many proposals emanating from these nonparticipant observers fail to meet the perceived needs of the residents of these areas and therefore cooperation of the residents is usually not forthcoming. No program, whatever its merits, can be a realistic solution to such social problems without the cooperation of those for whom the solution is designed. Not only must the residents of such areas participate in and be an integral part of the research from the outset, but the researcher must share their perceptions and, at the very least, have an empathic awareness of their problems. For it is only by direct observation and experience that an accurate picture of the individual and the social variables affecting him can be adequately ascertained; and these variables are equally important in understanding prisoners, the mentally ill, and the physically handicapped as they are in understanding delinquents and ghetto dwellers. The need for knowledge of the socially disadvantaged acquired in real-life settings is especially important at the present time in order to facilitate the creation of programs that are based upon an intimate knowledge of these people and their problems.

Although emphasizing the need for naturalistic observations and experiences, the value an exhaustive review of the technical literature can have in selecting the social problem for investigation should not be minimized. The review should include the literature from every discipline that might contribute to an understanding of the problem. In addition to reviewing the literature, the social problem and its possible solutions should be discussed with scientists of the various disciplines who are interested in one or more aspects of the problem. And, most important, all aspects of the problem should be discussed in great detail with representatives of the population where the problem is most prevalent.

These three sources of information—field observations and experiences, review of the literature, and discussion of the problem with scientists and others with relevant experience—serve as background material for the selection of a research problem. Not only does such information aid the experimenter in problem selection, but it also illuminates the whole of the problem for him. It is a truism that individuals must distill from their experiences, observations, readings, and discussions those variables that are most important in contributing to particular problems. The insight into the role of these key variables in solving the problems results in the formulation of meaningful hypotheses which can be subjected to experimental test. But the identification of the problem's important variables is not the only use for the knowledge gained in the problem-selection period, for inferences from the results of any subsequent experiment will be only as valid as the experimenter's knowledge of the problem. The information gained in exploring the problem will serve, in the future, as the background material for making inferences from any experiment conducted (pp. 199–210).

The problem-selection survey will probably reveal several important social problems that need to be subjected to experimentation. In selecting the one problem to be investigated, the researcher is strongly influenced by his own interests. For despite the global nature of social problems and their general interest to every researcher concerned about his society, the selection of a particular problem requires such an investment in time and energy—usually of several years' span— that a great deal of consideration must be given to the long-term interest the problem has for the investigator. Thus, his own interest must be one of the most important factors in finally determining the choice of a problem.

Observations, experiences, readings, and discussions appropriately precede every experiment in social innovation, but they are most valuable as an aid in selecting the first problem to be investigated. Once the first research has been completed, the choice of a new investigable hypothesis usually emerges as a direct result of the information gained from it. The longitudinal nature of social innovative research and the mass of data collected present the researcher with information not available from any other source. Accordingly, the completion of the first research is usually the clue to the second, the second to the third, and so forth.

Integrating all the aforementioned sources of information and considering his own interests, the researcher tentatively selects a problem and attempts to conceptualize different social subsystems that would have, in his judgment, a high probability of solving it. Each conceptualized subsystem is thought of as a total social organization, clearly defining the rights and obligations of its members, able to be meshed into society without instigating such social upheaval that society automatically rejects the new subsystem.

In order to provide the most adequate test of new subsystems, it is necessary to utilize existing social practice as a baseline comparison program. This is not only logically necessary because institutionalized practices should not be changed if they cannot be improved, but it also increases the probability of gradualness in change—a situation most socially desirable. In the examples to follow, therefore, the first subsystem in each paradigm is that currently established as the usual social practice.

Let us first take some examples from the so-called rehabilitative institutions such as mental hospitals, prisons, and homes for delinquents. Recent studies show that two of the most important problems are those of chronic institutional residence and recidivism (Fairweather, 1964, p. 3; State of California, 1965, pp. 90–94). These studies reveal that the highest rate of recidivism, especially with mental patients and prisoners, occurs among those individuals who have been institutionalized for the longest time or who have had the most releases. The researcher now conceptualizes different subsystems that might alleviate the high rate of return to these total institutions. Arbitrarily selecting prison recidivism as the example, and without a detailed exploration of the variables which must be controlled and of other experimental necessities which are presented in later chapters, the programs presented in Paradigm 1 might be suggested for comparison. Each of these six subsystems attempts to explore the effects upon recidivism of two variables, namely, time in prison and the nature of the extramural situation. Thus the two variables manipulated in Paradigm 1 are the amount of time in prison and the community situation to which the ex-prisoner returns.

Paradigm 1: Social Subsystems for Reducing Institutional Recidivism for Criminals

Subsystem 1. (Control) Usual time in a selected prison program and return to the community through the usual methods—parole officer, etc.

Subsystem 2. Usual time in a selected prison program and return to a work situation where meaningful jobs have been established for the ex-prisoner in an industrial setting.

Subsystem 3. Usual time in a selected prison program and return to a peer group subsociety of ex-prisoners where a living situation combined with the operation of a business is provided.

Subsystem 4. Minimum time in a selected prison program and return to the community through the usual methods —parole officer, etc.

Subsystem 5. Minimum time in a selected prison program and return to a work situation where meaningful jobs have been established for the ex-prisoner in an industrial setting.

Subsystem 6. Minimum time in a selected prison program and return to a peer group subsociety of ex-prisoners where a living situation combined with operation of a business is provided.

Similar to recidivism and clearly associated with it is the problem of continuous institutional residence. It is an extremely important problem for total institutions, particularly mental hospitals. Current studies have shown that the probability of relatively permanent hospitalization increases with the amount of time one has been hospitalized in the past. Thus, after being hospitalized one year the probability of continuing hospitalization the next year is greater than it was after one month. After several years of hospitalization the probability approaches 1.00 (Fairweather, 1964, pp. 274–275; State of California Department of Mental Hygiene, 1963). Therefore a program that would have the highest probability of significantly reducing chronic hospitalization for the mentally ill might be one that initially minimizes the length of hospitalization. The subsystems presented in Paradigm 2 would have as their members mental patients hospitalized for the *first* time. Again, the meticulously defined design and sampling aspects have been deleted so that the social subsystems will not be encumbered with detail. (These research refinements will be discussed in Chapters 6 through 11.) Subsystems presented in Paradigm 2 explore the effects of the mental hospital and posthospital situations upon the prevention of chronicity. The two variables manipulated here are time in the hospital and the community situation to which the discharged mental patient returns.

Paradigm 2: Social Subsystems for Reducing Chronic Mental Hospitalization and Recidivism

Subsystem 1. (Control)	Mental hospital treatment and release to the community in the traditional manner (outpatient clinics, etc).
Subsystem 2.	Mental hospital treatment and returning the patient to a community program appropriate for him. For example, the patient might be returned to his family or sent to a community dormitory where living and working or educational programs are provided. He can return to the hospital if necessary, but he returns to the community setting as soon as possible.
Subsystem 3.	General medical and surgical hospital with a neuropsychiatric ward where patients remain only a few days until mitigation of the acute phase of illness and until a diagnosis is made; release to the community in the traditional manner (outpatient clinics, etc.).
Subsystem 4.	General medical and surgical hospital with a neuropsychiatric ward where patients remain only a few days until a diagnosis is made and mitigation of the acute phase of illness has occurred; then they return to the appropriate community setting described in Subsystem 2. Later on they can return to the hospital if necessary, but as soon as mitigation of the acute phase of the illness occurs they again return to the community setting.

The plight of children who are unable to cope with the usual social demands of their age group can be taken as another example of a pressing social problem. Some of these children can be classified as neurotic or psychotic, others as delinquent, some as socially disadvantaged, and still others as mentally retarded. Parents and schools are frequently unable to establish a consistently meaningful program resulting in socially acceptable behavior and academic achievement for such children. Assuming appropriate sampling, design, and statistical techniques, Paradigm 3 presents different social subsystems which could be compared for their effects upon changing behaviors and perceptions. One should recognize that these programs are initially broad in order to maximize the possibility for differences to appear. When such differences do appear, further studies can more precisely define those variables contributing the most to the differences discovered in the broader studies. It should also be noticed that the three variables manipulated here which might affect social adjustment and education are the living situation, peer group identification, and professional guidance.

Paradigm 3: Social Subsystems for Improving the Academic Achievement and Social Adjustment of Problem Children

Subsystem 1. Living at home and attending public school.
(Control)

Subsystem 2. Living at home and attending special school.

Subsystem 3. Living at home, attending special school, and receiving special professional help.

Subsystem 4. Living at home only on weekends, with school group on week nights, and attending public school.

Subsystem 5. Living at home only on weekends, with school group on week nights, and attending special school.

Subsystem 6. Living at home only on weekends, with school group on week nights, attending special school, and receiving special professional help.

Subsystem 7. Visit home monthly, living the remainder of time with school peer group, and attending public school.

Subsystem 8. Visit home monthly, living the remainder of time with school peer group, and attending special school.

Subsystem 9. Visit home monthly, living the remainder of time with school peer group, attending special school, and receiving special professional help.

As another example of the use of controlled experiments in contributing to the solution of social problems, one might explore the possibility of training high school drop-outs to achieve their maximum social adjustment. Assuming appropriate experimental techniques, Paradigm 4 presents eight different subsystems for comparison. The social subsystems presented in Paradigm 4 involve different conditions of training and community living and working arrangements as the key variables to be manipulated.

Paradigm 4: Social Subsystems for the Training of School Drop-Outs to Their Highest Level of Achievement

Subsystem 1.   No training and residing in the community.
(Control)

Subsystem 2.   Training in a center followed by release to the community with no special planning.

Subsystem 3.   Training in a center followed by placement in industrial jobs.

Subsystem 4.   Training in a center followed by a peer group living situation and industrial job.

Subsystem 5.   Training in a center followed by a living situation where participants also operate a business.

Subsystem 6.   No training, with placement in industrial jobs.

Subsystem 7.   No training, but living in peer group situation with industrial jobs.

Subsystem 8.   No training, but living situation where participants also operate a business.

As a final example of an important social problem where controlled experiments are clearly needed, let us turn again to the field of education. Many pressing problems are amenable to experimental social innovation, such as the following. (1) What are the most appropriate teaching methods for different student groups? (2) How can social integration best be accomplished? (3) How can adult illiteracy be reduced? (4) What is the most appropriate high school curriculum to educate the future citizen? (5) Do independent study programs, such as honor programs, help or hinder student social, personal, and intellectual development? (6) What are the effects of various kinds of technical and liberal arts training upon the personality, achievement, and humanitarian values of the student? (7) What are the effects of such traditional programs as school guidance upon the personality, achievement, and humanitarian values of the student? (8) What are the results of introducing schooling before six years of age upon the individual and his society? Let us take an example where controversy is continuous—the advantages and disadvantages of grouping children in classes according to their ability. Leading authorities do not agree on the merits of such a division (Katz, 1964; Conant, 1959, p. 49). Paradigm 5 presents a simple comparison of two different compositions of student groups that might yield some direct empirical evidence useful for the resolution of this disagreement.

Paradigm 5: Social Subsystems comparing the Effect of Group Composition Upon the Academic Achievement and Social Adjustment of Students

> Subsystem 1.   Heterogeneous groupings of students.
> Subsystem 2.   Homogeneous groupings of students.

It is possible, of course, to initiate more global experiments in real-life settings.   Suppose, for example, that the experimenter wished to take selected blocks in the Negro ghettos and establish different social subsystems as proposed solutions to their problems.   The most productive solutions as determined experimentally could then be carried out on a larger scale.   Or, again, there is the possibility of sampling small communities in poverty-stricken areas and instituting different self-help social practices as community projects.   Their effects could be compared before committing society to a course of social action.

In all the examples just presented, these two basic assumptions have been made.   (1) Adequate experimental sampling, design, and measuring techniques would be utilized; and (2) each of the subsystems clearly defines and maintains status and role constancy for the duration of the experiment.

The presentation of these five paradigms is intended only to serve as examples of possible social innovative experiments.   They are suggested in order to stimulate the reader to think along similar lines about social problems with which he is familiar.   They are clearly not finished experimental proposals.   Nonetheless, they demonstrate the outline of a method for establishing and comparing different social subsystems.   These paradigms should make it obvious that social acceptance of such research proposals is necessary if they are to be experimentally established and investigated.   Once the problem to be investigated is tentatively selected, it is necessary to explore the feasibility of establishing such programs on an experimental basis before the experimenter commits himself totally to the research endeavor.   The researcher now becomes pragmatic.   He explores the possibilities of carrying to a successful conclusion a study of the problem tentatively selected for investigation.

He must first consider the nature of the social setting in which he plans to execute the research.   Here, he is concerned about the availability of a representative sample (pp. 108–121) and the receptivity of management to his proposed research endeavor (pp. 51–62). If the research is to be carried out successfully in an institution, it must be compatible with prevailing institutional social practices so that the research program can be conducted without disrupting the social organization of the institution to such a degree that the research or the institution itself would be jeopardized. Experiments that require gross deviations from accepted institutional practices are exceedingly difficult, if not impossible, to carry out. Indeed, where possible such researches should be done in newly created situations where no traditions exist. But if the research must be carried out in an ongoing institutional setting, it is most important that a series of experiments which gradually subject new practices to empirical exploration are planned. As with all social innovative experiments, the accepted social practices of the involved institution form one of the social subsystems to be investigated (p. 26).

Budget considerations become another immediate and pressing concern of the researcher, because in these large-scale endeavors the experimenter must be able to obtain the necessary staff, space, computer time, and other needed research accoutrements. The researcher must also anticipate the type of data he is likely to obtain and to satisfy himself that appropriate statistical techniques exist or can be created to process the data that will be collected.

Consideration of the issues that need to be resolved by each experimenter prior to final selection of the problem can be summarized in the following sixteen questions.

1. Will the appropriate community institutions cooperate in carrying out the research?

2. Can the administrative commitments necessary to insure the establishment and continuation of the study be obtained?

3. Can an effective mechanism be established to manage appropriately the administrative and interpersonal problems that inevitably will arise during the course of the experiment?

4. Can budget for the project and office space for the research personnel be obtained?

5. Is it possible to get an adequate research sample?

6. Are there meaningful operationally definable variables and criteria?

7. Can instruments to measure them be developed?

8. Is it possible to control or equate the different experimental groups on important variables?

9. Is there an adequate design and statistical treatment for the type of data that can be collected?

10. Can field procedures be established so that data collection can take place?

11. Are computers and other needed equipment for data analysis available?

12. Can the hypotheses be stated in such a way that rejecting or not rejecting them leads to meaningful conclusions?

13. Will the results provide information which can be utilized in formulating hypotheses about future research?

14. Is there an adequate outlet for publication of this longitudinal research?

15. Will it be possible to publish research results that have negative as well as positive implications for existing practices?

16. Can all alternative subsystems created be put into operation?

These questions can be classified into two general categories: those requiring commitments from social institutions and those regarding research procedures. Both will be discussed in detail in later chapters, but for the purposes of problem selection these administrative and research questions should be explicitly answered in the affirmative as a condition for final selection of the problem. If the answer to any of the questions is uncertain or unclear, the researcher should continue his inquiry until a definitive answer is given. If, finally, the answer to one or more of these questions is negative, the researcher should consider selecting another important social problem or shifting the site of the research project. This is necessary because the personal and monetary commitments required for the experiment are so great that anything less than a clearly stated interest in and commitment to the solution of the problem on the part of the involved social institutions would not warrant this investment in time and energy.

If all these questions can be answered in the affirmative, the researcher can then finally select the problem and formally state it in terms of testable experimental hypotheses. The questions concerning the research procedures can be answered by the experimenter, but the commitments necessary to insure the establishment and continuation of the experiment can only come from the involved social institutions. It is now necessary to find out if such commitments can be obtained.

Chapter 4

Obtaining Administrative Commitments

Experiments in social innovation are typically long-term, longitudinal studies which require the maintenance of experimental conditions for extended periods of time. This necessitates continuous administrative support from those agencies involved in the research program. There is also the necessity to maintain the staff's morale so that their personal commitment to the research goals is maintained from the beginning to the end of the experiment. Because of these features, such experiments require considerable support and understanding from society. The type of support depends on the situation in which the research is done. When a research is completed wholly within a single institution, such as a hospital, prison, or school, commitments can usually be limited to that particular institution. On the other hand, when the research is done in a residence or work situation which is not isolated or differentiated from the community, such as rehabilitation programs involving daily work in industry or living in houses, hotels, or dormitories located in the downtown or the residential areas of cities, commitments must be obtained from the related community agencies, such as city councils, labor unions, and industries. The number and type of commitments is even greater when the subsystem to be explored includes both a rehabilitative institution and the community. Examples of such subsystems, in this case involving criminal institutions, mental hospitals, and the community, are presented in Paradigms 2 and 3 of Chapter 3. To clarify the processes involved in obtaining these reciprocities, it is most informative to discuss institutional and community commitments separately.

In the Institution

First, let us explore the manner of obtaining the needed administrative commitments when the research is completed solely within one institution. After the problem has been selected, the next step is to obtain definitive commitments from institutional management which will permit the successful conduct of the research program. Administrative personnel are rarely aware of the needs of experimenters concerned with social innovation because in their experience when research has been done at all it has proceeded independently of the service in the institution (p. 11). Illustrative examples of conflicts that can arise when innovative research takes place in a service organization are presented by Smith (1961), Meyer and Borgatta (1959), and Moss, Freund, and Broadhurst (1959).

In rehabilitative institutions such as mental hospitals and prisons, norms of procedure which define research and service as separate entities have usually been established. The physical location of the research is generally in a separate building or on different floors from the location where treatment or rehabilitative programs take place. Often there are separate research and service budgets. There are often separate research and service professional positions. Even within a given discipline, such as psychology, two individuals with equivalent backgrounds, including academic degrees, may be labeled differently—one as a clinician (service person) and one as a researcher. Because of these institutional traditions, management tends to perceive professional personnel as either research or service personnel, but rarely as both. Researchers themselves have been inclined to emphasize this artificial dichotomy because recently much more prestige and money have been given to research activities. Institutional researchers frequently isolate themselves from institutional problems. In prisons and mental hospitals, for example, they often define their role as "pure" researchers and carry out their activities independent of the rehabilitative programs which are the primary responsibility of such institutions. Because of these traditional institutional practices, it is difficult for administrative personnel to understand that social innovative research is *research-in-service*.

Accordingly, it is the first task of the researcher to articulate to management that his experiments involve a wedding of service and research—a novel idea to say the least. This is particularly important because the data for some of the research must come from interviews with management personnel themselves. Since management has been spared any personal involvement in research in the past by the very nature of its isolation from institutional procedures, such revelations by the researcher are often met with surprise and resistance when initially proposed. It is the researcher's responsibility to discuss fully with management the need for such research, being certain to indicate how it can warrant the time and effort that service and management personnel will be asked to give. If the researcher cannot clearly elucidate how the proposed research might help solve some of the vexing problems faced by that institution or aid in the accomplishment of its goals, it is highly unlikely that thoughtful management personnel will give approval to the program.

The approval is all the more important because the very essence of experimental social innovation is that it requires changing the service function in those units where the research will be conducted. Therefore the *control* of those units must be delegated by management to the experimenters.

Because the historical role of research in institutions has been parallel to and independent of service, care must be exercised in clearly communicating to management the importance of insulating the service units to be used for research from any institutional practices that would destroy the research. Thus management should be told that it is imperative to officially label one or two residential and working areas as research units and to isolate them from the remainder of the institution. In a mental hospital these may be wards; in a prison they may be cell blocks; and in a home for delinquents they may be cottages. Since experiments in social innovation are well controlled and involve small numbers of matched persons, it is typically necessary to isolate only one or two such units from the major institution. These units will establish programs quite different from those in the remainder of the institution. Management must also be informed that once experimental procedures have been initiated and the research has begun, the innovative procedures cannot be changed until the research has terminated without destroying the project itself. This requires the continued protection of these research units from administrative practices that would necessitate such changes in the research program. This protection, in turn, always requires effective management support.

Another aspect of current research practice frequently contributes to the administrator's misunderstanding of the reciprocities involved in these experiments. Because of the prestige given to research by society at this time, and particularly since the advent of large-scale research grants, some administrators have developed a willingness to commit themselves to research without full knowledge of their obligations. This has often been labeled the "Yes-No" phenomenon by researchers. It is given this title because researchers are told by management, particularly when specific questions are not asked, that management is indeed interested in a research program. Upon attempting to implement the program and to obtain adequate space, sample, and other necessities, the answer becomes "No." Thus in this situation the commitment to research has been misunderstood by both the researcher and management. In these cases it seems that management has a general interest in the prestige and money research may bring to the institution without an understanding of the reciprocal responsibility of managerial personnel themselves for support of the research. For this reason, when discussing research proposals with institutional management, the researcher should ask concrete, meaningful questions stated in terms of money, space, and other needs with which administrators are familiar.

Another possible source of misunderstanding with institutional management arises from the frequently held preconception that the research staff will bring additional services to their institution without cost to the institution itself. This is sometimes believed possible by administrators when large research grants can be obtained for exploring a given problem. In such a case management often views the research budget as a supplement to the institutional budget which can be used to pay for the existing service programs rather than as funds for meeting new research needs. When this is the perception of management, conflict will almost inevitably arise in the course of the experiment because the expected increase, usually in service personnel, does not occur. When this happens, initial research agreements are often not honored. To prevent such misunderstandings the experimenter should clearly describe the use of the research budget to management.

Publicity for a research project, particularly when a large grant is involved, is another possible area of conflict between researchers and management. It is usually important to management that much publicity be given these research projects. Since the experimenter is attempting to generalize to future situations where publicity will probably not be an important variable, it is sometimes necessary for research purposes that the project be protected from such publicity until the action phase has been completed. Here again the needs of the researcher can be at variance with the institution, and it becomes imperative that agreements concerning publicity be made prior to the onset of the experiment (p. 191).

There is another problem frequently faced when the research is carried out in an institution. This involves publication rights. Quite often administrators, particularly if they are professional people interested in the research being conducted, expect to have their names appear on the publication without any material aid in the research except for making the necessary administrative arrangements. This can be devastating to researchers, and it has brought about the demise of more than one project. The role of administrators in scientific publication should be clearly agreed upon prior to the research effort. Perhaps the most forthright statement on this matter is made in the American Psychological Association's publication, *Ethical Standards of Psychologists* (1953, p. 126).

"Administrators are expected to take or be given credit for authorship of professional reports only when they have made significant contributions to the conduct of the research or to the writing of the report."

Many of the possible conflicts between the administrators of institutions and experimentalists involved in social innovation can be anticipated and prevented by initial agreements with management. These agreements are based upon the mutual commitment of both management and the investigator to the research endeavor. To accomplish this, the researcher should request a meeting with top management people and present the proposed research in great detail. After presenting his research proposal, he should pointedly ask management the following questions.

1. What will be the amount of the research budget?
2. Will management grant the researcher the authority to select institutional residents to go to the research unit when this is required for sampling purposes?
3. If important individuals within the institution complain about the research unit simply because it receives special consideration, will management continue supporting it?
4. Will management be willing to provide needed personnel?
5. Will space be provided the research team?
6. Will there be arrangements for computer analysis of the data?
7. Will management respect its commitments and not request the researchers to violate the research design or to participate in the usual institutional procedures when to do so would curtail their full-time research effort?

These questions are especially important since they give the researcher a yardstick for evaluating what is likely to happen in the future when tensions arise, if they do, as a result of the project.

On the other hand, the researcher must assure management of the following.

1. He will not violate any of the existing institutional norms except those agreed upon by both parties as an inherent part of the research.

2. He will give periodic progress reports to management.

3. He will not change any of the agreed upon procedures without specific permission from management; upon the emergence of any unforeseen difficulties involving the institution, he will request a meeting with management to discuss these problems.

The establishment of these reciprocities between management and the research team is essential not only to clarify the obligations of each, but also to provide a mechanism for continuing communication between these two parties, each of whom must be interested in finding solutions to the social problems that are the responsibility of the involved institution.

It is also of extreme importance that all agreements should be made between the researchers and the top management official of the institution. In the hospital setting, this would be the manager, superintendent, or director; in a prison, the warden; in an educational institution, the principal, president, and so on. Active support of top management is essential for experiments in institutions. The person with the highest status in an institution may not necessarily feel bound to the commitments made by subordinates. Recently, failure to secure such an agreement with the superintendent of a home for delinquent girls brought an abrupt termination to a research program agreed upon by an assistant superintendent. Such a failure could readily have been prevented had the initial agreements been made with the superintendent himself or with an individual or body appointed by him.

In the Community

When the locus of the research is the community rather than a single clearly defined institution, the agreements become more complex because many institutions and individuals become involved. This occurs because once the research has moved to the community, the research organization itself becomes a part of the community and its relationship to other community institutions must be established.

Thus research subsystems creating work situations in the community, as proposed in Paradigms 1, 2, and 4 of Chapter 3, cannot be established without agreements with labor, industry, law, medicine, education, government, and other affected social institutions. If the sample is mental patients, for example, adequate medical coverage must be arranged with community-based medical persons.

The most important first step for setting up a research program in the community, then, is obtaining agreements from the affected community institutions. To accomplish this, it is important to bring together leaders of relevant local industry, unions, representatives of the legal profession, medicine, insurance, the press, and others to clearly present the need for the research and to elucidate its goals. Thus representatives of the community institutions can become, if they wish, an integral part of the research effort. In this regard they may serve as members of a community research committee.

The need for clarifying the role relationships between the research organization and its community partners exists because no typical organization created within the society has social innovative research as its primary function. Thus universities and colleges, whose mores tend to isolate them rather than integrate them with the community, usually have not established the legal apparatus to subsume work and living groups in the community under their legal jurisdiction. Mental hospitals, homes for delinquents, prisons, and the like are similarly limited. The need to establish community research centers which could provide legal staff to make these contractual arrangements is discussed in Chapter 14.

In obtaining commitments from society's institutions, a major role is played by a third party—the agency granting the research funds. There are many private and federal agencies which are responsible for selecting projects to be financed. The costly nature of experiments in social innovation usually makes it imperative that the researcher apply for a grant. He, therefore, must consider the most appropriate agency to support the research that he wishes to pursue. For example, if he selects the mentally ill as his population he might choose to request research support from the National Institute of Mental Health or some private organization that provides funds for experiments in treating mental illness. On the other hand, if his problem were most easily classified as vocational training, he might request support from the Vocational Rehabilitation Agency or some appropriate private agency in this field.

The choice of the agency from which to make requests for monetary support is made increasingly difficult by the fact that the agencies granting research money, particularly federal agencies, have arbitrarily divided social problems by population. Thus the mentally ill, prisoners, the socially disadvantaged, the physically handicapped, for example, are considered different populations in this classificatory scheme despite their similar marginal statuses. There are therefore limitations placed upon the research by the agreements that are possible with one granting agency. One particular limitation becomes apparent when the researcher decides that a combination of populations may be experimentally advisable. For example, current work in mental illness shows the advantages of heterogeneous populations for creating problem-solving groups (Sanders, MacDonald, Maynard, 1964; Maynard, 1964). It might well be that each group, for maximum productivity, morale, and self-satisfaction, should be comprised of members selected from chronically hospitalized mental patients, those acutely ill in remission, neurotics, paraplegics, paroled criminals, marginal employables, delinquents, school drop-outs, the blind, drug addicts, and alcoholics, arranged in certain proportions. The advantages of such a research population are the potential unique contribution each member could make to the unit as a whole. However, it is exceedingly difficult to finance such a project because it includes populations arbitrarily designated as different by administrative authorities so that they have become the responsibility of different agencies. The agreements that the researcher can make with any one agency may limit the research populations available to him (p. 221).

Most social innovative researches are not confined exclusively to a single institution or to the community. In the course of pursuing answers to critical social problems, the experimenter usually cannot observe the superficial boundaries that separate the community from the isolated institution. Instead, in studying the problems of marginal man the purpose of the experimental subsystems is usually to provide a series of statuses with increasing responsibility which brings the institution and the community together into one unitary system. In Paradigms 1 to 5 of Chapter 3, the social subsystems contain prisons, mental hospitals, homes for delinquents, and educational institutions, all of which may be linked inseparably with living and working situations located in the community. The typical experimental subsystem in social innovative research is likely to be one that destroys arbitrary boundaries between total institutions and the community. Because of this, agreements for research programs usually involve reciprocities with both a selected institution and representatives of the larger community.

Such a program is currently under way in the treatment of the mentally ill (Fairweather, Sanders, Maynard, and Cressler, 1966). It may be helpful to take this research as a model and to explore its administrative agreements in great detail. In an earlier study (Fairweather, 1964), it was established that chronic mental patients organized into groups according to certain principles could and did solve problems in much the same manner as other groups. It was proposed therefore that groups of these chronic mental patients could be moved as units into the community where they would work and live in their reference group. An experiment was proposed to explore the proposition that membership in these community groups would reduce recidivism and chronicity as well as improve the former patients' perceptions of themselves. Adequate arrangements were made for controlling important variables, acquiring a representative sample, creating the measuring instruments, and preparing a social innovative design. After the research had been carefully planned in all phases, appropriate commitments to implement it were sought.

The first step was to discuss fully the research proposal with the hospital psychiatrist on whose ward the research would be initiated. It is important to note here that the psychiatrist had been intimately involved in the original hospital research project establishing the feasibility of creating problem-solving patient groups. Because of his own research experience and interest in the proposal, he agreed to support the research effort on his ward. The proposal was then submitted to the hospital research committee whose members agreed that it was a desirable experiment and further agreed to commit the hospital to engage in it. The director of the hospital was a member of the research committee and became an investigator of the research project with a clearly defined status. The principal investigator, who was jointly a member of the hospital staff and of a local university, applied for a grant through the university. The granting agency sent a site visit committee to the hospital, where the entire research proposal was reviewed and the hospital director affirmed the hospital's commitment to the research. The agency approved the grant.

Since the experimental social subsystem involved the establishment of a discharged patient-managed business in the community, it was necessary to secure a residence and a place of business and to make all legal arrangements for the upkeep of both. To accomplish the establishment of the business, the university contracted for the management of the proposed business with a local nonprofit corporation which had been engaged in rehabilitative efforts with mental patients for the past several years. The corporation had agreements with labor unions and other local organizations which made the formation of a gardening and janitorial business relatively easy to accomplish. The university then leased a dormitory in the community to house the discharged patients. A research staff was hired by the university. Equipment to perform the gardening and janitorial work, such as trucks and power equipment, were purchased or leased by the university.

The nonprofit corporation which had signed the management agreement with the university insured the discharged patients, who now were its employees, for liability and workmen's compensation as well as bonding them. They formed a subcorporation for the discharged patients' business. The ex-patients were then able to conduct business under their own name. The discharged patients, as part of their new business, contracted for jobs, kept their own business records, advertised in the local papers, established their own bank accounts, purchased new equipment and supplies, kept their work equipment in repair, and, generally, operated a rather extensive business. For their living arrangements, they purchased and prepared their own food, kept the dormitory in repair, scheduled appointments for their members to visit the doctor and, in the main, contracted with the representatives of food handling, medical, and other community organizations to meet the needs of their members. The extensive contractual arrangements and the agents necessary to *establish the subsystem so that it could be studied in the community setting* are presented in Figure 4.1.

Close scrutiny of Figure 4.1 shows the complexity of the agreements that were required to establish the social subsystem in the community. Also, it should not be overlooked that the longitudinal nature of research in social innovation may require the renegotiation of contractual arrangements during the course of the experiment. Some of the agreements presented in Figure 4.1 were renegotiated during the course of the experiment. The most simple change involved the renegotiation of some of the insurance contracts, necessitated by the cancellation of the existing ones.

When the experiment is conducted solely within the community, the investigator should make certain that he has made arrangements for the following necessities prior to the onset of the research project.

1. An adequate research budget.
2. The appropriate personnel.
3. Work space for the research team.
4. Arrangements for computer analysis of the data.
5. Contracts with all community organizations with which the members of the research staff or the innovated subsystems will have a relationship.

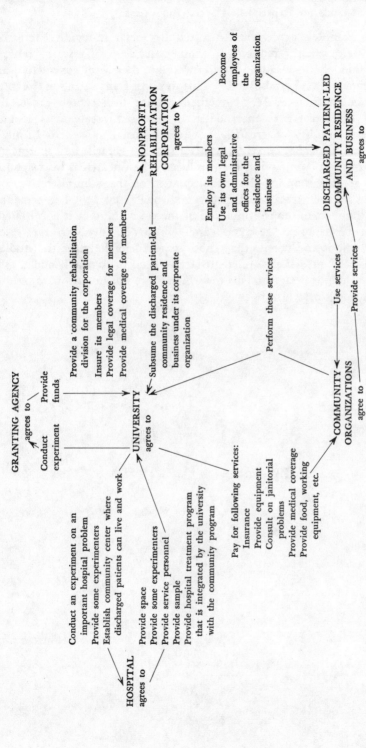

Figure 4.1. Contractual arrangements among the cooperating institutions.

The complex agreements required by social innovative research could be drastically reduced in number and scope if research centers which had the legal authority to formulate their own contractual arrangements were established. This proposed organization is fully discussed in Chapter 14. Nonetheless, until such centers are established, the researcher concerned with social innovation must assume the responsibility of creating a research social subsystem through whatever means are currently at his disposal. He will find that at no point in the planning and the conduct of the research is his responsibility greater than in the establishment of the administrative apparatus for the experimental program through contractual agreements, for without them the continuation of the research, once it is initiated, cannot be assured. Many research endeavors, involving far fewer organizations and people than those required for longitudinal studies where social subsystems are created, have been prematurely ended as a result of minor disagreements for which there was no adequate resolution through prior arrangement.

Chapter 5

Forming the Research Team

After achieving the agreements that are necessary for the conduct of the selected research program, it becomes essential to form the research team that will execute the social innovative experiment. It is essential that all individuals involved in the research realize that such experiments require a *team* effort. In order to establish and maintain social subsystems, a great many people must coordinate their activities over extended periods of time. The research program itself constitutes a social subsystem whose purpose is to establish, preserve, and investigate the innovated subsystems. In organizational characteristics and devotion to task, the research team has many of the same requirements for its members as manned space teams have for their members. Both established new systems and evaluate them; both require the integration of different professional persons into a research effort where each member makes his own particular contribution to the team's goal; and both require a complete and total ego-involvement in the task. To enhance each member's dedication to the research effort, it is important that all the members be involved in the experiment from its beginning.

The team should be formed before the planning phase of the research so that every member can participate in designing it. Participation is important because the ideas of every member can substantially aid in the final design of the experiment and, equally important, the planning sessions serve to increase the ego-involvement of the research staff in the project itself. Once an individual's ideas have been incorporated in the experimental plan, his interest in the research is maximized, a most necessary condition in longitudinal studies. Participation in the planning phase also gives the team members a more comprehensive perception of the project and thus provides a trial period so that each individual can review his own interest and become acquainted with other members of the team. Should any researcher's interest or behavior be detrimental to the research effort, a determination can be made prior to the action phase of the research and termination of his association can be completed before the experimental subsystems are placed in operation. Keeping the same research team from the beginning to the end of the research is particularly important in social innovative experiments because once the action phase begins all conditions should remain as constant as possible. One dissatisfied team member can easily destroy the total research effort by altering his role while the subsystems are in operation.

The problem selected for investigation will in large measure determine the composition of the research team. For example, if the subsystems concern educational institutions, several educators would be on the team. Every experiment, regardless of its subject matter, involves a study of the internal processes of the subsystems, the effect of the subsystems on the surrounding community (external processes), and the perceptual and behavioral processes of the individual members who are participants in the subsystem. To accomplish this at the present time, several social science disciplines must be represented on the research team. Logically, each researcher should be a multidisciplinary individual. This may be possible in the future, after research and training centers are established (pp. 213–228), but for the present the team should be comprised of members from the involved disciplines. For many experiments dealing with social innovation, selected service personnel may need to be included on the team. Thus in Paradigm 1 (p. 44) guards, probation officers, and other directly involved personnel would be on the team. Their statuses and roles would be clearly established from the beginning, and, in common with all other research team members, they would be included in the planning of the research.

Members of the team, in addition to their professional qualifications, must be personally compatible with each other. The attitude of the researcher is as important as his professional qualifications. There is no room for unbridled individualism here. Those people who find working with others difficult, those who wish to do their own research quite independent of what others do, those who are preoccupied with the importance of their own ideas, those who are prestige seekers, and those who have a stereotyped perception of the role of the researcher and are therefore unwilling to perform such mundane activities as scoring instruments when it is essential to completion of the project should not become involved in such longitudinal experiments. The experimenter must make a total personal commitment to the goal of the research. This is important mainly because at any time during the course of the experiment an emergency may require that he play a research role quite different from his major role. He must be able and willing to accept such an obligation from the outset.

Also, the experimentalist should have a high degree of motivation and interest in the social problem to be investigated because he must be willing to devote several years of his life, if necessary, to finding a solution for it. The possession of this attitude and the willingness to make such a commitment usually eliminates from consideration those individuals who have a temporary curiosity about the problem or those who are attempting to use a research project solely for personal gain.

Another important attitude of research personnel is skepticism. Inseparable from a commitment to finding solutions to the selected social problem is a healthy skepticism about the proposed solutions. Such an attitude is best summarized in the statement, "I don't know." It is exceedingly important, since social innovative research is multidisciplinary and essentially empirical in nature, that those individuals who are committed to a single approach or theoretical position do not become involved in these experiments. Such experiments incorporate variables from many disciplines and as the basis for formulating hypotheses the experimenter uses theoretical knowledge which he should hold very lightly, particularly since he is concerned with the vast complexities of social systems.

In order to achieve the necessary identification with the entire research effort, each member must become ego-involved with the research and the created subsystems. Every person on the team should have both a research and service role, even if it is only minimal. In the hospital rehabilitation program (Fairweather, 1964), for example, the nurses completed research forms for medication and, along with the nursing assistants and the social worker, rated the performance of the patient task groups and their leaders. Such involvement in the research aspect of the program, even when the personnel are mainly concerned with the service function, contributes invaluable research data and, in addition, creates a personal identification with the program. It is equally true that the research project staff should participate in the service phase of the program, although such participation may be quite minor.

This may be illustrated by describing the role of one researcher who participated in the community experiment previously mentioned (p. 34). In order to permit observations of the work and living situation of the janitorial and gardening service operated mainly by discharged chronic mental patients, a research team member, a psychologist by training, was initially appointed coordinator of the community program. He spent from 2 to 12 hours each day, depending on his duties, in the community working and living situation. In this role, he had to learn all the statuses, roles, and procedures involved in the operation of a janitorial and gardening service. He had to review periodically the bookkeeping done by the member business manager, drive some of the work crews to their jobs in a truck, consult about a job training program for new members, establish and enforce procedures to make certain that each member was taking his prescribed medication, and generally perform the managerial duties of the organization.

This was the service aspect of his job. The research side of his job involved the daily rating of the job performance of each work crew, keeping a log of daily observations that were pertinent to the research, periodically administering written tests, scheduling interviews for the members, and pursuing other activities concerned with data collection and daily observations. After eight months in this position, as required in the research design, he returned to the hospital setting where the institutional part of the research was being carried out. Here, his role, established in the research design, required that he lead a ward service team comprised of a social worker, nurses, and nursing assistants. In this role he led group discussions to evaluate patients, collected research information, rated patients and groups along with other service personnel, scheduled patients for interviewing, entrance and exit testing, and the like. After eight months in this role the action phase of the project was completed and he returned to the administrative and data processing center of the project. Here he aided in the scoring and computer processing of the data. Finally, he wrote, along with other researchers who shared his experiences, a report in which observations and analyzed data were presented.

This illustration suggests some of the role characteristics of the social innovative researcher, including the breadth of his interests, work, and commitment. It should be obvious from this example that a total team effort will require the researcher, upon occasion, to yield his own interests to those of the overall program. Although identification with the project may be enhanced by participation in the research and service phases of the study, it should be further strengthened by rewarding each researcher as much as possible for his individual effort. To accomplish this, every experimenter should have an independent and clearly defined role consistent with his special interests. Thus the researcher just mentioned joined the project staff with a special interest in the sociological processes of the community dormitory. He wrote the section in the experiment's publication describing these processes. A distinct role can also be established by assigning a particular aspect of the work as the responsibility of one individual. Again, in the study just mentioned, one person was assigned the collection of all follow-up data, another did all of a certain type of interviewing, and a third was responsible for the budget.

Generally, complete role clarity, although desirable, cannot be fully achieved because the needs of a project at any one moment may require a change in role. A researcher initially very interested in his work in a particular project eventually may find it incompatible with other interests and terminate his association with the project. If this should occur, another person in the research organization may need to be shifted to this position which, of course, will require a complete change in his role. Because of unpredictable developments like these, the researcher's commitment must be to the total project rather than to any one aspect of it.

As with all team efforts, interpersonal difficulties will arise. Some can be prevented or, at least, reduced in advance by utilizing the appropriate organization procedures; some, it would appear, cannot. Foremost among the possible areas of conflict is that of publication. It is most important that all details about authorship be agreed upon as soon as possible after the formation of the research team. This is an important detail of the planning phase. All such agreements should be made *prior* to the onset of the research program. They should be in writing so that there can be no misunderstanding about the reciprocities involved. Furthermore, the agreements should set forth the alterations to the initial agreements that may be needed should the prospective authors not fulfill their obligations. Especially important here are the changes in authorship that will occur should a researcher leave the team prior to completion of the project.

Not all conflicts, however, can or will be reduced by role clarification and agreements, for those individuals interested in social innovative research are characteristically interested in problem solution. For this reason, problems that arise during the course of the experiment are likely to be solved by any member present at the moment unless the role responsibility for such problem solution has been clearly defined at the outset of the experiment. The very personality characteristics essential for excellence in this type of research may therefore interfere with the team effort unless adequate lines of communication and coordination of activities among the various research members are established early.

Recruiting members for the research team is not an easy process. Recruiters ought to be as concerned about the prospective researchers' motivation, interests, personal compatibility, and ethics as they are about his professional qualifications. The process of selection for an initial research team may be different from that used for subsequent teams, because there are, at this time, few social innovative researchers. Therefore, to provide for future researchers, each team, once formed, must establish its own training program. Such programs should eventually provide a pool of researchers that could form new teams. Currently, in the absence of training programs that supply social innovative projects with trained multidisciplinary researchers, such teams must be formed from available personnel (pp. 224–228).

Although the composition of each team is specific to the problem selected, several general considerations seem to be warranted regarding such teams. The most important of these is that the total spectrum of knowledge about the social problem must be represented on the team. Ordinarily, the following areas may be represented in either a full-time or consulting capacity: sociology, psychology, medicine, law, statistics, economics, social work, political science, education, and history. The determination of whether an area needs to be represented on a full-time or consulting basis depends upon the nature of the social problem. In Paradigm 5 (p. 48), for example, the subject matter is the educational system. Educators would certainly be needed here on a full-time basis while medicine and law might be represented as consultants, to be involved only when medical or legal problems arise. Nonetheless, all members, whether full-time or consulting, should participate in the planning sessions because each may perceive from his own point of view variables that have not been previously recognized by the other members. Of course, it would be inappropriate and deleterious to the total research effort to represent specialists who, after discussion and thought, appear to have no essential contribution to make to the study. A meaningful role for each member of the team, full-time or consultant, is essential if the research program is to establish and maintain goal-directed behavior. This ideal model of a social innovative research team, however, is rarely achieved under actual field conditions. Rather, some compromises usually must occur because budgets limit the size of the staff independent of its needs.

It may therefore be informative to explore the composition of a research team in an actual field situation. The research involved the community-hospital rehabilitation program previously mentioned as an example (pp. 65–67). Table 5.1 presents a list of the personnel

Table 5.1. Personnel Participating in the Hospital-Community Study with Their Primary Institutional Affiliation

Hospital		University		Nonprofit Rehabilitation Corporation
Service	Research	Consultants	Research	Service
One psychiatrist One social worker Two nurses Four nursing assistants	One chief social innovative experimenter (principal investigator) One experimental assistant	Legal Accounting Insurance Statistical Computer Medical Janitorial	One chief social innovative experimenter (principal investigator) Two social innovative experimenters Three experimental assistants	Board of Directors

69

and the institutions with which they had their primary affiliation. The table shows that the chief social innovative experimenter was the only individual listed under more than one institution. He had primary affiliations with both the hospital and the university. The janitorial service operated by the former mental patients and the granting agency, presented in the administrative diagram (p. 61), do not appear here because none of the research or service staff personnel had their primary affiliation with them.

The team leader is presented in Table 5.1 as the chief social innovative experimenter. It cannot be overemphasized here that the team leader must himself be a trained social innovative experimenter thoroughly familiar with the administrative, training, and experimental needs of the team. This is particularly important since the team members will repeatedly come to him over the course of the experiment for guidance and decisions about all research aspects. Individuals without experience in such experiments, regardless of their other professional qualifications, are typically not sufficiently grounded in the day-to-day operations of experimental subsystems in action to manage successfully a social innovative research program.

The team leader selected the problem for investigation and made arrangements for management commitments. He was responsible for the total research effort and had both administrative and research duties. His research duties, in addition to selecting the problem, included the final selection of the design, supervision of the creation or selection of the measuring instruments, establishing appropriate sampling procedures, choosing the appropriate statistics, supervising the computer analysis of the data, and so on. As previously mentioned, all of these decisions were made by him *after* thorough discussion with the team members.

Hiring of the research team was his first official act after obtaining administrative and budgetary commitments. Other administrative duties included making arrangements for office space, computer time, supplies, and, most important, keeping the experimental conditions constant during the action phase (p. 90). The team leader delegated most of the aforementioned obligations, but whether he did or not, he was finally responsible for all administrative and research activities. Among his administrative duties, one of the most important was that of maintaining the research group itself. He attempted to provide each person with as unique a role as possible, a morale factor mentioned earlier, and, upon occasion, was the arbitrator of disputes within the staff. Most importantly he established lines of communication among staff members so that interpersonal problems could be solved before they grossly affected the research effort. Examples have been given of the role of the team leader and the coordinator of the community program (pp. 65–67) for the community experiment. In addition, the composition of the research team which carried out that experiment included several other persons. Two experimental assistants, one from the hospital and one from the university, had many duties, mainly concerned with the daily operation of the research program. They prepared correspondence for other researchers and for relatives of the former mental patients who now operated the janitorial service. They mimeographed testing forms, administered tests, interviewed staff, hospitalized patients, and former patients, and prepared budget requests. In all these duties they followed the research schedule, making certain that the many programmed procedures occurred on time. Here again each assistant had a set of duties that were his individual responsibility.

Two other assistants were hired after the project had begun. They were trained by the researchers to coordinate the service activities of the janitorial and gardening service. The introduction of these individuals was planned at the outset of the research (p. 184). They replaced the experimenters in administering the janitorial and gardening service. Interviewing, testing, and other more technical matters were still performed by the experimenters, but the collection of certain research data, such as keeping a log of selected events and rating the work crews, was done by the assistants.

The service personnel—psychiatrist, social worker, nurses, nursing assistants—were employees of the hospital, who, along with one of the researchers, established and implemented on a daily basis the hospital aspect of the research effort. In addition to their primary service duties, each played a role in the research effort. The psychiatrist met periodically with the team leader to discuss patient sampling requirements, medication, and other research matters. The social worker, nurses, and nursing assistants served as members of an evaluation team which rated patient task groups on the ward. In this capacity, they worked closely with the researcher who was assigned to the ward. This team also contributed other research data without which the experiment could not have been completed.

Consultants also had an exceedingly important role in the overall project. They served in this capacity because their duties, although essential, did not require full-time assignment to the project. Thus the *accounting consultant* periodically audited the books of the janitorial service. The *legal consultant* was contacted when problems of a legal nature arose. On one occasion the janitorial service was sued by a dissatisfied customer, and this was handled through the legal department. The lawyer recommended the appropriate malpractice and personal liability insurance for the research staff and the former patients who operated the janitorial service; he drew up the management agreement between the university and the nonprofit corporation under whose auspices the former patients worked; he also arranged for the lease of the dormitory in which the former patients lived. His duties, broadly conceived, included the legal representation of the research staff and the former patient members. The *insurance consultant* followed the recommendations of the legal consultant in obtaining appropriate coverage for these two groups. Certain carriers, for example, will not insure former mental patients, whereas others will, and his specialized knowledge made him aware of this. The *medical consultant* served as the house physician for the members of the former-patient group. He prescribed medication, was on emergency call, gave physical examinations, and generally met the medical needs of the ex-patients residing in the community dormitory who operated the janitorial and gardening business. The *janitorial consultant* recommended supplies for the work teams of the dormitory, proposed new work procedures, demonstrated new products, and advised the workers about all the janitorial aspects of the work situation.

These consultants were involved in the *service* aspect of the community dormitory where the janitorial and gardening services were located. The statistical and computer consultants, however, were needed for the research aspect of the experiment. From the outset of the study, the *statistical consultant* had been actively involved in all research planning. He advised about design, appropriate instruments, and correct analytic procedures. Although it is the final responsibility of the principal investigator to select and implement the statistical procedures, it is frequently necessary, because of the complex nature of the design and data involved in a social innovative experiment, to seek the knowledge of a theoretical mathematical statistician. The *computer programmer*, on the other hand, worked directly with the principal investigator and was responsible for punching computer cards, carrying out the analyses on the established programs, and presenting the data to the principal investigator upon final analysis. It is important to note here that all of the consultants whose positions have been described worked full-time elsewhere, and consulting ordinarily required only a few hours of their time each month.

The *nonprofit corporation*, appearing in Table 5.1 as the Rehabilitation Corporation, provided the janitorial service with corporate membership. Since this corporation already had obtained agreements with local industries and unions because its primary function was the rehabilitation of mental patients, a management agreement between the university and the corporation provided the appropriate relationship with community business and unions. In addition, the corporation provided an organization through which workmen's compensation and other needed insurance could be obtained. In the daily operation of the research project, whether in the hospital or the community, no individual associated with the nonprofit corporation had a service or research role, but its Board of Directors were kept fully informed of the business activities of the janitorial and gardening service. Annual audits and other business information were provided to it as necessary to fulfill its legal obligations as a nonprofit corporation. Simply stated, the nonprofit corporation provided the janitorial and gardening service with a corporate affiliation that integrated it into the work community.

As with the organizational structure shown in Figure 4.1, the institutional affiliation of the research personnel presented in Table 5.1 again reveals the need for cooperative relationships among the many institutions that are often involved in social innovative experiments. The university and the hospital, as shown in Table 5.1, needed to have the closest relationship because personnel from both organizations served in the research effort. The personnel involved in the research, whether their primary institutional affiliation was with the university or the hospital, had to have a strong identification with the research program. Each institution had to recognize the need for this identification and promote it, for the primary identification of each member of the social innovative research team, whether they were predominantly service or research personnel and regardless of institutional affiliation, was with the research effort and not with their departments within the institutions or with the institution itself. The research transcended the institution.

An identification with such a research project is most difficult when an institution or department within the institution is predominantly a service organization. The hospital personnel, shown in Table 5.1, were permitted by their department heads to perform some research duties as long as such duties did not interfere with their service function. The nurses, for example, not only dispensed medication and performed the other usual service functions required by their status, but they also completed research forms and carried out other research functions. However, they were administratively responsible to the supervisor of the nursing service and not to the research team leader. It is therefore clear that conflicts might have developed between the nursing supervisor and the research team leader had there been no appropriate prior agreements with department heads, as mentioned in Chapter 4. Such agreements are obviously essential to the successful conduct of social innovative experiments.

Another important consideration regarding the selection and assignment of service personnel when such a research is conducted within an institution is that the department heads are aware of the cooperation and dedication required of researchers in such projects. Occasionally the department head of a service organization may agree to allow service personnel to be involved in such a research project and then assign to the research program personnel who do not wish the assignment or who have had difficulty in adjusting to their previous service position. Individuals so assigned rarely become identified with the research effort and frequently oppose it. Therefore, it is exceedingly important that service personnel volunteer to participate in the research. Also, a trial period during which they can request a release from the project or during which the team leader can request their transfer should be provided. The practice of arbitrarily assigning service personnel to a research program on a nonvoluntary basis may only insure the program's failure.

A team research effort also requires that no one individual be indispensable to the total effort. Thus team members should be able to substitute for others on the team in the event of an emergency. It is also important that social innovative research be a full-time pursuit for the researcher. Except for consultants, whose positions are defined as part-time employees, all other researchers should have full-time positions with the research team. Such positions help obtain identification with the project and clearly define the reciprocal obligations.

Organization of a multidisciplinary social innovative research team thus appears to involve several requirements which distinguish it from the typical process of forming interdisciplinary research groups. As soon as the necessary administrative agreements are completed, prime consideration must be given to the maintenance of identification with and ego-involvement in the research effort over a long period of time. From this requirement stem the other essential rules of thumb to be used in forming the team. These may be summarized as follows.

1. An experienced team leader should recruit all team members, involve them from the planning phase of the experiment, specify as clear and unique roles as possible for all, no matter how minor, and make sure that each is a volunteer with the appropriate full-time or part-time commitment to the project.

2. Because of the current lack of trained multidisciplinary researchers, team members must be drawn from existing academic disciplines and professions. Nevertheless, the team should consider the training of a new generation of such researchers as one of its major responsibilities in order to insure a supply of such trained people in the future.

3. The social problem selected for investigation and experiment will determine the areas of knowledge requiring representation on the research team, as well as the extent to which such representatives need to make a contribution to the study. Some areas will suggest the use of consultants rather than full-time research team members, while other areas will suggest the necessity for organizational mechanisms (such as the nonprofit corporation mentioned in the illustration) to implement the research effort.

4. From the outset of involvement in the study, research team members should have written agreements concerning their reciprocal obligations and responsibilities, including that related to ultimate publication of the results of the social innovative experiment.

5. Finally, certain ideal personal characteristics of such researchers seem essential to the success of experimental social innovation. These include the personal capacity to get along with others on the team so that smooth interpersonal relationships facilitate the long-term research effort; a dedication to teamwork in which individual contributions are seen in the light of team needs rather than as personal successes; the capacity to manage dual loyalties, especially in the situation where the research is carried out in an institution, so that a harmonious balance between institutional and team identifications is achieved; the capacity for flexibility in role performance so that research and service functions are carried out easily, successfully, and simultaneously because of a readiness to serve in any capacity advancing the experiment; skepticism about any particular approach to social problem solution being the only approach that could be adopted; and an unequivocal interest in the social problem selected

for investigation and its empirical solution by the application of experimental procedures.

These requirements draw upon what is at the present time a limited fund of experience in the conduct of social innovative experiments. Many others will arise from the nature of the social problem under experimental investigation. As such teams attack important social problems in the future with the same vigor with which space exploration is currently being conducted, both the solution of such problems and the mobilization of human resources thereby involved will become more efficient and effective. The guidelines given in this chapter are intended to provide an initial framework for that mobilization which daily appears more and more critically needed.

Chapter 6

The Functional Definition of a Social Subsystem

The goal of social innovative experiments is to compare the effectiveness of new social subsystems in solving a selected social problem. The social subsystem, which is the unit of research in experimental social innovation, can only be clearly understood in terms of its functional properties. When the experimenter attempts to establish a social subsystem as an alternative solution to a given social problem, he is primarily interested in the outcome of that subsystem. But the outcome of a subsystem is dependent upon the individuals who participate in it and the social context in which it is operative. It is the functional relationship between outcome, participants, and social situation that the social innovative experimentalist uses to operationally define a social subsystem. This generic relationship may be stated in the following manner: *The outcome of any social subsystem is a function of its participants and its social situation.*

This functional relationship is not new among theoretical propositions offered to explain human behavior. For example, Tolman (1935) proposed a general formula for behavior, $B = f(S, H, T, P)$. This general formula proposes that behavior (outcome) is some function of the environmental stimulus set-up (social situation) and three other variables specifying the condition of the behaving organism (participant characteristics). But Tolman usually devoted most of his attention to the participant variables. Lewin (1936, pp. 11–12) gave more importance to the social situation. He defines behavior (outcome) as a function of the person (participant characteristics) and his environment (social situation), $B = f(PE)$. In an even more systematic way, Brunswik (1943, 1956) has argued for the inclusion of participant and environmental variables in any formulation of behavior, with particular reference to the planning of psychological experiments. And recently Hammond (1948, 1954) and Holland (1966) contended that responses which occur in psychological testing situations or in interviews are influenced by the relationship between the examiner and the respondent, and also that they must be considered in the context of the wider social background provided by the culture in which the testing or interviewing takes place. In all of these examples, it is the implicit or explicit assumption that the variables which must be explored in order to understand human behavior are those of outcome, participants, and the social situation.

The paradigms presented in Chapter 3 can now be classified in terms of a formula which shows functional relationships among the three variables. They are presented in Table 6.1. Paradigms 1, 2, and 4 vary the social situation while holding the effects of the participants constant. In the case of these three paradigms, the experimenter should be able to logically attribute any differences in outcome to differences in the social situation. Paradigm 5 holds the social situation constant and varies the participants. Any differences in the outcome between subsystems in Paradigm 5 should be attributable to differences in the participants. Paradigm 3, on the other hand, varies both the social situation and the participant dimensions. Results here should logically be attributable to differences in social situation or participants or to some relationship between these two dimensions. Thus the outcomes of any social subsystem are its products and may be attributable to its particular social situation, its participants, or both.

The experimenter may conceptualize the social situation and the participants as the dimensions of a subsystem. They are most often the variables that are manipulated to bring about changes in outcomes. The outcomes of subsystems are specific to the kind of social problem for which one is seeking a solution. For example, if the social problem is education, the social change outcome criterion may be academic achievement; if the social problem is postprison adjustment, the social change outcome criterion might be reduction of recidivism.

Participant variables are those that describe the attributes of the sample of participants, such as age, education, medical history, attitudes, and expectancies.

The social situational variables may be classified as those that are internal and those that are external to the social organization. Internal social processes are those intrinsic to the subsystem, such as group morale, type of work, and fiscal processes. The external processes are those that impinge upon the subsystem and result from the subsystem's interaction with the larger environment. They

Table 6.1. The Relations of the Variables in the Paradigms Presented in Chapter 3

	Outcome .... is a *function* of	Social Situation .... and	Participants
Paradigm 1	Reducing criminal recidivism	(a) Time in prison and (b) Community situation	Equivalent
Paradigm 2	Reducing chronic mental hospitalization	(a) Time in hospital and (b) Community situation	Equivalent
Paradigm 3	(a) Improvement in academic achievement and (b) Social adjustment	(a) Living situation and (b) Professional help	With or without peer group
Paradigm 4	Highest level of personal achievement	(a) Conditions of training, (b) Community living and (c) Working arrangements	Equivalent
Paradigm 5	(a) Improvement in academic achievement and (b) Social adjustment	Equivalent	Heterogeneous and homogeneous group compositions

Table 6.2. Some General and Specific Outcome Criteria in Experimental Social Innovation

General Criteria	Criteria specific to problems of:		
	Mental health, criminality, delinquency, drug addiction	Education	Poverty, race, urban development
Satisfaction	Recidivism	Academic achievement	Employment
Self-regard	Behavior control	Social adjustment	Living standards
Morale	Employment		Family cohesion
Cost of maintaining subsystem			Integration
			Housing and living conditions
			Criminal behavior

involve variables such as the state of the economy and the subsystem's interaction with other institutions.

Social subsystems are operative in a dynamic society, and for this reason the behaviors, perceptions, or social organizational variables cannot be rigidly assigned to particular categories that transcend time. Thus the behaviors, perceptions, or social organizational variables that are categorized as outcome in one study may not be categorized in the same class in subsequent studies. For example, employment, the use of leisure time, or self-satisfaction may be more important to a society in some years than they are in others. Thus in the 1930s employment might be society's outcome criterion for its educational system, whereas in the 1970s it might be the use of leisure time. *The experimenter's categorization of measures as outcome is contingent upon the condition of the society and its needs at the time the experiment is done.* Although outcome, participant, and social situation variables are presented independently in Tables 6.2, 6.3, and 6.4 for clarity, it cannot be overemphasized that such a classification is arbitrary and that the variables listed as outcomes can change with changing social conditions and different experimental needs.

The Social Change Outcome Criterion

The experimenter should first be concerned about the possible outcomes of the created social subsystems. This is so because social subsystems are created to solve social problems and the outcome of the subsystems determines the degree to which they solve the problem they have been established to ameliorate. Outcome, of course, may be defined in many different ways but the primary outcome—that for which the subsystem was established—is designated as the *social change outcome criterion*. Table 6.2 presents some general and specific outcomes. A discussion of their measurement may be found in Chapter 9.

The selection of a particular social problem determines in large measure the social change outcome criterion, because the criterion should represent a solution to the problem. The solution, however, must arise not from the experimenter's definition but rather from a consensus of the individuals charged by a society with the responsibility for finding a solution to the social problem. It is necessary, therefore, that those agencies financing research programs along with other responsible members of society agree about the outcome criterion.

Although the experimentalist is usually interested in many outcomes, such as improvement in morale, productivity, and self-enhancement, he should initially define the social change outcome criterion. To do so, he assesses society's consensus about what it considers to be an appropriate solution to the problem. Take the Job Corps of the U.S. Antipoverty Program as an example. If there is consensual agreement among those members designated by society as responsible for the program that its end product should be productive employment in the community for those who participate in the program, the criterion for the success of the Job Corps training program should be productive employment in the community. This is society's definition. The experimentalist may be interested in the participants' attitudes toward future employment, expectancies about employment generated by the subsystems, the skills learned by participating in the subsystems, changes in achievement test scores, and so forth. This information can be documented and correlated with the social change outcome criterion, but it is not such a criterion and should not be substituted for it.

Another example can be found in the recidivism of criminals and of those hospitalized for mental illness. If the representatives of a society who are responsible for the rehabilitative programs of both prisoners and long-term hospitalized mental patients agree that the criterion for successful rehabilitation is a reduction of recidivism, then the outcome criterion becomes just that—reduction in recidivism. The social change outcome criterion is, therefore, determined by the representatives of a society and by the experimenter only in his role as a member of that society. The experimenter, of course, can and should be interested in the effects of the subsystem upon a wide variety of behaviors and perceptions. He should collect information on these interesting and important variables and correlate them with each other and the criterion. But since social innovative experiments are not value-free, the experimenter accepts the notion that the representatives of a society are charged with the responsibility of solving the problems that the created subsystems are designed to ameliorate. Accordingly, the representatives are responsible for discovering a solution to the problem that is acceptable to society. The social change outcome criterion should, therefore, reflect their consensus about an acceptable solution.

Other measures selected by the researcher to represent his interests should be collected and correlated with the criterion as an integral part of the study. It should be clearly understood that the selection of the criterion by society's representatives in no way limits the variables that the experimenter may explore. This technique merely insures that the information most important to a society, namely, that information about which its representatives are most concerned, is collected and its relationship to any other aspect of the research can then be ascertained—a situation that might not apply if the researcher were solely responsible for the definition of the criterion. Because the social change outcome criterion reflects the consensus of a society's representatives, it can usually be stated in terms of real-life behavior. For the experimentalist, this has important consequences because some current research studies question the relationship between real-life behavior and perceptions about it. Although Deutscher (1966) has recently summarized some of the studies showing a certain discrepancy between words and deeds, other recent researchers question whether a positive relationship of *any* significant magnitude exists between specific behaviors and verbal attitudes (Fairweather, Moran, and Morton, 1956; Forsyth and Fairweather, 1961; MacDonald, 1964, pp. 148–149; Fairweather, 1964, pp. 273–282).

For example, in a particular experiment, the researcher might readily choose expectancies about employment as the criterion. If these recent studies are valid, this choice would yield little information concerning job performance—a likely social change outcome criterion. So it is most important that information about the outcome criterion (job performance in this case) be obtained as a primary focus of the research rather than attempting to infer about performance from attitudes or expectancies actually assessed in the experiment. As successive experiments are completed, the social change outcome criterion becomes empirically elaborated. Successive correlational analyses (pp. 164–179), which show the interrelationships of the various measures, are used to accomplish this. To elaborate the criterion, those measures not related to it can be excluded while those with high relationships can become an integral part of it. In this way, experiments can generate information that may be used to shape a new social change criterion consensus. The role of the experimenter in social innovation is thus to provide new information derived from experiments, which can be used by a society's representatives to help formulate a somewhat more scientific consensus. His responsibilities as a scientist and as a citizen merge at this point. When research information indicates that the criterion in use needs redefinition, it is the experimenter's obligation to request that the agents of society make such a change, and it is indeed his obligation, in his role of educator, to help shape a new consensus. Of course, these responsibilities are an inherent part of the citizen's role in any democratic society.

The selection of the criterion has other important consequences which may lead to a clearer definition of the social problem. For example, one social change outcome criterion might be the employment of minority group members. If this should be the case, subsystems need to be established to provide employment opportunities. The results might further clarify the many facets of such a problem. Suppose that employment was not accepted by some of the members even when it was offered. At that point, the use of employment as a criterion would have illuminated a hitherto unknown facet of unemployment—namely, the unwillingness of some of the problem population to accept employment even when it was offered. If this happened, the problem of employment might then be viewed as many-faceted and requiring different solutions, only one of which would provide a situation in which employment is available. The choice of such an outcome criterion as employment would have illuminated this.

A recent experiment in treating mental illness (Fairweather, 1964), concerned with reducing the recidivism rate of discharged mental patients, demonstrates this principle quite clearly. Remaining out of the hospital was the social change outcome criterion. Many measures concerning hospital behaviors and perceptions, such as social behaviors, attitudes, and expectancies about the future were also used. A subsequent cluster analysis of 120 different measures that could have been related to the outcome criterion showed that the criterion was significantly related to only a few posthospital measures and to only one of the within-hospital measures. The empirically established relationships are shown in Tables 11.1 and 11.2. A glance at Table 11.1 shows that employment in a low status job, a supportive community living situation, short stay in the hospital, and cooperative behavior in a group are the only measures of the 120 that were substantially related to recidivism. Table 11.2 shows the low relationships between the seven other created clusters and the elaborated social change outcome criterion. These results can now be used to give a more specific empirical description of the outcome criterion.

The social change outcome criterion, therefore, can become more completely described by successive experiments which show the empirically derived relationships between experimental measures and the criterion. It should be emphasized that the new attributes do not redefine the criterion but, rather, elaborate it. Any redefinition of criterion must occur by social consensus because in actual social change, society, not the experimenter, finally determines the outcome criterion it will accept. It is, therefore, the experimenter's responsibility to clearly determine the social consensus about possible outcome criteria at the time he proposes the experiment.

While it is not the researcher who ultimately chooses the criterion, it is he who reveals the results of the experiments. It is his responsibility to set forth the empirically established relationships of the experimental variables with the criterion and to make them available to those members of society who *can* redefine the criterion. Using Tables 11.1 and 11.2 as examples, the experimenter presents the information to those members of society who are responsible for planning treatment programs for the mentally ill. Low as well as high relationships should be reported. As Table 11.2 shows, such phenomena as social interaction within the hospital, positive attitudes about a treatment program, and high aspirations about the future are not related to posthospital adjustment. On the other hand, the supportiveness of the community living situation to which the patient returns, staying in the hospital a minimum amount of time, and being a cooperative group member are related. The experimenter presents this information to the responsible agents of society. He does not use it independently to alter or redefine the social change outcome criterion, because orderly social change cannot reasonably occur unless it represents a society's consensus about an acceptable solution for the social problem.

Participants

While the importance of empirically determining the attributes of the social change outcome criterion needs to be emphasized, the criterion cannot be considered independent of its relationships with the two manipulative dimensions of an experiment—the participants and the social situation. Table 6.1 shows the need for equivalent (matched) groups to participate in each subsystem of some experiments and the need to systematically vary such participants in others. In either case, the experimenter must first clearly define the attributes of the participating sample so that they can be assigned to the subsystems according to the research plan.

Although certain key variables can usually be employed to match marginal individuals (pp. 113–116), ascertaining these key variables does not fully define the sample participating in the experiment. For a complete description of the participants, it is necessary to accumulate information about their many characteristics. Certain demographic features such as age, religion, education, family, employment, and socioeconomic situation should be obtained. It may also be important to describe the sample on selected test scores. The experimenter may wish to have information on tests of intelligence, achievement, interests, occupational preferences, and personality. And there are also rather specific items of information such as minority group membership, residential area, and language spoken. A list of the most common participant variables is presented in Table 6.3. Procedures for making samples of participants equivalent on these variables are presented in Chapter 8. Methods for ascertaining and measuring the attributes of any sample can be found in Chapter 9.

Table 6.3. Participant Variables

Demographic

    Age
    Education
    Employment history
    Social class
    Marital status
    Medical history
    History of institutionalization
      (prison, mental hospital, etc.)
    Military history
    Socioeconomic status
    Family history
    Race
    National origin
    Membership in societies
    Religion

Personality characteristics

    Behavior description
    Test scores
    Ratings

Intelligence

    Test scores
    Educational achievement
      (grades and awards)

Social Situation

The outcomes of subsystems are not only contingent upon the participants but also upon the subsystem's social situation. To achieve meaningful problem-solving comparisons between subsystems, the situation *in which* they are operative should be the situation to which one wishes to generalize. For example, if the problem concerns the community employment of marginal groups it is axiomatic that the situations in which research is conducted are those where the participants can be employed in the community. Results of educational, rehabilitative, and work programs established in situations dissimilar to those to which the researcher wishes to generalize probably will not yield information that is directly applicable to problem solution. Table 11.2 illustrates this principle very well. Behavioral adjustment in the hospital did not generalize to post-hospital adjustment. This is primarily because of the differences in role requirements between the hospital and the community situations —a hypothesis validated in a subsequent study (Fairweather, Sanders, Maynard, and Cressler, 1966).

It is therefore of exceeding importance that *the social innovative experiment is conducted in a situation where the social change outcome criterion is operative.* Thus, if the social change outcome criterion is community employment, the research situation should contain, at least as one facet, an employment opportunity in the community setting. This is necessary because many variables other than those accounted for in the experiment, such as minority group membership and sex, can determine employment. If the experiment is conducted in a situation where there is no social change outcome criterion operative, the effect of extraneous variables, such as minority group membership in the case of employment, might lead the experimenter to infer that the experimental variables—employment training procedures, for example—have not prepared the participant for employment, although, in fact, the probability of receiving employment was slight regardless of training.

The social situation within which the subsystems are operative can be described by its internal and external processes. The internal processes include the subsystem's internal economics, its social structure, and its group dynamics. The external processes include the manner in which it is related to the community through function, position in the social and economic structure, and interaction with its social surroundings. A list of social situation variables that are operative in most social subsystems is presented in Table 6.4.

Table 6.4. Social Situation Variables

Internal processes	External processes

Type of social organization:
   Structure (pyramidal, etc.)
   Size
   Composition
   Degree of autonomy
Type of work performed (social, productive)
Work units (group, individual, etc.)
Status relationships (rights and duties of each member)
Group processes
   Morale
   Norms
   Reinforcement system
   Communication system
   Cohesiveness
   Status role relationships
    (leadership, etc.)
   Performance
Fiscal processes (manner in which economic matters are handled)
   Income
   Costs
   Rate of pay
   Profit and loss statements
   Bookkeeping procedures
Membership
   Voluntary
   Involuntary
   Turnover
	Time
	Social climate
	State of the economy
	Socioeconomic description of neighborhood
	Assessment techniques in program
	Geographical location
	Folkways and mores of the institution or community
	Publicity
	Relationship to other community institutions
	Economic support
	Legal agreements, etc.
	Relations among subsystems in experiment

Procedures for making subsystems comparable on the social situation dimension as required in Paradigm 5 of Table 6.1 can be found in Chapter 7. Measurement of the internal and external processes is presented in Chapter 9.

Internal Social Processes

One aspect of a subsystem's internal functioning is its own fiscal processes—the way in which it handles monetary matters within its organization. These are the *statuses* and *operations* which are purely internal to the subsystem and which do not directly involve the wider social environment. They constitute the subsystem's financial management. Some members of the subsystem (including staff, consultants, or members) will usually have certain fiscal responsibilities as part of their status. For example, in the community project (p. 34), the member executive committee alone can grant loans to members out of a fund accumulated from part of the job revenue. Similarly, the member in charge of the kitchen and dining room was delegated the responsibility for buying food and kitchen supplies, whereas certain consultants decided on other expenditures.

These statuses generate certain *operations* of budgeting and accounting which are necessary to make the financial decisions and dispositions. The budgeting, for example, allocates certain money to purchasing food, buying equipment, and leasing property. Accounting operations are simply means of ensuring that the budget is followed by the persons responsible. All these operations are carried out by members of the subsystem who have those duties as part of their statuses. To use again the example of the community project, a differential wage scale has been established (or budgeted) for the three grades of members—supervisors, assistant supervisors, and workers. One member holds the position of business manager and does the bookkeeping. Consultants are responsible for checking the bookkeeping and auditing the subsystem's books.

The defining characteristic of these internal fiscal processes is that they all deal with money after they are in the subsystem and before they leave it. Monetary transactions between the subsystem and its social environment (including income from work and from supporting institutions as well as output into the economy of the wider society by spending) form the external economic processes of the subsystem, which will be discussed later.

Another internal process variable which requires description and measurement is the social structure of the subsystem. It defines all of the formal statuses of the organization and their interrelationships. Here again, the statuses will vary with the type of subsystem created; however, it is most important that each status is clearly and accurately defined and its relationship with other statuses is described so that the organizational structure of the subsystem can readily be conceptualized by the reader. The organizational chart also shows the formal lines of authority among the members. This is done by placing those in the highest power positions highest in the vertical organization of the chart. A detailed account of the many types of organizational structure including important publications can also be found in Chapter 9.

But structure is the static concept of the subsystem's internal processes describing its formal organization. Once the subsystem has been established, the structure is relatively constant. On the other hand, the subsystem's group dynamics describe the active aspects of its internal processes. Each dynamic property can be treated as a variable, because it can change with time and with changes in other dynamic properties. Usually dynamics, when contrasted with structure, must be measured longitudinally because of their changing qualities. This is particularly true in real-life groups where membership is frequently transitory. Take the dynamics of leadership as an example. In a group there is a high probability of new informal leadership with the departure and arrival of members. As the new members arrive and the old ones depart, the informal leadership of any group usually changes. Whether this is reflected in the formal structure is dependent upon the degree to which the formal structure reflects the informal structure. Nonetheless, it is necessary in describing the dynamics of the groups' internal processes for the experimenter to be able to trace longitudinally the emergence of the new leaders and the departure of the old. Leadership, of course, can and does change within groups having the same membership, but the likelihood of such changes increases with increased group turnover. Many other variables which should be measured can change with the turnover of members. They include such processes as group performance and morale. Techniques for the measurement of group dynamics can be found in Chapter 9.

External Social Processes

In addition to the internal processes of the experimental social situation, external processes also need to be fully described and measured. Each subsystem is implanted in an ongoing larger social organization whether it is an institution, the community, or both. The establishment of subsystems can and will affect the larger social organization and it, in turn, will affect the subsystems. It is important therefore for the experimentalist to study the effects of the interaction between the subsystems and the larger social organization. He is here mainly concerned with processes external to the subsystem. If the subsystem is located in an institution, the researcher attempts to measure the effects of the subsystem upon institutional personnel, inmates, the structure of the institutional organization, and so on. Attitudes and expectancies of inmates and staff toward the participants in the subsystem, effects of the subsystem upon the formal social organization of the institution, and critical incidents which occur during the course of the experiment as the result of these effects all describe events that are external to but impinging upon the subsystem. The specific attributes that should be described, however, are again very dependent upon the type of institution in which the subsystems are implanted. If, for example, the experimenter creates a new educational subsystem, he may be concerned about its effects on other teachers, pupils, and the school board. On the other hand, if the subsystem is a prison, the effect of the new subsystem upon staff, inmates, and parole policies should be investigated. A specific list of the areas of measurement which the experimenter can ordinarily use to describe external processes when the subsystem is implanted within an institution and techniques for measuring them can be found in Chapter 9.

If any aspect of the subsystem extends into the community, the effects of this implant are also part of its external processes. The subsystem will have an effect upon the neighborhood where it is located and upon the individuals with whom it has contact, whether socially, in the pursuit of business, or in its daily living functions. For example, if the subsystem provides a residence and employment for its members, researchers should document its effect upon the business community, other workers, the unions, and other community organizations as well as documenting the effect of the residence upon the neighborhood.

Another aspect of a subsystem's external processes is its economic relationship to the larger community. Different subsystems will have different economic variables operative because of their different function. There are profit and nonprofit subsystems; subsystems that produce a saleable product and subsystems that do not; subsystems that are subsidized by the government and those that are not; and so forth. Clearly, the economic variables that are important to the operation of one subsystem may not be important in another. The experimentalist therefore must determine those economic variables important in the subsystems that he is comparing and describe them as accurately as possible, using common terms such as income and assets. Generally, the cost of living for each individual, income received, and equipment needed are important research records. Particular attention should be given to economic variables that can be used in a comparative manner. Institutions are frequently concerned with the daily cost per inmate and comparative subsystems established as alternatives to total institutional living should, therefore, keep cost records so that the subsystems can be compared on per capita cost. Whereas the economic variables that are important in the particular research situation must be determined by the researcher, there are several measures that are common to most subsystems. Their measurement is described in Chapter 9.

To summarize, the three attributes of any subsystem which should be clearly defined, described, and measured are those of its participants, the social situation in which the subsystem operates, and the outcome criterion on which it is evaluated. The degree to which any subsystem can be replicated depends upon the degree to which these dimensions are clearly defined and measured. And the value to society of any social subsystem depends upon the degree to which the outcome criterion upon which it is evaluated represents a consensual solution to a pressing social problem.

Chapter 7

Making Social Subsystems Comparable

Any social subsystem can be made comparable with any other subsystem by controlling the effects of selected variables. However, unlike a laboratory research situation, variables here cannot be eliminated from consideration simply by deleting them from the experimental situation, because researches must occur in a natural social setting. Social innovative experiments therefore have, as the usual mechanism to control extraneous variables, the equating of the created subsystems on those variables the experimenter does not wish to evaluate at the moment. As a first step in making subsystems comparable, the experimenter may draw upon his own knowledge of the social problem to identify and define those variables that enter into the social organization of the relevant subsystems.

He is typically interested in the effect upon that social organization of a limited number of important variables. He may, for example, be concerned about the effect of different groupings of people, such as homogeneous and hetrogeneous ability groupings of elementary students, upon their perception of others and upon their class performance, or about the effect of guaranteed postprison employment upon prisoner recidivism, or the effects of other sample groups or social situations on a variety of outcome criteria. In order to ascertain the effects of particular participant and social situation variables on the outcomes of a subsystem, it is necessary to isolate their effects from the whole of the social organization. Tables 6.3 and 6.4 contain a number of variables, any one of which could affect the outcomes of a social subsystem. Since the experimenter is usually interested only in evaluating the effects that a few of these variables have upon the social change outcome criterion, it is necessary to control all other identifiable variables that might affect the outcome. Logically and ideally, this can be accomplished by equating each subsystem for every variable except those whose effects the researcher wishes to evaluate. Suppose, for example, the researcher is interested in the effects of guaranteed postprison employment upon criminal recidivism. Two matched groups of prisoners could receive the same conditions of incarceration, such as living in the same cell block, working in the same place, and being imprisoned for the same length of time. Upon release, the experimental group could be placed in employment while the control group could be continued under the traditional practices of the prison, provided that guaranteed employment was not its usual practice. For even more information about the effects of guaranteed employment upon criminal recidivism, postprison employment could be varied in a graded series so that different experimental groups would have equivalent prison programs but different conditions of postprison employment, such as different places and types of work, as presented in Paradigm 1 (p. 44).

Making subsystems identical on all variables except those one wishes to evaluate enables one to distill the effects of the experimental variable or variables of the subsystem. To make subsystems comparable, so that the effects of the selected experimental variable or variables can be readily ascertained, the experimenter equates the comparative subsystems on important variables whose effects he is not interested in evaluating at the time. It is here that the experimenter's knowledge of the social problem, usually accumulated through extensive personal observation, is so important. He must decide, in collaboration with the research team, which are the important variables that must be evaluated or equated for control. For example, the experimenter may wish to discover the effects of different methods of teaching upon the achievement of the participants. Since current studies indicate that residence based on socioeconomic factors may affect intellectual performance (Katz, 1964), the experimenter would wish to have areas of equivalent socioeconomic status in which to activate the programs. On the other hand, the experimenter might decide to evaluate the effect of such areas upon the performance of students, in which case he would offer the same educational program in different socioeconomic areas. The participants or social situation variables—criminals, students or educational programs, socioeconomic areas, and so on—can be either independent variables (experimental), dependent variables (outcome), or one of the variables equated (controlled) so that their effects are constant in each subsystem. Equating subsystems for important variables so that they are constant in each one results in controlling sources of extraneous variance.

It is also important to recognize that the variables of the first experiments involved in a particular social problem are more crude than they will be when knowledge has been accumulated. Thus, in the prison example just given, the postprison employment situation is considered a variable that differentiates one subsystem from the other. If an experiment shows that postprison employment does significantly affect the recidivism rate (outcome), the experimentalist may then wish to utilize different employment situations as variables in subsequent studies so that the type of work situation that contributes most to reduction in recidivism can be ascertained. The experimenter may, for example, compare group with individual work situations, money with peer group acceptance as rewards, and other more refined variables. The variables are also more crude in the initial researches because they are carried out in order to ascertain the effects of gross differences between subsystems. Again, referring to the prison study just mentioned, from a logical point of view it is first essential to determine whether postprison guaranteed employment significantly reduces recidivism. If it does, then more finite comparisons concerned with type, amount, and other more refined attributes of particular employment situations can be explored. If it does not, other promising broad variables which might reduce recidivism can be explored. This essentially follows the decision-making paradigm of successive approximations to problem solution as suggested by recent writing in decision theory (Luce and Raiffa, 1957).

There are, of course, certain variables, unique to specific situations, which the experimenter may not wish to control, but would rather observe and measure so that he can later determine their relationships through statistical associative techniques. One example would be the use of drugs in treating the mentally ill or drug addicts. The amount and type of these biochemical agents are determined by the prescription of physicians. Thus individuals participating in the experimental subsystems may receive different dosages depending upon their particular needs. If the drug or drug dosage is not varied systematically by the physician as an integral part of the program, accurate records must be kept. An analysis of these records would reveal whether drug or drug dosage has had an impact upon the population of the subsystem. If the effects of such variables appear exceedingly important, systematic studies under appropriate supervision can later be accomplished. Upon occasion, however, there are events that occur only once and for this reason escape reliable quantitative measurement (pp. 192–193). In such instances the experimentalist must rely upon observation rather than precisely controlled conditions for information. With adequate planning, however, such instances can be relatively rare.

While the variables that are to be manipulated or controlled in any experiment must be determined by the nature of the social problem under investigation, there are general classes of variables that are relevant to all social innovative experiments. These variables are those defining the sample participating in the subsystem, those internal to the subsystem, and those external to the subsystem. Tables 6.3 and 6.4 present lists of common variables in these three categories. A detailed discussion of these variables appears in Chapter 6 and techniques for measuring them in Chapter 9.

A careful examination of Tables 6.3 and 6.4 shows that any one of the listed variables could affect the performance of the subsystem. Any variable, molar or molecular, that might affect the performance of a subsystem, must be treated either as an *independent* (experimental), *dependent* (outcome), or *equated* (controlled) variable in the social innovative experiment. That is why it is useful here to closely examine how the three classes of variables can affect the subsystems and how these effects can be controlled.

Participant Variables

The first important category of variables which affects such a subsystem is obviously the sample of people who participate in it. This includes all individuals, whether professional staff, service personnel, or the participating members themselves. Because experimental social innovation occurs in institutions or community settings where a research staff establishes the subsystems, the staff has roles and statuses in the subsystems, at least during their developmental phases. Therefore, the experimentalist needs to be cognizant of the population characteristics of the staff as well as those of members participating in the subsystem.

It is also important in this connection to examine some of the methods that can be used to equate subsystems for participating members. As shown in Table 6.1, the experimenter often wishes to vary internal or external social process variables to find how they affect the outcome. In such a case, the subsystems typically need to have equivalent member populations. Table 6.3 presents demographic, personality, and intelligence characteristics which can be measured. Then a score can be assigned to each member of the sample. After such scores are ascertained, individuals can be matched on the appropriate characteristics and then they can be randomly assigned to the different subsystems. Each population experiencing a particular social problem usually has a few *defining attributes* which, when equated, make the sample of the subsystems comparable. A detailed discussion of matching procedures for samples is presented in Chapter 8.

Determining the nature of an individual's membership in the subsystem is also exceedingly important, particularly whether such membership is voluntary or involuntary. Prisoners, elementary and high school students, some of the mentally ill, and others are involuntary members of subsystems. For experimental purposes, it is important that membership in the different subsystems be equivalent. Thus one cannot logically compare on outcome and processes two subsystems, one with voluntary and the other with involuntary membership, because the two conditions of membership might differentially affect both the outcome and process measures. The condition of membership in an experimental sample is an increasingly important problem with the advent of the new antipoverty programs whose members are usually voluntary. In such cases, it is possible to generalize only to other voluntary populations (pp. 204–205).

Each subsystem usually has a staff of professionals who participate in the subsystem. They serve as leaders, consultants, and in other statuses. Because of this, it is necessary to equate staffs for each subsystem. Even though individual staff members are matched on variables such as age, education, socioeconomic level, and so on, they are likely to behave differently as groups. The experimenter must be cognizant of this difference in group behavior because staffs usually play a dominant role in experimental social innovation, particularly where total institutions such as prisons and hospitals are the research setting. When the experimenter wishes to compare subsystems with established statuses and roles, it is essential that the individual demographic characteristics and team styles of the staffs be equated for each subsystem.

When there are several staffs, they may be rotated through the subsystems in a prearranged order, spending equivalent time in each, so that the effect of the staffs and the order in which they serve in the subsystems is equated. This methodological technique is called counterbalancing and is fully discussed by Lindquist (1953, pp. 162–163). It is frequently the case, however, that time and money will not permit the large number of staffs necessary to achieve adequate counterbalancing. In such instances, each research staff should spend an equivalent amount of time in every subsystem even though the order in which the staffs participate in the subsystem, first in one and then the other, cannot be varied to eliminate the effects of such a rotation. However, the effect of the order in which the staffs serve can be somewhat minimized by having each staff spend a rather lengthy and equivalent period of time in each program.

The result of switching staffs in order to equate the staffs' roles in the subsystems is presented in a recent publication (Fairweather, 1964, p. 33). There, only two staffs were available for the two experimental conditions. Obviously, one staff had to appear in one of the experimental conditions first so that the order in which the staffs participated in the subsystems could not be equated. However, the two staffs were switched from one program to the other in order to provide equal time in each. It was found that the change in staff morale accompanying the switch was more pronounced when one subsystem was valued more than the other. Nonetheless, the immediate effects of the change were largely dissipated in about three months. From this information, therefore, it appears that staffs serving in the same experimental condition for periods of six months to a year, provided they spent equal time in each subsystem, would greatly reduce the order effects. Also, it is possible to analyze the experimental measures in small time increments, such as months, and then to compare the different months for the effects of the switch, giving particular attention to those months immediately prior and subsequent to the switch.

This example illustrates that experiments in social innovation must, upon occasion, rely upon careful observation rather than the more desirable controls, because time and money do not permit experimental procedures that could readily be accomplished in the laboratory. It is questionable whether most research budgets could afford the number and varying compositions of staffs that are necessary to meet counterbalancing procedures, regardless of how desirable this procedure might be. Extensive observation and measurement are substituted for experimental control in these instances. An example of this technique is discussed by Vitale (1964, pp. 218–230).

Social Situational Variables

Internal Processes

The second category of variables that can affect the subsystem is the social situation. One class of its processes are those that are internal to the subsystem and describe and define its dynamic properties. A list of these internal social processes can be found in Table 6.4. One or more of these processes can constitute the independent variable or variables of the social subsystem. Thus the effects of vertical or horizontal social organization, of different reinforcement systems, and, particularly, of different status and role relationships define differences between the internal processes of the created subsystems and are often the independent variables in the social innovative experiment. These internal processes, however, are not independent of one another; indeed, a recent study reveals that three common dimensions explain the structure of group dynamics. They are morale, leadership, and performance (Maynard, 1966). In any naturalistic social setting, certain of these process variables are the result of the social organization and cannot be independently varied. Among these are performance, cohesiveness, attitudes, and morale. To elaborate, let us take morale as one example. It is the product of the social subsystem and it is difficult to conceive of a naturalistic social situation where the researcher could create beforehand a precise experimentally required amount of morale so that it could function as an independent or equated variable. Those variables that can be experimentally manipulated and, therefore, can be independent or equated variables are those that can be varied *prior* to the onset of the experiment.

Table 7.1 presents the internal process variables classified into those

Table 7.1. Experimentally Manipulatable and Nonmanipulatable Internal Social Process Variables in a Naturalistic Social Setting

Manipulatable—Varied (Independent or Equated Variables)	Nonmanipulatable—Resultant (Dependent Variables)
Size	Performance
Composition	Cohesiveness
Type of social organization (horizontal, vertical, etc.)	Attitudes
	Morale
Type of work (social, productive, etc.)	
Work organization (team or individual)	
Norms	
Reinforcement	
Communication	
Leadership	
Statuses and roles	
Degree of autonomy	
Voluntary or involuntary membership	
Fiscal processes	
Program (time spent in activities)	

that can be experimentally manipulated (independent or equated variables) and those that are the products of the system (dependent variables). If the experimenter desires to make internal social processes equivalent—constant for each experimental population—in order to vary the population or external process variables, then all manipulatable variables must be equated for the experimental subsystems. On the other hand, when the experimentalist desires to explore differences between the internal social organizations of the subsystems he must clearly identify those internal process variables he is equating and those he is experimentally varying. For example, in the hospital study the member and staff roles were varied for the two subsystems while keeping other internal variables constant.

". . . In the traditional program, all problems regarding the patient are taken up with him as an individual matter. His role is very clearly a subordinate one in which he relies upon the staff for their final decisions without any voice about possible courses of action. On the other hand, the social system of the small-group treatment program clearly delineates the patient's role as that of participant in group discussion and recommendations . . . .

"The different roles for the patients, in turn, required different roles for the staffs . . . .

"On the traditional ward, the psychologist was responsible for scheduling the patients' daily activities, discussing problems with them . . . . In this program, the role of the social worker usually involved contacts with relatives and discharge plans for selected patients . . . . The nurse dispensed medication, kept accurate accounts of patients' behaviors, assigned beds to new patients . . . and, in general, carried out the nursing function with the help of the nursing assistants.

"On the other hand, the roles were quite different on the small-group ward . . . . Once a week, each of the four task groups of patients met with staff and presented their recommendations to them. The staff, then, adjourned to a room where the recommendations were discussed and either accepted, rejected, or amended. Usually the psychologist led the discussion but had no vote . . . . The nurse, social worker, and nursing assistants voted upon each recommendation of the patients' task groups. When discharge plans for their members were completed by the task groups, an appointment was arranged for the potential dischargee with the social worker. During this meeting the plans were discussed and were approved, disapproved, or changes were recommended. The decision reached was presented in writing to the task group. The psychologist received notes from the various task groups which concerned task group recommendations about their members, requests for appointments, and requests for consultation during the task group meeting hour. In addition to the usual medical responsibilities and membership in the staff evaluation team, the nurse and nursing assistants frequently placed notes in the task groups' boxes informing each of the task groups about problem behavior of task group members . . . ." (Fairweather, 1964, pp. 31–32.)

Subsystems are also typically equated for programs—time spent in the prescribed activities—except for those differences required to evaluate the independent variables. An example of equating subsystems for programming in order to make subsystems comparable may also be found in the hospital experiment just cited. The two subsystems in the hospital experiment (traditional and small group) were equated for their programs except for those aspects of the subsystems that constituted the independent variable. Table 7.2 presents these two programs.

"This table shows that the only differences between each day in the treatment programs, with regard to patient assignments, are the hours from 8:00 to 9:00 and from 11:00 to 12:00 on the small-group ward. During those two hours, the task groups met on the ward. From 8:00 to 9:00 they engaged in a ward housekeeping task, and from 11:00 to 12:00 they held task group meetings during which decisions and recommendations about group members were discussed. To provide a control for these two hours, patients participating in the traditional program had work assignments. The differential use of these two hours in the treatment programs provided the time and the social atmosphere for the development of problem-solving task groups, which is the major experimental variable in this study." (Fairweather, 1964, pp. 28–29.)

External Processes

The third category of variables that must be controlled or varied are those external to the subsystem. Table 6.4 lists them as time, social climate, state of the economy, socioeconomic area in which the subsystem is implanted, geographical location (urban, suburbs, rural), social location (institution or community), the measuring techniques in the experiment, and relationships to other community institutions. The social climate concerns the degree of acceptance of the sub-

Table 7.2. Program for the Two Social Subsystems

	Small-Group Ward	Traditional Ward
A.M. 6:00–6:30	Lights on in dormitory	Lights on in dormitory
6:30–7:30	Bedmaking, shaving, bathing	Bedmaking, shaving, bathing
7:30–7:55	Breakfast	Breakfast
7:55–8:00	Medication	Medication
8:00–9:00	Task group ward housekeeping	Individual work assignments
9:00–10:00	Ward meeting hour	Individual work assignments
10:00–11:00	Recreation hour	Ward meeting hour
11:00–12:00	Autonomous meetings of task groups	Recreation hour
P.M. 12:00–12:05	Medication	Medication
12:05–12:30	Free time	Free time
12:30–1:00	Lunch	Lunch
1:00–4:00	Individual work assignments	Individual work assignments
4:00–5:30	Ward activity— patients' choice (recreation, shower, socialize, etc.)	Ward activity— patients' choice (recreation, shower, socialize, etc.)
5:30–6:10	Dinner	Dinner
6:10–9:00	Off-ward recreation, i.e., library, dance, etc.	Off-ward recreation, i.e., library, dance, etc.
9:00–9:05	Medication	Medication
9:05–10:00	Free time	Free time
10:00	Bedtime	Bedtime

system by those in whose area it is implanted. If the experimenter wishes to evaluate the effect of social climates he may vary them and measure their effect on some selected outcome criterion. To achieve this, he might compare the same social subsystem implanted in an institution or community hostile to it and in another institution or community friendly to it. Repeated measurements over a period of time might reveal how the social climate in which they are implanted affected the subsystems and how the subsystems, in turn, affected it. Usually, however, the experimenter wishes to equate the social climate in which different subsystems are placed so that he can measure the effect of participant or internal social process variables. Accordingly, the experimenter attempts to locate the two subsystems in the same institution (school, prison, hospital) and community locations. He would implant the subsystems in the same area, particularly if different areas of the institution or community have different social definitions, such as those of closed contrasted with open wards in a mental hospital or industrial contrasted with residential areas in a community.

Closely associated with social climate, and sometimes indistinguishable from it, is the variable of geographical location. This variable, like social climate, may be varied or equated. Here, the experimenter needs to consider the state, county, and city similarities or differences, the urban or rural nature of the setting, and, if urban, the socioeconomic area of the city in which the social subsystem is to be located. Suppose, for example, that two elementary school subsystems were created and placed in two schools where the social change outcome criterion was academic achievement. It would be of great importance that both schools be located in the same city and in the same socioeconomic neighborhoods if the experimenter was attempting to control socioeconomic environment and geographical location by equating them.

This presents another important place for control in social innovative experiments. It also points up a difficulty. In making social subsystems comparable, it is often necessary to locate them in as similar an environment as possible while, at the same time, preventing the social interaction of the different subsystems' participants so that the effects of one subsystem do not contaminate the others. Particular care, then, must be given the location of the subsystems. If located in the same environment, there must be sufficient geographical or social distance among the subsystems to prevent the contaminating interactions. One method of accomplishing this is to place the subsystems within the same socioeconomic area but separated by sufficient geographical distance so that the people living in the subsystems use different community facilities—stores, and so on. Thus, the probability of their interaction is very small indeed. On the other hand, if the geographical area where one subsystem is located is too small to accommodate more than the one subsystem, others can be located in geographically separate areas where the same socioeconomic conditions exist. Krech, Crutchfield, and Ballachey (1962) present a socioeconomic index developed by Tryon which can be used for this purpose. It is especially valuable because scores for different geographical locations can be directly obtained from census data.

One variable external to the subsystems impinges upon them as one attempts to investigate them: this variable is the measuring procedures employed. Tests, interviews, ratings, and other assessment devices are the measuring tools of the experimenter. Equivalent procedures should be applied to all experimental subsystems, since the assessment techniques are not usually independent or dependent variables. To accomplish this, the same individual should do the testing, rating, or interviewing for all participants in every subsystem. The room where the testing and interviewing takes place should be the same for people participating in all the subsystems. The instructions should be the same. The hospital study just mentioned also gives an example of this.

". . . the recreation hour was a rather laissez-faire situation. Patients were informed that they could do anything within the confines of the ward that they wished to do, and with whomever they desired during this hour. To describe the patients' behavior during the recreation hour, the Location Activity Inventory . . . , developed at FDR Veterans Administration Hospital in Montrose, New York, was selected and extensively modified to accomplish the desired comparisons. The *same* trained rater recorded patients' behavior for both wards . . . ." (Goldman, 1964, p. 49.)

Time is another important variable that may substantially affect most social innovative research. It is important that all subsystems are activated and terminated on the same date. Fluctuations in economic and political climates, as well as attitude changes among the citizens, will influence the conditions present at any given moment. Information gained in one time period may not be comparable to that gained in another. To take but one example, community subsystems that use employment as a criterion measure would yield quite different results if some subsystems, activated during a general depression, were compared with subsystems that were operated during a period of prosperity. It is, therefore, necessary to compare subsystems during the same periods of time. In this regard, experimenters who do not establish comparative subsystems but, rather, attempt to use a single subsystem as its own control by measuring the outcome criterion at different moments of time, cannot logically attribute any changes found solely to the variables operating in the subsystem, because processes that occur between measurements can affect some conditions that might, in turn, change outcomes. About this matter Cochran and Cox (1957, p. 14) have said:

"If a control is required, it must be an integral part of the experiment so that results for the control are directly comparable with those for the other treatments. This point tends to be overlooked in experiments with human subjects when it is difficult or troublesome to assemble the desired number of subjects. For example, if a new drug is to be tested in some ward of a hospital, the recovery rate in the ward before the drug was introduced is not a satisfactory control, nor is the recovery rate in a different ward where patients happen to be receiving the standard drug. An observed difference between the effects of the new and the standard drug might be due to differences in the severity of the disease or in the type of patient or in other aspects of the medical care in the two time-periods or the two wards . . . ."

The use of comparative subsystems opening and closing on the same dates is the only manner in which the outcomes of subsystems can be logically compared.

There are also the traditions of the institution or community where the subsystems are operative. Different institutions or different units within an institution frequently have quite divergent mores and folkways. Thus, for example, one prison may parole inmates as quickly as possible while another, with a norm of maximum custody, may rarely parole prisoners at all. In mental hospitals, the ward social climate is established by the staff—one ward climate may be authoritarian, another democratic, and yet another laissez-faire—so that two wards within the same mental hospital may have drastically different social climates. In order that the experimental programs are operated under the same conditions, the different subsystems should be activated in the same institutions and in the same living and working areas. The two subsystems of the hospital study can again be used as an example.

". . . The two wards were located in opposite ends of the building, and, consequently, their floor plans proved to be almost mirror images of each other. These plans included a porch, dayrooms, a number of ward and staff offices, two large dormitory areas, and their adjacent lavatories.

". . . by the time the program was under way, the wards were equally well equipped with books, magazines, playing cards, dominoes, checkers, and other recreational items. A 21-inch television set and regulation pool and ping-pong tables had long been established features on both wards." (Goldman, 1964, pp. 45–46).

The wards were, however, physically separated by a locked hallway of approximately 100 feet.

It is also necessary to control the publicity given the experimental program, especially that publicity which might unduly affect the subsystems. This is particularly important when new subsystems are started, because inferences from the experimental results will be made to future situations where, usually, little or no publicity will occur. Furthermore, such publicity may affect the participants in one subsystem and not those in another. This is most likely to happen when a society has an immediate interest in the new subsystem but not in the old subsystem that is the control condition. Publicity also frequently arouses the interest of lay people who may wish to visit the experimental residences and talk with the participants and, in this and other ways, interfere with the experimental procedures. For these reasons it is important that the experimenter limit publicity about the experimental program until *after* the study has been completed.

Since the nonmanipulated variables of a social innovative experiment can be from any of the three classes of experimental variables (participants, internal, and external social processes) the experimenter assumes that constancy of population and external social process variables, when combined with constancy of manipulatable internal social process variables, will yield similar results in performance, cohesiveness, attitudes, and morale (the nonmanipulatable variables) for all experimental subsystems. Despite this assumption by the experimenter, it is imperative that all of these variables, whether manipulatable or nonmanipulatable, be measured throughout the course of the experiment, so that the subsystems can later be compared on any chosen variable at any given time and its relationships with all other measured variables can be determined (pp. 164–179).

The control and manipulation of these three classes of variables—participants, internal, and external social processes—constitute the means through which social subsystems are made comparable. It is this aspect of the research planning that requires great attention to detail and it is also the aspect of the planning that clearly reveals the experimentalist's knowledge of his subject matter. It cannot be overemphasized that the variables presented in this chapter are those *usually* present in natural social situations but it is not an exhaustive list and there are many variables, not mentioned here, that are operative in specific situations. The procedures of identifying, controlling, or evaluating them as independent, dependent, or equated variables is the task of the experimentalist and should be directed to the specific social problems with which the experiment is concerned.

Making the subsystems comparable is frequently the phase of experimental social innovation that is most discouraging to the researcher, for it is here that the complexity of social problems comes clearly into focus. The large number of variables which can affect outcomes and processes and which, therefore, must be taken into consideration in the research planning, comes forcibly to the experimenter's attention. This awareness can be extremely discouraging and it may very well be that the complexity of social phenomena has prevented the growth of experimental methods for social innovation. The experimenter cannot ignore these variables if he values the results of his research efforts. However, their complexity should not serve as an excuse for failing to conduct such experiments. With considerable planning and effort, the important variables can usually be managed in a way that permits a test of the experimental hypotheses. And even though complete control of experimental variables is probably never attained in practice, it is the logical model upon which inferences rest. Thus all subsystems in each experiment must be made as comparable as possible on those variables that need to be controlled. This close attention to adequate control in the planning phase of the experiment will be rewarded at its conclusion, because such attention to detail will eventually lead to the most accurate inferences possible under the natural field conditions of a social innovative experiment.

Chapter 8

Defining the Population
and Obtaining the Sample

At any given moment there is a certain number of people experiencing a particular social problem in their society. The number of individuals in the whole of a society who are participants in a given problem represents the *population* for that social problem. Thus there are a certain number of chronically mentally ill, socially deprived, school drop-outs, and other marginal persons in the entire country who are participants in its many social problems at any one particular time. These populations overlap and change from moment to moment as the result of several variables, such as population increases, economic conditions, and changing attitudes. Because the social innovative experimenter wishes to establish subsystems that have general applicability, he attempts to select from the total problem population a *sample* that is *representative* of it.

A sample that is to be representative of those individuals experiencing a given social problem—one that yields valid information about the effects of a social subsystem in solving the social problem for the affected population—must be selected at random. To attain randomness, the experimenter must exercise no choice about the selection of individuals within the framework of the sampling procedures chosen. Exercising such a choice makes useless the probability tables from which inferences about the effectiveness of the subsystems will later be made. It is easy for social innovative experimentalists to ignore the principle of random selection because random samples are often difficult to attain. Such difficulties are particularly pronounced when the research is completed in institutional settings, since appropriate sampling procedures require institutional commitments to new solutions for their problems. Experimental necessities for innovative solutions are quite often in conflict with existing institutional norms (pp.

31–33). Nonetheless, the experimentalist must strive for random selection although even with perfect cooperation—a condition rarely achieved—it is doubtful that randomness ever occurs in naturalistic settings.

Concerning random selection under field conditions, Snedecor (1956, pp. 7–8) states:

"Randomness in sampling is perhaps never quite attained in practice. It is nevertheless the mathematical model on which most statistical theory rests, and since the theory must be used in drawing conclusions from work-a-day samplings, it is to the interest of the investigator to approximate, as closely as feasible, the ideal conditions. The better the approximation, the more nearly correct will be the inferences drawn."

The selection of the problem is the first step in determining the population with which the experimenter is concerned. For example, if the experimenter chooses to study the effects of heterogeneous and homogeneous groupings of students upon academic achievement, by this choice he has limited his population to students. He then may decide that he is interested in the effect of these different group compositions on the performance of elementary school students. And then later he may be concerned only with elementary students in suburbs around large urban communities where middle class and upper middle class families reside, because his information might show that homogeneous (the track system) and heterogeneous groupings occur most frequently in these settings, and they are a continuous source of difficulty there. The problem therefore has immediately limited and defined the population with which the experimenter must be concerned.

In order to select a sample which meets the conditions of randomness, it is necessary after problem selection to define the characteristics of the population which will provide the participant sample. The experimenter defines the population by describing its attributes. He needs to know the distributions of age, socioeconomic status, health, educational level, and other demographic information of the problem group along with their behavioral and biological characteristics. These attributes define the problem population. Such information comes from three main sources. They are personal experience, surveys, and historical records.

Becoming acquainted with individuals who are experiencing the social problem the researcher wishes to investigate is an important first step in gaining information about the attributes of the experimental population. For example, several weeks of observation and discussion with those in a mental hospital make the experimenter keenly aware that people living in closed wards behave differently than those in open wards, despite other similarities in case histories. This then is a key attribute differentiating the two groups that cannot usually be obtained from surveys but must be taken into account in sampling procedures.

As another example, the experimenter interested in school problems should spend time observing the students in different schools. He may find gross differences in teaching methods, teacher and pupil behavior, health, and values among schools located in different socioeconomic areas. Accordingly, the experimenter may use this information to establish stratified sampling procedures for children from the different socioeconomic areas. On the other hand, he may use this information to define more clearly the population he is interested in. He may, for example, perceive the problem as more acute for pupils in one socioeconomic class than for those in another. Thus he may become concerned about the lower socioeconomic group, and if he then had interpersonal contact with them, his direct experiences might enable him to more adequately describe the lower socioeconomic population so that procedures could be initiated to appropriately sample this group. Other examples of observations in prisons, rehabilitation centers, and slums could be made. But it is imperative that the experimenter have immediate experience growing out of empirical observation to acquaint him directly with the defining attributes of the research population. This direct experience is a necessary but frequently ignored condition (see pp. 40–41).

An additional but not substitutive source of information that may be used to determine the characteristics of the population under consideration is the survey. Questionnaires may be given through interview or the mails to determine many of the demographic characteristics of the population under consideration. The data from these questionnaires may be utilized to define further the attributes of the problem population. Information from the problem population, family, friends, employers, associates, etc., can yield valuable defining information. Other sources of information, such as school records, census data, and hospital files, may be used to supplement the descriptive information collected from observations and questionnaires.

In addition to his own experiences, surveys, and other records, it is important that the social innovative experimentalist discuss the nature of the population characteristics with individuals who have extensive experience in day-to-day contacts with them. The experimenter who wishes to establish subsystems for the blind should discuss their behaviors, perceptions, and living situations not only with the blind, but also with those who daily live and work with them. The defining attributes of the problem population result from a collation of all these sources. A list of the most common descriptive information obtained from them that is most useful in describing research populations can be found under participant characteristics in Table 6.3.

After the population has been defined, it is then necessary to select a *representative* sample from it to participate in each experimental subsystem. Representative samples are needed because if differences are found when comparing the outcomes of the subsystems, the experimenter will want to generalize the observed results to the problem population from which the samples were drawn. Many and varied sampling procedures have been established to accomplish this. A complete discussion of them is outside the scope of this book, but the essential characteristics of sampling techniques as applied to experimental social innovation will be briefly presented. For a more detailed discussion of the complex problem of sampling, surveys, and experimental design, the reader is referred to Yates (1949) and Cochran (1963).

The sampling techniques utilized by the experimenter must be those that yield the most information from a relatively small sample. This is necessary because the social subsystems with which the experimentalist must work are expensive and difficult to establish. Usually the experimenter has a limited budget that he uses to establish living and working situations in either institutions, the community, or both. Furthermore, when new subsystems are established requiring living arrangements, a frequent occurrence with marginal groups, there typically will be very limited space. It is important, therefore, that the experimenter utilize the most efficient sampling procedures possible consistent with an adequate research design. To receive the most accurate information for his research investment, the experimenter, whenever possible, uses matched samples as participants in the created subsystems. Matched samples, contrasted with unmatched samples of equal number, increase the probability that accurate inferences about the outcomes of the subsystems can be made from the research results by minimizing the effects that different participants can have upon outcomes. Reducing differences between participating samples is particularly important when the experimenter is attempting to establish the effect of social situation variables upon outcomes.

To control for the effect that different participants might have on the subsystems' outcomes, then, it is most efficient to match individuals who will participate in the subsystems and then to assign each of them randomly to one of the experimental subsystems. The gain in efficiency and information brought about by using matched samples compared with unmatched samples is discussed by McNemar (1962, pp. 82–86), and the techniques of random assignment to the different subsystems (conditions) can be found in Snedecor (1956, pp. 9–14) and Dixon and Massey (1957, pp. 33–35).

Before matching procedures can be initiated, however, it is necessary to define the key variables on which the participants should be matched. If the experimenter has been living and working with such individuals, has conducted surveys, explored records, and discussed the problem of his selected population with people who have experience in the field, he should be able to identify the key defining variables of the population. He can then collect items of information that describe these variables. He obtains descriptive statistics (usually means and standard deviations) about these population items. Since his geographical location may limit the representativeness of his sample, the descriptive statistics he collects can then be compared with national figures, if they are available. Comparisons of the sample with national statistics on key defining variables give the experimenter information about the representativeness of his sample.

It is important, however, to caution the experimenter about the use of national statistics collected by others. The experimenter should meticulously investigate the manner in which the national data were collected and how the statistics were computed before using them for comparative purposes. This is particularly true with national statistics about marginal groups, where descriptive statistics are sometimes distorted because of social factors like prejudice; on other occasions they may be distorted because of the data collection and computation of the statistic itself. An example of the latter was found in the computation of the annual irregular discharge rate (leaving the hospital against medical advice) among tuberculosis patients by Moran, Fairweather, and Morton (1956). They discovered the following:

"A small group of individuals, probably no more than 10 or 15 percent of all people hospitalized for tuberculosis, appear to constitute the entire irregular discharge problem. This small group, through repeated irregular discharges, builds up the reported annual irregular discharge rate to almost 50 percent."

This is the type of computation that must be clearly understood before comparisons with national statistics can be appropriately made.

It is most important that complete demographic information is obtained for the sample population and is presented in any publication of the research results (p. 209). This is necessary because future researchers may wish to replicate the study or compare the sample with other samples.

Since the experimenter wishes to generalize from a finite sample to the problem population, it would be desirable if the sample could be drawn from the national population. Suppose the experimenter is establishing different subsystems for the newly formed Job Corps. Let us further suppose that he is interested in males between the ages of 18 and 21 who are in lower to lower-lower socioeconomic positions. Tryon's method of cluster analysis, applied to census data, provides a means of scoring census tracts on the basis of socioeconomic variables (Krech, Crutchfield, and Ballachey, 1962, pp. 319–326). Those falling into lower and lower-lower socioeconomic levels can thus be identified. Then, appropriate sampling methods are applied to the national geographical areas involved, using procedures such as those developed by organizations doing national surveys like the Bureau of the Census (1947). In this way, individuals from different geographical areas can be matched on key variables and each of the matched participants can then be randomly assigned to the created social subsystems. This desirable national sampling procedure, however, is usually not available to the social innovative experimenter. Often he must obtain his sample under far less than ideal conditions. He may, for example, have access to the population of only one institution or, at best, several institutions within one geographical area. Although the experimentalist always attempts to compare the descriptive information of his sample with national figures and continuously advocates replications in order to discover the generality of his findings, he still must establish his sampling procedures within the framework of the practical limitations imposed upon him by his own social situation.

Because the social innovative experimenter is usually interested in marginal populations, his sampling procedures are typically less complex because key defining matching characteristics of these populations are often limited in number. Simplification of matching procedures occurs because most marginal groups have a few well-defined attributes that clearly differentiate them from other social groups and, in addition, are slow to change over time. For example, most chronically hospitalized mental patients receive high dosages of tranquilizing medication, without which they become grossly disorganized—hallucinated or deluded—and they have long hospital residence; culturally and socially disadvantaged persons have low educational achievement, have high rates of school drop-outs among adolescents, are frequently Negroes, and have high rates of unemployment; the blind and the physically handicapped also have obvious differentiating features. Because of the representativeness of these attributes for particular marginal groups, it is frequently possible to generalize quite widely from a small sample of participants who are carefully matched on these key features.

In a recent experiment, for example, the effectiveness of four psychotherapeutic treatment programs was compared for three different groups of mental patients (Fairweather et al., 1960). Previous experience and research information indicated that different patient groups (neurotics, acute and chronic psychotics) might respond differently to the four treatment regimens. Research information further suggested that patients of different ages might also respond differently to the treatment conditions. Accordingly, patients in groups of four were matched on age, diagnosis, and length of hospitalization (the three key variables) and each member of the group was then randomly assigned to one of four treatment situations. By matching on the three key variables, the participants in each treatment were also matched on other important characteristics, such as education, level of employment, and occupational status. The degree of similarity that was achieved by matching on these three defining variables is shown in Table 8.1.

Further examples may be found in other areas for social innovative research. Katz's recent article (1964) suggests that to be comparable, students should be matched on educational background with special reference to socioeconomic level, and a summary article by Holland and Richards (1965) indicates the need to consider past academic achievement (grades) in any matching procedures applied to students. Thus grades and socioeconomic level are two key variables that need to be considered when creating relatively equivalent groups that might participate in different school social subsystems. Another example may be found in the relationship between recidivism and chronicity in a criminal population (State of California, 1965, pp. 90–94). The number of previous incarcerations is one key variable that must be considered when matching populations in order to

Table 8.1. Comparison of the Four Treatment Groups on Demographic Characteristics [a]

Variable	GG	G	I	C	Test of Significance
Matching variables					
Diagnoses					
% character disorders	12.5	12.5	12.5	12.5	
% neurotics	20.8	20.8	20.8	20.8	$\chi^2 = 0$
% psychotics	66.7	66.7	66.7	66.7	
Mean age	36.25	33.17	34.21	34.92	$F = \ldots$ [b]
Mean weeks of prior NP hospitalization [c]	51.6	49.2	53.8	54.8	$F = \ldots$
Concurrent variable					
% receiving tranquilizing drugs	54	58	58	42	$\chi^2 = 1.58$
Demographic variables					
Education					
Mean grade completed	10.5	10.6	11.0	11.2	$F = \ldots$
Race					
% white	79	75	75	75	$\chi^2 = .17$
% Negro	21	25	25	25	
% pensioned for NP illness	67	50	67	58	$\chi^2 = 1.52$
Mean age of first NP hospitalization	28.5	27	29	31	$F = \ldots$
Employment					
Mean % time employed in past 10 years	71.5	75	68	71	$F = \ldots$
Mean weekly salary of last job	74.3	63.2	68.5	62.7	$F = \ldots$
Occupational status					
% professional-managerial	12.5	20.8	25	16.7	
% skilled trades, sales, clerical	33.3	20.8	20.8	20.8	$\chi^2 = 2.48$
% unskilled workers	54.2	58.4	54.2	62.5	
Marital status					
% currently married	25	33	25	25	$\chi^2 = .53$
% single or divorced	75	67	75	75	

[a] GG—Group living; G—Group psychotherapy; I—Individual psychotherapy; C—Work.

[b] The F ratio value . . . indicates that the within-group variance was greater than the between-group variance.

[c] NP—Neuropsychiatric.

explore the effect of innovated rehabilitative programs. These illustrations all indicate that when knowledge is accumulated about a particular problem, it is often found that samples can be equated by matching the participants on a few important key variables. It is the experimenter's knowledge of the variables that noticeably identify a particular population which aids him in creating the matched samples.

These procedures are sufficient if the subsystems within which the individuals are to participate are closed social systems without input or output of members. However, such is rarely the case in naturalistic settings. In these settings the experimentalist usually draws his matched pairs, triads, etc., at the beginning of the study in order to achieve equivalently matched participants at the outset. Matching procedures and random assignments are thus only the first stage in a multistage sampling process that continues over time. After the initial matched sample is obtained and the subsystems become operative, the major sampling problem becomes one of securing additional matched participants while, at the same time, preserving the dynamic naturalistic properties of the social subsystems.

There are, of course, many multistage sampling procedures which can be adopted to assure randomness and adequate matching that will increase the possibility of attaining representative, matched samples to participate in the created subsystems. If the research is carried out in an institution, arrangements for a sampling pool can be made. After the initial matching procedures have been completed and assignments to the subsystems have been made, the subsystems can then be put in operation. At the same time, a building to house incoming participants can be located at a considerable distance from the building where the research is being conducted. New participants can live in this unit for an equivalent and prearranged time during which demographic and other information is obtained from them. The new residents can then be matched in pairs or groups of individuals, depending on the number of subsystems, and randomly assigned to one of them. The advantage of this procedure is that it guarantees a matched sample while also controlling for the influence of the time variable. The disadvantage of the pool system is that it requires considerable administrative commitment and the establishment of a separate unit in which the new members of the sample can reside prior to their assignment. However, these multistage sampling procedures are most important when the research is done in an institutional setting. Examples of the use of a sampling pool for matching purposes can be found in Sanders, MacDonald, and Maynard (1964, pp. 197–198) and Maynard (1964).

Another multistage procedure may be employed when management cannot support the establishment of a residence where matching procedures can take place. The first stage consists of the matching and random assignment procedures just described. They are followed by a second stage consisting of simple random assignment to the experimental subsystems. The procedure merely requires that after initial matching and random assignment each new candidate for participation in the created subsystems is assigned to the study on admission, without bias, to any of the subsystems. This procedure is less precise than the two-stage matched procedure used when a sampling pool is available, because it depends upon chance phenomena to continue the equivalence of the matched samples achieved in the first stage. Nonetheless, this less efficient technique is sometimes necessary in institutional research where research procedures are frequently perceived as interfering with ongoing service programs and where permitting the initial matches is distressing enough to institutional management. An example of first stage matched and second stage random assignment may be found in Fairweather (1964, pp. 33–36). A more detailed discussion of management commitments required to establish appropriate procedures may be found in Chapter 4.

Multistage sampling procedures are also used in community settings where assignment is accomplished by making agreements with the appropriate institutions for a random selection of matched participants prior to their leaving the participating institution. Here the experimenter may be concerned with mental hospitals, prisons, and other total institutions. Several such institutions may cooperate in the overall sampling by each contributing a specified number of matched participants to the study. These participants may be matched and then randomly assigned to the different community subsystems upon release from the institution. Thus a continuing flow of matched participants can be provided without the necessity for establishing a sampling pool by close cooperation with the involved institutions.

Although the administrative commitments are more extensive for institutional research, community subsystems usually have an additional sampling problem that does not exist in the institution. Total institutions—mental hospitals, prisons, and so on—assign their residents to the programs established by the institution. Usually such assignments are involuntary. Individuals are assigned to experimental programs without the approval of the participants. Schools, particularly elementary and high schools, frequently assign students or require certain courses so that there is little or limited choice by the student concerning his courses or the method of teaching. On the other hand, participation in community subsystems, particularly those that involve living and working situations, requires that the participants volunteer to live and work in the program of the subsystem. The experimenter therefore often has the variable of voluntary or involuntary participation as a differentiating feature of community research compared with institutional research.

Volunteering is a sampling problem that is especially important in social innovative experiments. Most new rehabilitative programs, for example, require that individuals volunteer to participate in them. The logical question that immediately arises is whether or not the volunteers are a representative sample of all the individuals experiencing the problem. An exploration of differences between volunteers and nonvolunteers can be undertaken by surveying the differences and similarities in their attributes or by establishing a nonvolunteer comparative group. Nevertheless, direct generalization to the nonvolunteer groups is logically untenable. Generalization can only logically be made to other volunteers (pp. 204–205). This is exceedingly important, especially with those new antipoverty programs that depend upon volunteers for their population, because generalization about the success or failure of such programs for society—even when other appropriate experimental conditions are met—can be considered applicable only to those who volunteer for them. If a well-conducted survey had established that only ten percent of a problem population had volunteered for the experimental program, it would be obvious that such volunteers may not be representative of the problem population. Hence subsystems that are satisfactory for these volunteers may or may not apply to the nonvolunteers, who, in this example, constitute ninety percent of the problem population.

When the researcher is concerned with a heterogeneous population, subgroups of which might respond differently to the created subsystems, a sampling procedure that divides the population into these subgroups should be employed. This process is called stratification. In such a case, each subgroup may be treated as a separate population from which a representative sample is obtained. The experimenter may wish to divide his population into different age groups, different educational levels, or different degrees of social deprivation, if his evidence suggests that each subgroup may respond differently to the innovated subsystems.

In a previous experiment (Fairweather et al., 1960), the researchers' observations and other information about the population indicated that neurotics, short-time psychotics, and chronic psychotics might respond differently to different treatments. The experimental sample was therefore subdivided into those three strata in order that the three different diagnostic groups could be independently compared. This stratification is presented in Table 8.2. It shows that the three diagnostic groups were significantly different in the demographic characteristics of weeks of previous hospitalization, pension for mental illness, employment, and marital status. Furthermore, the results of the study showed that the chronic psychotics and neurotics made a significantly poorer community adjustment after treatment than the acute psychotics. Thus by using stratification procedures, the demographic differences that appear in Table 8.2 were highlighted and a differential response to treatment by the three diagnostic groups was established. This example illustrates that increased information can often be found when a sample is stratified into subgroups. By combining matching procedures with stratified sampling techniques, the social innovative experimenter can achieve a great deal more information from small samples than can be obtained from simple random assignment. Further detailed discussion of stratified sampling procedures may be found in *Sampling Techniques* (Cochran, 1963, pp. 87–153).

In addition to comparing the subsystems, the experimenter frequently wishes to explore the effects of the subsystems upon neighbors or others with whom the participants interact—those external to the subsystems. To evaluate these effects he may wish to interview or have questionnaires completed by residents of the area in which the subsystems are located. If the research is completed in an institution, he may be interested in the attitudes of professional groups and inmates not included in the sample. All of these sources of information must be appropriately sampled. Stratified or simple random sampling techniques can be utilized, depending upon the population sampled, the information needed, and degree of precision required. Generally, the appropriate sampling techniques are those of the survey, a discussion of which is beyond the scope of this book. The interested reader is again referred to Cochran (1963).

A problem for which there is no final and definitive solution, since an answer to it is dependent upon the influence of so many

Table 8.2. Comparison of the Three Diagnostic Groups on Demographic Characteristics [a]

Variable	N	PS	PL	Test of Significance
Matching variables				
Mean age	36.09	34.41	33.31	$F = ...$ [b]
Mean weeks of prior NP hospitalization	25.34	20.47	111.22	$F = 45.91$ †
Concurrent variables				
% receiving tranquilizing drugs	37.5	56.3	65.6	$\chi^2 = 5.27$
Demographic variables				
Education				
Mean grade completed	11.03	10.34	11.09	$F = ...$
Race				
% white	81.3	65.6	81.3	$\chi^2 = 3.94$
% Negro	18.7	34.4	18.7	
% pensioned for NP illness	37.5	59.4	90.6	$\chi^2 = 19.46$ †
Mean age of first NP hospitalization	31.19	29.75	25.88	$F = 3.06$
Employment				
Mean % of time employed in past 10 years	79.22	83.50	51.09	$F = 17.02$ †
Mean weekly salary of last job	68.06	73.72	56.13	$F = 2.37$
Occupational status				
% professional-managerial	12.5	21.9	21.9	
% skilled trades, sales, clerical	34.4	18.8	18.8	$\chi^2 = 3.32$
% unskilled workers	53.1	59.3	59.3	
Marital status				
% currently married	28.1	46.9	6.2	$\chi^2 = 13.39$ *
% single or divorced	71.9	53.1	93.8	

[a] N—Neurotics; PS—Short-term psychotics; PL—Long-term psychotics.

[b] The F ratio value . . . indicates that the within-group variance was greater than the between-group variance.

* .01 level of significance.

† .001 level of significance.

situational variables, is that of sample size. The experimenter is continuously faced with this problem. If all the population characteristics are known, an estimate of the sample size necessary to yield a statistic with a preselected level of statistical confidence can be obtained (Snedecor, 1956, pp. 60–62; Cochran, 1963, pp. 71–86).

Usually, however, the social innovative experimentalist does not have the type of information that permits him to estimate the sample size—particularly when he begins his experiments with social problem populations.   Therefore, he frequently must make an arbitrary decision about the size of the sample that is necessary for subsystem comparisons to yield information with an acceptable degree of statistical confidence.   When sufficient information about the population is not available to estimate the sample size required in the manner presented by Snedecor (1956) and Cochran (1963), it is suggested that the researcher have at least fifty matched participants in each of the subsystems.   This number is arbitrarily recommended because certain practical considerations, in addition to the statistical ones already mentioned, typically enter into the determination of sample size.   When members participating in a subsystem live in one dormitory, the size of the dormitory itself is a variable in the social subsystem.   A current experiment in a community dormitory indicates that fifty participants at any one time might very well be the upper limit for a social subsystem where dormitory living is involved (Fairweather, Sanders, Maynard, and Cressler, 1966).   With two subsystems this provides a minimum sample of 100.   Although the size of this sample is arbitrary, matched populations of at least fifty pairs or over usually yield sufficiently valid comparative and associative statistics.   This is particularly true when initial survey material shows the sample to be representative of the parent population.   The sample size, at least the minimum permissible size, should be determined prior to the onset of the experiment.   Whatever the sample size, however, its *representativeness* is its most important characteristic.

Chapter 9

Concepts and Procedures
of Measurement

The experimenter must now prepare instruments with which he can measure the attributes of the experimental subsystems' three dimensions—participants, social situation, and outcomes. Before instruments can be selected or created, however, it is essential that the researcher have an understanding of the concepts that are basic to measurement, particularly those that are used in the construction of scales. The general discussion presented here is liberally sprinkled with references so that the interested reader can easily find a more thorough presentation of the rationale and computational procedures of measurement.

It is most important that the investigator be cognizant of the fact that units of measurement for the data of social innovative experiments represent the entire spectrum of measuring scales. Generally viewed, there are four types of scales into which most social innovative data can be classified. They are the nominal, ordinal, interval, and ratio scales. Detailed definitions of these four types of scales appear in Stevens (1951) and Siegel (1956, pp. 22–30). They may be summarized as follows: *Nominal* scales are "naming" scales which specify only membership in a category. Examples are diagnostic labels such as schizophrenic or tubercular and social group membership lists such as occupational groupings like lawyer or physician. No quantitative relation is defined between any of the categories. The only formal property of this scale is equivalence within a category, that is, all members of a group are equivalent in membership. *Ordinal* scales do specify a quantitative relation among different categories (or points) of the scale, but are limited to statements of equivalence and inequality. Thus of two values *a* and *b* on an ordinal scale, one may specify only the relations "equal to," "greater than," or "less than," with no statement of the distance between unequal values. Any set of scores which may be ranked from least to most or best to worst makes an ordinal scale. An *interval* scale is formed when the distances between any two points are known for all values on the scale. Scales to measure temperature are of this type. A *ratio* scale is one which has an absolute zero point as well as all the characteristics of an interval scale. Examples are scales of mass and velocity.

Since social processes are real-life phenomena, they usually require nominal or ordinal scaling. Indeed, it is questionable whether interval or ratio scales can empirically exist with most social data, at least as these variables are now conceived. Because of this, it is usually appropriate that the experimentalist plan to create nominal or ordinal scales. Of the information which the researcher utilizes, only standard psychological tests and other investigator-constructed questionnaires and some demographic information such as age may have actual interval or ratio measurement, and even here such precision of scaling is questionable. Because of this, the experimentalist needs to categorize his information carefully so that scales appropriate for the data can be constructed. It is also important to note here that the classificatory nature of most social innovative data often requires the use of nonparametric statistical techniques, a subject more thoroughly discussed in Chapter 10.

The type of scale involved is only one of the many considerations that the experimentalist is concerned with when he enters the arena of measurement. It is important to consider here two concepts frequently associated with measurement that have historically emanated from the construction of psychological tests. These are the concepts of validity and reliability. While a detailed discussion of these two concepts of measurement cannot be presented here, it is important to examine briefly their place in the measurement of social subsystems. Excellent discussions of the concept of reliability and validity as typically used in psychological test construction are available in Anastasi (1961, pp. 105–149), Ghiselli (1964, pp. 207–253, 335–369), and Guilford (1954, pp. 373–410).

Historically, the concept of validity has been given many different definitions which can be ranked from the very empirical to the very theoretical. *The validity of a measure in the field of social innovation is simply an empirical matter because it can be defined as the magnitude of its correlation with the social change outcome criterion.* As discussed in Chapter 6, the social change outcome criterion represents the consensus of a society's representatives about an acceptable solution to a given social problem. The social change outcome criterion, then, is the only valid criterion measure as far as society is concerned. Accordingly, the validity of any other measure obtained during the course of an experiment can be ascertained by determining its correlation with this criterion.

The use of the correlation coefficient (pp. 164–169) to determine the validity of other measures is also necessitated by the nature of social process data, which is, of course, multifaceted. Because the data pertain to academic disciplines that have historically treated such facts independently, the relationships of any one discipline's variables to those of the others are usually unknown. It is very difficult therefore to conceptualize the relationships among variables from different disciplines before the experiment begins. Thus an empirical correlative approach becomes necessary not only to discover the relationships of the variables with the social change outcome criterion (validity) but also to determine the dimensionality of the measures themselves. The validity of any measure used in a social innovative experiment can be determined by its correlation with the social change outcome criterion, and the same set of computed correlation coefficients, along with the other intercorrelations, can be used by the researcher to determine the empirical dimensions of all experimental measures. This can be accomplished through factor or cluster analyses, techniques that are discussed together with correlations in Chapter 11.

Reliability, another concept mainly developed from the creation of psychological tests, concerns the measuring instrument itself. More specifically, a measure's reliability is the degree to which the same scores would obtain if it were possible to repeat the measuring procedures under the same conditions. Empirically, the reliability of a given measure is computed through using various correlative techniques (pp. 164–169). It is determined by the degree of association between distributions of scores. There are at least two general means of achieving these sets of scores and determining their reliability. The first is to secure two measures on the same sample under equivalent conditions and determine the correlation between the two distributions; the second is to have a sample of raters for the same phenomenon and to utilize a statistic which computes the degree of consensus among the raters. A correlation coefficient is used in the first case and the coefficient of concordance, W, is a statistic that can be utilized for the latter purpose (p. 169). A high reliability, represented by a correlation coefficient of .95, for instance, demonstrates that very similar scores are obtained when the measure is given under the same circumstances. For a highly reliable instrument, therefore, it is quite probable that the distribution of scores obtained on one measurement would be approximately equivalent to those obtained on a second.

The concept of reliability, however, has a somewhat different meaning when applied to certain social subsystem measures because of the nature of the measures and the social situation in which measurement occurs. When the measure is a test, for example, the reliability of that test can be determined by the first method mentioned. On the other hand, it is frequently the case that the measure is a behavior rating obtained in a real-life setting where the behavior itself occurs only once. In these circumstances the researcher cannot repeat the measure, so he uses the second method—a consensus about the behavior that occurred in lieu of the usual correlation. In such cases, the "reliability" of the instruments, as far as experiments in social innovation are concerned, is more appropriately considered a consensus among judges. Because these different types of "reliability" are applicable to particular measures utilized in social innovative experiments, the concept of reliability will later be discussed independently for each instrument along with a discussion of the measure itself (pp. 134–143).

Equipped with an understanding of the concepts and computational procedures related to scaling, validity, and reliability, the experimenter is now faced with the pragmatic problems of constructing scales and utilizing them in collecting the research data. The selection or construction of measures for social subsystems depends, of course, upon the particular problem under investigation. The researcher develops measures that both describe and evaluate those aspects of the problems that the subsystems were established to solve. *It is most important therefore that the investigator select or create measures appropriate to the social situation under investigation, and that he not be rigidly bound to a set of measures simply because they have been frequently used and are available, or because they have high validity or reliability in other situations.* After selecting the particular concepts he wishes to measure, the researcher then explores the population of assessment devices that he might profitably utilize in the course of his experiment.

The population of items or measures, often referred to as the pool of scales or items, comes from many sources. The experimenter explores the literature because many measures pertinent to social problems have been developed for laboratory studies or other different but related situations. Another source of information for the collection of important measurable items is the worker in the field. In institutional settings, for example, the personnel who have daily contact with the inmates can often suggest important variables in the social situation or characteristics of the participants that scales could be constructed to measure (Fairweather et al., 1960). Discussions with other professional workers and administrators is another source of potential items for measurement. Most important, however, is the observation of the participants and intimate acquaintance with their daily living situations which give the researcher his most pertinent source of information for the selection or creation of items from which he can construct the scales. It is, however, from all these sources that the measuring devices are fashioned.

When scales that appropriately measure the attributes of the dimensions cannot be located, the researcher must construct them from his pool of items. He first decides, on a logical basis, which items will measure the research concepts. Items thought to measure the same concept are potential candidates for the scale. Once selected, all items are arranged so that the highest score for each item represents the highest value for the concept. Thus if the scale is designed to measure productive work, each item should be arranged so that its highest score is given to that item response corresponding to the greatest production. Items can then be arranged in groups that logically measure the same concept. This group of items is called a *scale*. The *scale score* is the sum of the items comprising the scale. This is one method of constructing a scale. When it is created by grouping items that logically measure the same concept, it is usually referred to as a *rational scale*. A second typical method for constructing scales is more empirical. These *empirical scales* are created through discovering the interrelationships of the items in the pool. To do this, the sample of items is treated by factor or cluster analysis (pp. 169–179). Those items comprising a factor or cluster are then used as scales. Both types of scales are useful for measuring a subsystem's parameters. A discussion of the creation of rational and empirical scales is presented by Guilford (1954, pp. 414–536) and Tryon (1966).

This cursory exploration of scale construction does not, of course, concern itself with many of the details of scale construction such as the following. How many items should a scale contain? How does the experimenter determine the interrelationships among the items in a scale? Are all items empirically, as well as theoretically, measuring the same concept? Are some items doing all the work in the scale? Can a scale be lengthened or shortened? What are the interrelationships among different scales?

Space does not permit a discussion of these detailed problems and some of the logical and statistical methods that have been developed to deal with them; however, the interested reader can pursue their discussion in several well-known books. A thorough discussion of scale construction may be found in Ghiselli (1964), Guilford (1954), Torgerson (1958), and Riley, Riley and Toby (1954).

In addition to selecting the concepts, constructing the scales, and determining their reliability and validity, the experimenter must also be concerned about the measuring procedures. He is first concerned about the degree to which the measuring techniques themselves will differentially affect the subsystems. It should, of course, be obvious that to keep the subsystems comparable, the measuring procedures utilized for one subsystem should be identical with those used in every subsystem to be compared, a matter discussed previously (p. 104).

Making the subsystems comparable for the conditions of measurement, however, does not insure that their naturalistic setting can be maintained—a condition necessary to each subsystem for maximum generalization from the experimental to comparable real-life situations. It is most important here that the techniques for obtaining the research information have as little effect as possible upon the natural living and working arrangements in the subsystems. This may be stated as *the principle of least interference.*

There are several techniques that the experimenter can employ to minimize the potential interference involved in the use of interviews, ratings, and other assessment devices. An interesting account of the ways in which measurement affects subjects, and techniques for reduction of these effects, is presented in a recent book, *Unobtrusive Measures: Nonreactive Research in the Social Sciences* (Webb, Campbell, Schwartz, and Sechrest, 1966). The most important technique to reduce interference is the establishment of data collection procedures as part of the subsystems' normal operations at the outset of their organization so that the participants will not perceive the measuring techniques as interfering. An excellent example of attention to the principle of least interference may be found in the ratings completed by Goldman (1964, p. 53). Here, daily ratings were defined as an integral part of the subsystems' procedures when they were established. Thus little interference with ongoing social processes was attributable to them because, after the initial curiosity of the participants was satisfied, the rating procedures were accepted as a part of the daily routine.

To reduce interference with ongoing social processes, it is important for the researcher to plan measurements as part of the tasks usually performed by the participants. It is desirable to obtain measurement only by interview or questionnaire—activities not usually associated with the naturalistic situation—when the measures are essential to the research and the necessary information cannot be derived from the usual behaviors of the participants in the subsystems. It cannot be overemphasized that any measuring procedure not essential to the completion of the usual tasks designed for the subsystem creates some interference with the naturalistic social processes. Albeit this interference is often minimal, it is important because it will limit the inferences that are applied to nonexperimental replicates of the subsystems where measuring techniques are not employed. Accordingly, the investigator should obtain his information whenever possible from measures that are interwoven into the fabric of the subsystems' real-life processes. An example can be given from the community study (Fairweather, Sanders, Maynard, and Cressler, 1966). In this case, ratings of the performance of the work crews are needed. Inspection sheets completed by the supervisor are required when every job is finished. These ratings are used by the crews as feedback information about their work and have a known utility because they are used to guide improvement in workers' performance. After the information is revealed to the crew, the ratings are retained by the staff as research records about the group's performance. This principle is also illustrated in a study conducted by Maynard in which rewards were associated with group performance in a naturalistic work situation. The feedback to the group on its performance occurred in the following way:

"As soon as the work of the groups had been evaluated on the Work Rating Scale, the ward psychologist computed the scores for each group and immediately posted it on the ward bulletin board. Usually all the scores were posted within an hour of the time the first group had finished and within a half-hour of the time the last groups had finished their work. The scores were posted in a way that displayed the cumulative reward gained by each group during the week . . . ." (Maynard, 1964, p. 65.)

When it is essential to evaluate the subsystems through the use of interviews, psychological tests, and questionnaires, the naturalistic conditions can be most adequately maintained by establishing the place where the tests or interviews are to be administered at some distance from the experimental situation. The hospital study gives an example of this.

"The paper-and-pencil assessment devices measuring patient change in the attitudes and perceptions . . . were administered when the patient entered and left the program. This testing was carried out in a specific building located approximately one block from the two research wards . . . ." (Fairweather, 1964, pp. 36–37.)

Particular attention has been given thus far to the concepts and procedures of instrument validity and reliability, scale construction, scoring techniques, and the procedures designed to obtain experimental data without unduly interfering in the naturalistic processes of the subsystems. Now some of the common assessment devices used by social innovative experimentalists should be explored.

In any social innovative experiment, measures must be taken of the attributes (participants, outcomes, social situation) of the subsystem described in Chapter 6. A meaningful analysis and evaluation of the subsystem can only occur if measures are taken on all pertinent variables: those equated or held constant must be measured to assure that the experimental conditions are maintained and those allowed to vary must be measured for comparative purposes.

The type of instrument or scale used for measuring any particular variable in the experiment must be suited to the object of the study and it must be consistent with the subject matter of the field experiment. Later in this chapter, examples of different types of scales will be shown in relation to the measurement of variables representing the different parameters of the social subsystem; but, before going on to that task, it is important to discuss in some detail the measurement of those variables which are the outcome criteria in a social innovation experiment.

Measuring Outcomes

The social change outcome criterion is typically a real-life behavior directly related to the solution of the problem being studied. Since the choice of items is to a large extent dependent on the social problem under consideration, the experimenter needs to choose criteria that a society's agents agree are a solution to the problem. For example, the social change outcome criterion for most rehabilitative programs— whether designed for the criminal, the chronic mental patient, or the physically handicapped—usually may be defined as adaptive social behavior. Items to measure such behavior deal with the amount and type of work, friendships, attained level of social skills, and so forth. In education, the social change outcome criteria are usually skills learned, grades, or other measures of academic achievement. Measures such as participant satisfaction with his role and future expectations are also important outcomes in some experiments. It should be noted here that outcome criteria are those specific participant and social situation variables which have been selected by a society as a solution to a social problem (pp. 81–85). Outcomes are usually measured by questions asked in interviews, written questionnaires, behavior ratings, and other records of performance such as grades. An example of some items from a questionnaire designed to assess the outcomes of sub-systems for the treatment of mental illness is presented by Wohl (1964, pp. 160–168).

The social change outcome criterion consisted of three areas of social concern about treatment effectiveness, namely, recidivism, employment, and the degree of illness. The questionnaire shows items assessing the criterion.

*   *   *   *   *

Name of Respondent_____ Date_____
Relationship to Respondent _____: _____

Questionnaire

Please complete each of the following statements by checking the phrase that best describes how this person is getting along. Check only one of each set. An example is given below:

Example: This person came to the hospital because he was a

    _____ Clerk
    _____ Plumber
    ___x___ Person who needed help
    _____ Electrician
    _____ Salesman

The phrase to check is *Person who needed help.* You will note a check opposite the term *Person who needed help.*

Now please fill out the following items by checking the phrase which best tells how _____ is getting along.

1. Since leaving the hospital, he (she) has:
    _____ Remained out of the hospital and is not receiving treatment for nervousness.
    _____ Been under a doctor's care for nervousness.
    _____ Been back in a hospital for nervousness.
        Give date or dates _____

2. Since leaving the hospital, he (she) has:
    _____ Worked full time (40 hour week).
    _____ Worked about 30 hours a week.
    _____ Worked some, but less than 20 hours a week.

_____ Worked some, but less than 10 hours a week.

_____ Been unemployed.

3. As I know him (her), he (she) usually behaves:

_____ Very normally.

_____ Usually normally, but with a few minor symptoms.

_____ Generally normally, but some symptoms show he (she) is not quite well.

_____ Not very normally and quite emotionally ill, but he (she) is able to get along.

_____ Emotionally very ill and disabled. I believe he (she) will soon have to be hospitalized.

*   *   *   *   *

Table 9.1 presents a summary of the types of scales typically used to measure some outcomes along with selected examples. A detailed dis-

Table 9.1. **Types of Scales for Measuring Outcomes with Selected Examples**

Type of Scale	Examples of Measures
Personal history	History of participant as a member of the subsystem
Behavior ratings	Check list of psychiatric symptoms
	Checklist of criminal behaviors
	Measures of behavioral performance
Psychological tests	Social adjustment measures (personality tests)
	Academic achievement tests
Essay and open-end questions	Measures of satisfaction, morale, and self-regard
Attitude and expectancy scales	Measures of personal attitudes and expectancies
	Morale and cohesiveness measures
	Attitudes of community toward subsystem
Economic records	Records of financial productivity of the subsystem
	Records of cost to community of maintaining subsystem
Administrative records	Academic records of participants while in subsystem
	Prison records of participants while in subsystem
Research journal	Narrative accounts of events related to any of the outcome criteria of experiment

cussion of the assessment devices with important references will be given in the section *Procedures for Measuring the Variables of a Social Subsystem* (pp. 133–144).

Measuring Participant Characteristics

In Table 6.3, the principal participant characteristics were listed as those pertaining to demographic information, personality, and intelligence. Demographic information is typically obtained through personal questionnaires and administrative records, such as clinical files and military histories. Personality characteristics are usually assessed through interviews with relatives, friends, and the participant; behavior in particular situations that reveals personality characteristics or behavior patterns; and psychological tests. Intelligence is often evaluated by school grades, performance on various aptitude and achievement tests, and awards received for outstanding academic performance. Table 9.2 presents the types of scales and some examples which are most frequently used to measure the attributes of the participants. Discussions of these techniques for measuring participant

Table 9.2. Types of Scales for Measuring the Participant Variables with Selected Examples

Type of Scale	Participant Variable Examples
Personal history	Historical background before experiment
	History as a subsystem member
Behavior ratings	Check list of psychiatric symptoms
	Amount of social activity
Psychological tests	Personality, aptitude, and preference measures
	Social adjustment measures
	Academic achievement tests
Essay and open-end questions	Autobiographical data
	Measures of satisfaction, morale, and self-regard
Attitude and expectancy scales	Measures of personal attitudes and expectancies
Administrative records	Academic records
	Prison records
	Medical records (drugs, illnesses, etc.)
Research journal	Narrative account of events related to participant variables

characteristics are presented with examples in the section *Procedures for Measuring the Variables of a Social Subsystem* (pp. 133–144).

Measuring the Social Situation

Internal Processes

Table 6.4 presents a list of internal social processes that are typically measured. The type of social organization is measured by determining the table of organization for the subsystem. The type of work performed is typically described and measured by the amount of productivity, organization of the work, individual or team work, and the status and role relationships among the work force members such as supervisor and worker. Group processes, the dynamics of the internal social organization, are measured by assessing such important processes as group morale, leadership, and performance, usually by behavior ratings, questionnaires, and other scales. A small group bibliography by Raven (1961), a section of a recent book by Miller (1964, pp. 123–272), and a recently published reference book by McGrath and Altman (1966) are excellent aids in selecting concepts and finding assessment devices for group processes. The internal fiscal processes are a matter of bookkeeping. They include such items as income and costs. A helpful survey of methods to analyze such fiscal data, termed cost-benefits analysis, may be found in Prest and Turvey (1965).

External Processes

These processes, which are also presented in Table 6.4, are most frequently described by interviews and administrative records. The effect of the implanted subsystem on the neighborhood is often evaluated through questions asked neighbors, business associates, and social companions in interviews and written questionnaires. Socio-economic descriptions of neighborhoods in which the subsystems are located, as well as the relationship of the subsystem to other community institutions, is frequently assessed by written questionnaires, interviews, census data, and community records. Examples of the types of scales used to describe and assess the social situation are shown in Table 9.3.

Procedures for Measuring the Variables of a Social Subsystem

Tables 9.1, 9.2, and 9.3 illustrate that a selected number of scales are used in the measurement of outcomes, attributes of participants,

Table 9.3. Types of Scales for Measuring Social Situation Variables with Selected Examples

	Social Situation Variables	
Type of scale	Internal processes	External processes
Behavior ratings	Measure of interaction of group members	Interaction with members of outside community
Essay and open-end questions	Suggestions and comments on social subsystem by members	Suggestions and comments on social subsystem by others
Attitude and expectancy scales	Morale, cohesiveness, and expectancy measures	Attitudes of community toward subsystem
Economic records	Monetary reward record (wages, fines, etc.)	Records of income from and output to community
Administrative records	Work performance rating Turnover of membership Table of organization	Visits by realtives and friends
Research journal	Narrative account of events related to internal processes	Narrative account of events related to external processes

and the social situation of subsystems. It is now important to describe in detail each of these types of measuring devices and to present appropriate references so the interested reader can pursue a further examination of them. For clarity, each type of measuring device is presented with special attention to the dimension or dimensions which it measures, the type of scale required by the data, the construction of rational or empirical scales, and the manner in which data can be collected. An example is given of several items from a representative scale. These examples and references are given to aid the experimenter in creating the assessment devices. The first technique, the personal history, is common to all social innovative experiments.

Personal Histories

1. *Dimension to which they apply:* Participants.
2. *Type of scale:* Nominal, ordinal, and occasionally interval or ratio.

3. Securing the pool of items: There have been many researches in different fields which have utilized extensive personal histories. Foremost among these is the U.S. Census questionnaire. A pool of items can be obtained by securing several different questionnaires that have been used in other experiments. For a helpful example, the reader is referred to Hughes, Tremblay, Rapoport, and Leighton (1960, pp. 443–544).

4. *Creating or selecting instruments:* From the pool of items, the experimenter chooses those that fulfill his experimental needs. The possibility of combining several items into rational or empirical scales is discussed elsewhere (p. 126).

5. *Techniques for scoring:* In order to score the items individually or to combine them into scales, it is necessary to be acquainted with the distribution of the items under consideration. For example, occupation, salary, and type of dwelling were used by Warner (1960, pp. 121–129) to construct a rational status scale. Age may be used as its numerical value, e.g., 10, 38. The type of scoring therefore will differ with the particular items depending upon whether they are from nominal, ordinal, interval, or ratio scales (pp. 122–123).

6. *Procedures for obtaining:* Questionnaires that have been completed by the participants themselves, or by their relatives, friends, employers, and other individuals familiar with their backgrounds. One may also utilize records from schools, hospitals, employers, and so on.

7. *Reliability:* In the case of historical information, the reliability of any item is enhanced when additional sources of information are utilized as a check against the informant. For example, school records, police records, and medical records may be compared with the information received from the interviewee. When the interviewee is the participant, it is also possible to check the information received from him with parents, friends, relatives, and acquaintances.

8. *Example:*

* * * * *

Historical Background

1. Name _____ 2. Code No. _____
3. Group _____ 4. ID No. _____
5. Permanent address _____

_____

6. Age _____ Date of birth _____

7. Race: W   N   Other

8. Marital status: Single   Married   Widowed
                       Separated   Divorced   Remarried

9. If married, occupation of spouse (specify): _____

_____

10. Education of spouse, highest grade completed: _____
    Specify any post-secondary training of spouse _____

*   *   *   *   *

Behavior Ratings

1. *Dimensions to which they apply:* Participants and social situation, internal and external processes.

2. *Type of scale:* Nominal or ordinal.

3. *Securing the pool of items:* Behavior ratings have been widely used in laboratory and naturalistic settings. Heyns and Lippitt (1954, pp. 370–404) describe such techniques. The Location Activity Index (LAI) developed by Hunter, Schooler, and Spohn (1962) and the Hospital Adjustment Scale (Ferguson, McReynolds, and Ballachey, 1953) are excellent examples.

4. *Creating and selecting the instruments:* Scales are constructed as described on page 126. Examples of creating behavioral rating scales can be found in Goldman (1964, pp. 45–77) and Maynard (1964, pp. 54–55).

5. *Techniques for scoring:* Usual procedures for the scoring of scales as described on page 126.

6. *Procedures for obtaining:* Trained raters typically make their ratings in the naturalistic setting. An example of this can be found in Goldman (1964, pp. 45–77) and Maynard (1964, pp. 54–55).

7. *Reliability:* Behavioral ratings sometimes have problems of reliability not encountered in psychological tests. Mainly they concern the degree to which the behavior is repeatable. In cases where the behavior is not repeatable, the usual method for determining reliability is the coefficient of concordance (pp. 168–169). Here several raters evaluate the same behavior and the coefficient of concordance gives their agreement. It is also possible to compute a simple percent of agreement among raters (Maynard, 1964, App. iii–iv). In certain well-controlled situations where behavior is repetitious, reliability can be determined by the more common methods. Such a situation is described by Goldman (1964, pp. 51–55). Upon occasion the rater may wish to combine the reliability with the scale score itself—a technique developed by Fairweather (1960, pp. 9–10).

8. *Example:*

*   *   *   *   *

Social Activity Scale [a]

Observer _____   Date _____

Group _____

Name	Social Behaviors [b]								
	1	2	3	4	5	6	7	8	9
	Path.	Sleep	Null	Func. NS	P.S. Act.	P.S. Behav.	SG	2 PG	3 PG

[a] A discussion of the Social Activity Scale can be found in Goldman (1964, pp. 58–71).

[b] Description of behaviors:

1. Path—Pathological
2. Sleep—Sleeping
3. Null—Unoccupied or apathetic
4. Func. NS—Functional nonsocial
5. P.S. Act.—Parasocial activities

6. P.S. Behav.—Parasocial behavior
7. SG—Social games
8. 2 PG—Two-person interaction
9. 3 PG—Three-person interaction

*   *   *   *   *

Psychological Tests

1. *Dimensions to which they apply:* Participants.

2. *Type of scale:* Nominal, ordinal, or interval.

3. *Securing the pool of items:* The experimenter may wish to use established psychological tests which can be obtained from the publisher. Certain personality questionnaires, self-sort personality devices, projective tests, achievement tests, intelligence tests, interest tests, and tests of occupational choice may be of value for the experimenter. Or the experimenter may create a pool of items from which he can construct his own questionnaire. Anastasi (1961) and Cronbach (1960) present thorough discussions of the different psychological tests.

4. *Creating and selecting the instruments:* Usually the experimenter can find an existing psychological test that will fulfill his needs. If not, scales can be created with subscales if desired (p. 126).

5. *Techniques for scoring:* Most standardized psychological tests have a manual or a set of instructions which provide the experimenter

with a description of the test, scoring techniques, and ways to interpret the test results. If an instrument is created, appropriate scoring techniques can be established for it.

6. *Procedures for obtaining:* When testing the participants, it is important that procedures are established for administering the instruments in a consistent and sequential pattern.

7. *Reliability:* Standardized psychological tests usually have information concerning the reliability of the tests in the booklet that accompanies them. If the experimenter creates his own tests, one of the standard methods of determining the reliability of that test can be used (pp. 124–125).

8. *Example:*

* * * * *

The Vocational Preference Inventory [a]
Developed by John L. Holland, Ph.D.

This is an inventory of your feelings and attitudes about many kinds of work. Fill out your answer sheet by following the directions given below.

1. Show on your answer sheet the occupations which *interest* or *appeal* to you by blackening Y for "Yes."
2. Blacken N for "No" for the occupations you *dislike* or find *uninteresting.*
3. Make *no* marks when you are undecided about an occupation.

1. Aviator	31. Power Station Operator
2. Private Investigator	32. Astronomer
3. YMCA Secretary	33. Juvenile Delinquency Expert

[a] Information about the Vocational Preference Inventory may be found in Holland (1965).

* * * * *

Essays and Questions Requiring Verbal or Written Answers

1. *Dimensions to which they apply:* Participants and social situation, internal processes.

2. *Type of scale:* Ordinal and nominal.

3. *Securing the pool of items:* Here again the researcher must determine what information is important and create questions to obtain it. The reader is referred to Vitale (1964, pp. 213–244) who discusses one instrument of this type.

4. *Creating and selecting the instruments:* The experimenter chooses those questions that fulfill his experimental needs.

5. *Techniques for scoring:* Verbal or written answers to questions or essays can be categorized in many ways. For example, the questions may be scored according to content. Procedures for this can be found in Berelson (1952), Cronbach (1960, pp. 65–66), and Anastasi (1961, pp. 564–590). This kind of analysis may be utilized for recorded tapes as well as questionnaires. Another type of scoring can be obtained by sorting the answers to the questions into prearranged categories from most to least characteristic (Stephenson, 1953, and Block, 1961). If the responses are verbal, this procedure ordinarily requires a typescript of the recorded tapes. If the answers are written, the answer sheets themselves may be sorted. An example of scoring questions by the Q-sort method may be found in Vitale (1964, pp. 214–215). There are also methods that can be used for scoring tapes without typescript. For instance, Tryon (1941a, 1941b) has created a technique for raters to directly categorize observations of behavior which also can be used to determine scores directly from taped recordings.

6. *Procedures for obtaining:* Data may be obtained by questionnaire or recorded interview. The training of interviewers is discussed by Hyman (1954) and Maccoby and Maccoby (1954, pp. 449–487).

7. *Reliability:* The reliability of Q-sort techniques is discussed by Vitale (1964, pp. 214–215). Methods of obtaining reliability for the direct scoring of tapes can be found in Tryon's discussion (1941a, 1941b). Generally, the responses can be scored or ranked by several judges and the usual correlative methods of computing reliability applied (pp. 124–125).

8. *Example:*

* * * * *

Name _____   Date _____
Group _____

On this page, there is a 3-part question. Please fill in each part as completely as possible.

1. What aspects of the small group program do you feel are beneficial to the group members?

2. What aspects of the program do you feel are harmful to the group members?

3. List below any ideas that you have which would make the program more helpful to group members.

* * * * *

Attitude, Expectancy, and Other Perceptual Scales

1. *Dimensions to which they apply:* Participants and social situation, internal and external processes.

2. *Type of scale:* Nominal, ordinal, or interval.

3. *Securing the pool of items:* The pool of items may be secured from a number of researchers evaluating attitudes, expectancies, etc. The researcher may profitably use the references of Anastasi (1961, pp. 528–556), Sherif (1965), and Miller (1964).

4. *Creating and selecting the instruments:* Here again scales and subscales may be created by the rational or empirical methods described earlier (p. 126).

5. *Techniques for scoring:* Individual scores can be obtained by summing the items in the various scales.

6. *Procedures for obtaining:* The testing procedures are the same as those used with psychological tests.

7. *Reliability:* Reliability can be ascertained by the usual correlative techniques (pp. 124–125).

8. *Example:*

*   *   *   *   *

Expectancy Scale

Name _____   Date _____

Group _____

Below are ten statements in which you are asked to guess how you will like your living situation in the community after you leave the hospital. Each statement can be completed in one of five ways. Please check the one phrase that most accurately reflects *your guess* about the future.

Example: I will like the food in the house where I reside in the community.

    ___x___ A great deal
    _____ Quite a bit
    _____ Somewhat
    _____ Only slightly
    _____ Not at all

The person completing this question believed that he would enjoy the food in his community home a great deal.

Please complete the following statements by choosing the *one* phrase which most accurately reflects *your guess* about the future.

1. I will like the place where I live.
   _____ A great deal
   _____ Quite a bit
   _____ Somewhat
   _____ Only slightly
   _____ Not at all
2. I will like the people with whom I live.
   _____ A great deal
   _____ Quite a bit
   _____ Somewhat
   _____ Only slightly
   _____ Not at all

* * * * *

Economic Records

1. *Dimensions to which they apply:* Social situation, internal and external processes.

2. *Type of scale:* Nominal, ordinal, interval, or ratio.

3. *Securing the pool of items:* The items selected depend upon those aspects of the subsystem's economic processes that are important to the social problem. Suppose, for example, the experimenter wishes to determine the cost and the income of a social subsystem where participants live and work. Following is a list of some items about which he will need information: personnel, travel, equipment, supplies (food, office, etc.), rent, utilities, insurance, professional consultants (medical, legal, etc.), wages, other income, and bookkeeping costs.

4. *Creating or selecting instruments:* From the list of economic items, the experimenter creates scales that measure those economic aspects of the subsystem in which he is interested. He may be interested, for example, in the economic position of individuals within the subsystem, such as individual cost or income. On the other hand, he may be interested in economic items for the entire subsystem such as total expenditures or total income.

5. *Techniques for scoring:* Scoring techniques here involve numerical representations of the monetary processes of a subsystem. For example, ratios of income to output, individual income, group income, etc., can be presented in numbers.

6. *Procedures for obtaining:* Detailed bookkeeping records for all costs and expenditures in research projects should provide the data for the construction of many of the scales.

7. *Reliability:* Reliability is determined by the bookkeeping procedures. Exceedingly important here are periodic audits which should result in accurate records about the economic aspects of the subsystems.

8. *Example:*

* * * * *

Daily Expenditures

Date	Name	Lodging	Food	Medical	Personal	Other

* * * * *

Administrative Records

1. *Dimensions to which they apply:* Participants and social situation, internal and external processes.

2. *Type of scale:* Nominal or ordinal.

3. *Securing the pool of items:* These records do not involve items in the usual sense. Rather, they are ordinarily frequency counts of records pertaining to health, such as amount and type of medication, visits to physicians, and illnesses. Other records about such matters as friendships, recreational activities, and membership in community social organizations are also classified here as administrative records.

4. *Creating and selecting the instruments:* The experimenter chooses those items of information that are important in describing the activities of the participants in the subsystems or the subsystems' social structures. If community subsystems have been established for the criminal, the mentally ill, or school drop-outs, records concerning their relationship with the community may be important. If this is the case, the experimenter may be interested in the places (restaurants, lodges, or clubs) in the community visited by the participants. The table of organization and the social structure of the subsystem are also important administrative records (Etzioni, 1961).

5. *Techniques for scoring:* Usually a record for each individual can be kept and scored on the amount of time spent in a selected activity or the frequency of such an activity—dinner engagements for example.

6. *Procedures for obtaining:* Health records may be obtained from the attending physician. Sign-out sheets may be utilized to record where a participant goes for recreation, for example, a bowling alley or the theater.

7. *Reliability:* Here, the experimenter keeps records of his own which can be checked for accuracy with such information as physicians' reports and the participant-completed sign-out sheets. For each administrative record, it is important to establish checks on its accuracy.

8. *Example:*

* * * * *

Tranquilizing Drugs

Name	Dates		Amount	
	From	To		

Total: _____

* * * * *

Research Journal

1. *Dimensions to which they apply:* All dimensions of subsystem.

2. *Type of scale:* Not applicable.

3. *Measurement:* This is primarily a detailed account of the life of the subsystem. It describes the global operation as well as stages of development, which are not covered by the formal measures. Critical incidents are reported here. For instance, one records here that members of the research team were replaced, the dates of new research phases, threats to the discontinuation of the program, and so forth. Certain critical incidents occur only once—such as a key

researcher quitting—and these incidents are *assessed in depth,* that is, all information available from all sources is collected and collated. It is important here to gain as much information about the incident as possible. An example of the use of a research journal can be found in Vitale (1964, p. 239). Flanagan (1956) presents techniques for measuring and recording critical incidents.

4. *Techniques for scoring:* Not primarily meant to produce formally scored items. The selected events that are recorded and described here may be categorized and scored according to frequency counts or content.

5. *Procedures for obtaining:* Daily records of observed events, motion pictures, tape recordings, and on-line computers can all be used to portray the subsystem in action.

Chapter 10

Selecting the Appropriate
Comparative Methods

The major purpose of establishing social subsystems as alternative solutions to important social problems is to compare their effectiveness in alleviating those problems. Even though the paramount comparison is made on the social change outcome criterion, it is essential that other comparisons be made on outcome variables and on those variables involving the internal and external social processes of the subsystems. This is necessary because it is important to understand and clearly communicate to others a comprehensive account of all the comparative results. Accordingly, various techniques are needed to portray an understandable and meaningful comparative picture. Broadly conceived, these techniques taken as a whole are the social innovative experimenters' comparative methods. They may generally be categorized as narrative-descriptive, graphical, and statistical.

Narrative-Descriptive Technique

Unlike cursory writing for scientific journals, narrative-descriptive accounts of the subsystems are essential in longitudinal studies where different social processes are involved. Graphs and statistics, the more formal comparative methods, cannot capture the dynamic qualities of social systems, particularly those involving changes over time. In the community study referred to earlier (Fairweather, Sanders, Maynard, and Cressler, 1966), the complex development of a work program could not be adequately portrayed without extensive descriptive narration. At the outset of this experiment, several questions were asked by the experimenter concerning the type of work program that could be developed with chronic mental patients living in a community setting. Some of the questions formulated at that time are the following. What type of work can the individuals perform? Can they be trained to improve their performance? What level of organization is required? Can they leave the living-working situation and take a normative work role in society? What work roles develop?

Clearly any two different subsystems could yield different results as answers to these questions. Although scales of measurement were developed to answer these questions comparatively, the total work situation has a history that needs complete and accurate narration in order to clearly present the entire comparative picture. An example of a descriptive comparison of two subsystems in a hospital study is presented by MacDonald (1964, p. 97).

"A second comparative example concerns the manner in which staff members were discussed by patients . . . . On the traditional ward, staff members were rarely disturbed by the criticism of patients . . . . On the small group ward patients evidenced far more spontaneity and affect in discussing a staff member . . . and this, consequently, led to much discussion . . . during the staff meeting that followed."

A second example is given by Tipler and Rankin (1964, p. 252).

"The first great change all personnel felt was the complete *silence* on the traditional ward. We had grown accustomed to activity and discussions from the patients and it was like another world on the traditional ward. We had plenty of time to read patients' charts and to become familiar with their behavior. We had to relearn the traditional communication patterns and adjust to the role of giving support, reassurance, and assistance in a one-to-one relationship again.

"The large-group meetings were a complete change. Here the patients were more quiet and many slept through the meetings. During this period of readjustment, we began to question our own usefulness and had a feeling of being superfluous. The patients accepted the staff change without undue concern."

Thus the narrative-comparative account of the two treatment subsystems provided a descriptive picture of the differences between them. Frequently, the narrative is punctuated by graphs or statistics where such techniques contribute to the clarity and completeness of the comparative picture. But whatever graphs and statistics are presented, the experimenter should be aware that narrative-descriptive accounts are the paramount feature in communicating the experimental findings.

Graphical Techniques

Graphical presentations of differences are another comparative method. Because of the static nature of most statistical methods, graphical presentations need to be used to show the longitudinal nature of the differences. Such graphs reveal *time trends*. Suppose, for example, that weekly measurements were taken for each experimental subsystem for two years. Let us further assume that the data can only be ranked (ordinal scale, p. 122) and that the experimenter wishes to compare the subsystems for the two-year time span. A nonparametric test (pp. 152–156) might be used to compare the cumulative scores for the entire two years, but this statistic would not show the weekly fluctuations of the scores. There may, for example, be a reversal of scores during some weeks of the two-year period which would not be apparent from the single statistic computed from the cumulative data. A graph of the weekly scores would quickly reveal any such reversals. Figure 10.1 presents illustrative graphs from the small group study (MacDonald, 1964, pp. 90, 93) showing two trends over time whose cumulative scores both yielded significant statistics. It is quickly apparent that the time trends are quite different. In the first graph the differences are decreasing, whereas in the second they are increasing with time. It is important to point out here that certain parametric statistics have been created for testing such time trends. However, as mentioned elsewhere (pp. 160–161), the experimental data, particularly that of the real-life social change outcome criterion, rarely meet the rather stringent assumptions required for the use of these trend analyses. Graphs are therefore often used in social innovative experiments in lieu of more formal parametric trend analyses. They are particularly useful in clarifying subsystem comparisons when nonparametric analyses are performed on cumulative data, as was the case with the graphs presented in Figure 10.1.

Other types of graphs can be used to present differences or similarities between subsystems in a precise and simple manner. These graphs are quite useful with social innovative data when the information is divided into two, three, or four distinct categories. *Bar graphs* are most often used for this purpose. Figure 10.2 shows a bar graph of

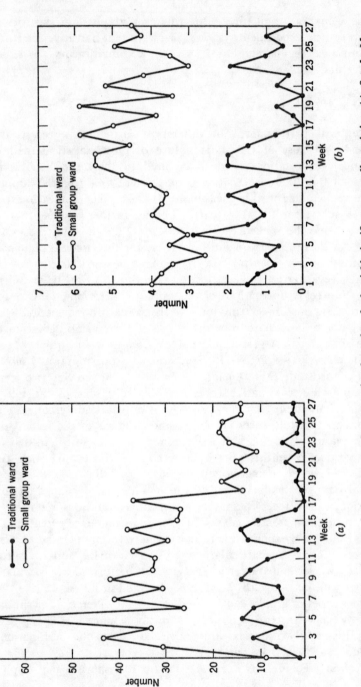

Figure 10.1. Different time trends for two sets of comparative data that both yield significant overall statistics. (*a*) Set 1. Mean number of times two or more patients were speaking at once for each treatment program. (*b*) Set 2. Mean number of topics with eight or more discussants for each treatment program.

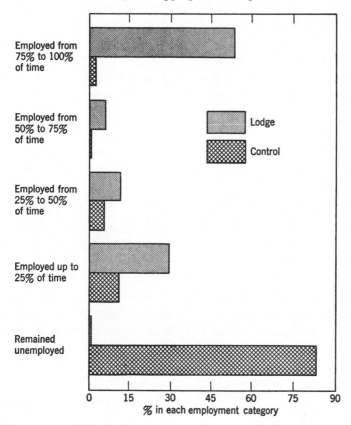

Figure 10.2. Comparison of the lodge and control groups on community employment for a six-month follow-up period.

the current community project comparing the employment of the participants in the two subsystems (Fairweather, Sanders, Maynard, and Cressler, 1966). These differences clearly are very great, and it is doubtful if any statistical test would materially add to the researcher's understanding of these experimental data or the inferences that he can make from them. Hence graphical representations of research data are particularly suited to experimental social innovation because of the longitudinal nature of the studies and because real-life data often can be expressed only on nominal or ordinal scales. Furthermore, graphs can present the data in such a simple manner that communication is enhanced. The interested reader may pursue a detailed discussion of the use of graphs elsewhere (Guilford, 1956, pp. 18–24; Moroney, 1956, pp. 19–33).

Statistical Techniques

Differences between subsystems are usually not as extreme as those in Figure 10.2, and the experimentalist then may use the more formal statistical methods to test hypotheses about differences between them. These comparisons are made by testing statistical hypotheses. It is important that the social innovative experimentalist have an understanding of the logic of testing statistical hypotheses. The interested reader may pursue a thorough and rigorous logical discussion of this matter in Lehmann (1959).

As an integral part of the planning phase for the experiment, the researcher should state his ideas about the outcomes of the subsystems in the form of hypotheses. These hypotheses can then be subject to test through the use of the appropriate statistical methods. Social innovative experiments have one unique characteristic that differentiates them from many other researches with respect to the hypotheses one is testing. This concerns the direction of the hypotheses. Comparative hypotheses about the outcomes of the social subsystems are *always* stated in terms that predict the created experimental subsystems will be more beneficial to the participants than the subsystem a society may be using currently (the control social subsystem). The social innovative researcher never entertains an hypothesis that predicts the created subsystems will have no effect or will have a harmful effect compared to the usual social practice (control), a matter discussed elsewhere (p. 200). In statistical parlance, this is termed a one-sided hypothesis and it has considerable effect in determining the inferences that can be made from the resulting statistic. Such situations give rise to one-tailed tests of significance (pp. 200–201).

In order to test a statistical hypothesis for a particular experiment, the researcher chooses the method most appropriate to his problem. When classified in terms of the data there are two general types of statistics—parametric and nonparametric. The differences between these two types of statistics involve the assumptions the researcher can logically make about some very basic properties of his data. Parametric statistics—although usually considered more powerful—require that the experimenter make more stringent assumptions about the nature of the research data than do nonparametric statistics. They also require more rigid suppositions about the distributions of the data and the units of measure. In general, parametric statistics require interval or ratio scales with normally distributed populations whose variances are homogeneous, whose data are based on inde-

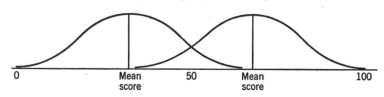

Figure 10.3. Two score distributions with different means.

pendent observations, and whose scale scores are additive. Nonparametric statistics, on the other hand, require that the researcher make fewer assumptions about his data. They are sometimes called "distribution-free" methods because they make no assumption about the population parameter and therefore are applicable to data that can only be categorized (nominal) or ranked (ordinal). Nonparametric statistics usually require less computational time than parametric statistics when small samples are used, an important consideration if computers are not readily available.

Statistical methods usually compare the central tendencies of the distributions of scores from the various subsystems, or they compare the distributions themselves. The mean and the median are the most common measures of central tendency. The mean is used when the score distributions are normal. It is simply the average score.

An example of two distributions with different means is presented in Figure 10.3. Differences in sample means are usually tested using parametric statistics. The median, on the other hand, is the middle score of a distribution. If, for example, one has 11 scores and ranks them from highest to lowest, the sixth score in the ranking is the median. This measure of central tendency is less influenced than the mean by extreme scores and by odd-shaped distributions. Medians are usually compared by nonparametric methods. An example of two distributions with different medians is presented in Figure 10.4. Some-

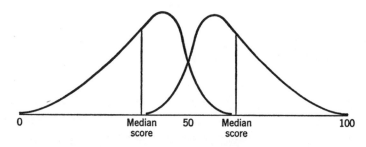

Figure 10.4. Two score distributions with different medians.

times the data are divided into so few categories that it is only feasible to compare the shape of the distributions. An example of two such distributions can be found in Figure 10.2. Usually nonparametric techniques are used to compare the differences between such non-normal distributions.

Nonparametric Techniques

Nonparametric techniques are the most useful comparative statistics for the social innovative researcher because his data rarely meet the assumptions for parametric statistics. Frequently, data from different academic disciplines can only be categorized and such information is amenable to nonparametric techniques only. In this regard, it often occurs that raters can only judge the relatively greater or less than value of an item; for example, more or less work is done, more or less effort is shown, and so forth. For a detailed discussion of the assumptions and use of parametric contrasted with nonparametric techniques the interested reader is referred to Siegel (1956, pp. 18–34), Moses (1952), and Edwards (1960, pp. 111–114).

Many references will be given for each statistic so that the interested reader can pursue, if he wishes, a thorough discussion of its underlying assumptions, mathematical derivations, and computational examples. This presentation of statistical methods is not intended to be exhaustive, but rather to furnish the reader with a general understanding of those methods that seem to have the most promise for use in evaluating social innovative experiments and to provide readable references where they can be explored in more detail. The use of nonparametric techniques for comparative statistical analysis requires a single score per participant, regardless of the statistic employed. This fact should be kept in mind during the ensuing discussion of such techniques, since the subsequent discussion of parametric techniques will also include the use of statistics involving more than one score per participant.

TWO SUBSYSTEMS WITH MATCHED PARTICIPANTS. Suppose the experimentalist wishes to compare two subsystems with matched participants when he has only one score per individual. This is frequently the case when the data are from ordinal or nominal scales and the researcher combines several repeated measurements into one cumulative score. Such a situation exists when, for example, repeated behavioral ratings or questionnaires are obtained. Let us further assume that matched sampling techniques, as presented in Chapter 8, have been used. Several nonparametric techniques are applicable in this situation. The *sign test* (Siegel, 1956, pp. 68–75; Moses, 1952; Dixon and

Massey, 1957, pp. 280–284) is commonly used when each of the matched pairs, one of whom participates in each subsystem, can be compared with each other in terms of having a more-than or less-than value on the comparative score (ordinal scale). In using the sign test it is not necessary to consider the size of the differences between the scores of the matched pairs but only the directionality (greater or less than). Thus in analyses where the scores for the matched pairs can only be arranged in greater- or less-than comparisons, the sign test is an excellent technique.

On the other hand, the experimenter may not only be able to compare each score of the matched pair in a differential manner, but, at the same time, the scores may also reveal the magnitude of the differences. Thus, for example, it may be possible to state that one of the paired scores is not only greater than the other, but that the difference between them is greater or less than the difference between another pair of scores. When this is the case, the *Wilcoxon signed rank test* for paired replicates (Siegel, 1956, pp. 75–83; Moses, 1952; Wilcoxon and Wilcox, 1964, p. 9) may be used. When the experimenter can assign direction (greater or less than) and specify the magnitude of the differences between any two scores (interval scale), and when the distributions are symmetrical though not normal, a more powerful test, the *Walsh test* (Siegel, 1956, pp. 83–87; Dixon and Massey, 1957, p. 342), can be used. There are, of course, other nonparametric tests for matched pairs when only one score per participant is available (Siegel, 1956, pp. 61–94; Dixon and Massey, 1957, pp. 280–299), but the experimentalist will find the three described here especially applicable to social innovative experiments.

TWO SUBSYSTEMS WITHOUT MATCHED PARTICIPANTS. It sometimes happens that the experimenter cannot establish appropriate sampling procedures to create matched pairs. Upon occasion it is so difficult to establish sampling techniques from which to create the matches that it is necessary for the researcher to utilize simple random assignment to the subsystems (p. 117). Although the advantages of matched samples are numerous, the practical problems involved in creating sampling pools and the like are sometimes too great to warrant their use (pp. 117–118). Then, the experimenter compares subsystems without matching the participants.

When these data fall into two categories, such as employed or unemployed, married or single, *Fisher's exact probability test* can be utilized. A detailed discussion of this test can be found in Siegel (1956, pp. 96–104). The *chi-square* technique is another test that can be used for unmatched, random samples. It is perhaps the most commonly used of all nonparametric techniques when the data are divided into discrete categories. Thus, for example, the hospital study compared the effect of the small group and traditional treatment subsystems with the *chi-square* technique (Wohl, 1964, p. 164). The data for each subsystem can be divided into two, three, or more discrete categories, provided certain assumptions about the minimum number of scores in each cell can be met. This technique as well as computational examples can be found in Siegel (1956, pp. 104–111), McNemar (1962, pp. 209–228), and Edwards (1954, pp. 366–372).

Another commonly utilized technique when the data yield distributions of scores is the *median test*. Note again, here, that no assumption about normality of these distributions needs to be made; however, they must have a distribution so that a median (central point) can be determined. In these cases, the common median for both sets of subsystems' scores is located and a two-way table comprised of those in each subsystem falling above or below the common median is established. This method is fully described in Siegel (1956, pp. 111–116) and Moses (1952).

When the data fall on an ordinal scale, that is, when they can be arranged in rank order, the *Mann-Whitney test* can be used. In this case, advantage is taken of the fact that an ordinal rather than a nominal scale exists. Computational procedures and a discussion of the logic involved can also be found in Siegel (1956, pp. 116–127). Data that fall on an ordinal scale can be compared by the *Wilcoxon rank sum test* for unpaired replicates (Wilcoxon and Wilcox, 1964, p. 7). In this test, the scores for all subsystems are first ranked and then compared by using the sums and the averages of the ranks.

When the distributions of the data are sufficient to yield cumulative frequencies, the *Kolmogorov-Smirnov test* can be used to compare the two distributions. At least ordinal scales are necessary to compute the statistic. Siegel (1956, pp. 127–136) presents a complete discussion of this test. Another test for two subsystems with unmatched participants yielding ordinal data is the *Wald-Wolfowitz test*. This test compares any differences in the central tendencies or distributions of the data from the subsystems. A discussion of it can be found in Siegel (1956, pp. 136–145).

MORE THAN TWO SUBSYSTEMS WITH MATCHED PARTICIPANTS. It is frequently the case, however, that the experimentalist wishes to compare more than two subsystems at one time when he has one score per participant. At the same time, his data may be from ordinal or nominal scales. It is therefore necessary for him to use a nonparametric technique. The data for an analysis may form a nominal scale or it may be dichotomous. In such a case, the *Cochran Q test* can be used. For a discussion of this test the reader is referred to Siegel (1956, pp. 161–166). If the data comprise an ordinal scale, the most common and useful technique for these comparisons is the *Friedman test* (Siegel, 1956, pp. 166–173; Wilcoxon and Wilcox, 1964, pp. 11–12). Essentially, this technique requires data that can be ranked for matched participants as far as the subsystems are concerned. For illustrative purposes, suppose that 100 matched participants were randomly assigned, 25 to each of four subsystems. Each subsystem would then have 25 matched participants. There are thus 25 groups of four matched subjects—one in each of the four subsystems that can be ranked 1, 2, 3, and 4. These ranks are used to compare the subsystems.

It is also possible to use the *Friedman test* to compare the interaction effects when different types of participants are involved in the experimental subsystems. This technique is very useful with group data when one wishes to compare group scores.

MORE THAN TWO SUBSYSTEMS WITHOUT MATCHED PARTICIPANTS. The *chi-square test* is most commonly used for this purpose. It tests the difference between frequencies within a category. The chi-square table can have several rows and columns. The columns could be the subsystems to be compared and the rows could be the categories of participants, such as high school and college students. The only difference between the comparisons of three or more subsystems and the two-subsystems comparison is an increase in the number of columns from two to the number of subsystems that the experimenter wishes to compare. Data for the chi-square test are ordinarily categories comprising a nominal scale. Excellent discussions of the chi-square test for comparing more than two subsystems can be found in Siegel (1956, pp. 174–179), McNemar (1962, pp. 228–236), and Edwards (1954, pp. 372–381).

The *median test,* like the chi-square test, can be extended to compare more than two subsystems. Here the measurement needs to be at least of rank order (ordinal scale). The median of the scores from all subsystems is located and a 2 (above and below the median) by N (number of subsystems) table is constructed from which the statistic is calculated. For underlying assumptions and computational procedures the reader is referred to Siegel (1956, pp. 179–184) and Edwards (1954, p. 390). As mentioned on page 151, this is the test for differences between the medians of the distributions for the subsystems.

The *Kruskal-Wallis test* can also be used to compare more than two subsystems. Here the distributions must be continuous (not necessarily normal) and the measurement on an ordinal scale. All participants in all subsystems are ranked from highest to lowest score, then the subsystems are compared on the rank scores. This test is concerned with the probability that the different subsystems have different distributions of scores. Computational examples, along with a complete discussion of this technique, can be found in Siegel (1956, pp. 184–196).

Despite their utility, there are some difficulties with nonparametric statistics that must particularly concern the social innovative experimentalist. Usually the repeated measures have to be summed into one score because there is no adequate nonparametric technique for repeated measures of the same participants. When this is the case, as it often is, the computation of the nonparametric statistic can be combined with graphs portraying the degree to which the computed statistic represents a constant difference over time.

Parametric Techniques

Occasionally the experimenter has parametric data, that is, the data are normally distributed (as shown in Figures 10.3 and 10.5), they are independent measurements, and the subsystems' score distributions have homogeneous variances. If this is not the case, it is still possible in some instances to transform the original scores into distributions whereby these assumptions can be made (Edwards, 1960, pp. 128–131). At any rate, when such assumptions can be met parametric statistics are the statistics of choice. Recently there has been a rather intense discussion about the degree to which these assumptions need to be met before parametric statistics can reasonably be used. For those interested, reference is made to a discussion by McNemar (1962, pp. 374–375) and to Norton's study, presented by Lindquist (1953, pp. 78–

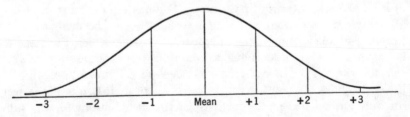

Figure 10.5. The relationship of the mean to 1, 2, and 3 positive or negative standard deviations.

86). As a general guideline, however, the scales should be interval or ratio before parametric statistics are applicable.

Although it is uncommon for social innovative data to be suitable for parametric tests, where such tests are applicable they are the statistical tests of choice not only because they are the more powerful tests but also because they offer statistical designs that can yield more information. This is particularly true when the scores are repeated measures on the participants or when before-and-after measures (pre and post) are a part of the evaluation.

Parametric techniques are concerned with testing for the significance of the differences between the means (central points) by use of the variances of the subsystems' distributions. A normal distribution with the mean and standard deviation is shown in Figure 10.5. The variance is the square of the standard deviation. A discussion of the mean, standard deviation, and variance can be found in Edwards (1954, pp. 33–43) and McNemar (1962, pp. 20–35). Let us now examine the parametric techniques that seem to be useful to the social innovative experimentalist.

TWO SUBSYSTEMS WITH ONE SCORE PER PARTICIPANT AND MATCHED PARTICIPANTS. The most common technique used for this purpose, when each participant has one score, is the *t test*. There are computational differences when the samples are matched and when they are not matched. The computation of the *t* test as well as its assumptions when the samples are matched can be found in Edwards (1954, pp. 278–288) and McNemar (1962, pp. 101–102).

TWO SUBSYSTEMS WITH ONE SCORE PER PARTICIPANT AND WITHOUT MATCHED PARTICIPANTS. The statistic of choice is again the *t test*. Its logic and the inferences are the same as the *t* test with matched pairs, but there is a difference in computation. The logic of its use and some computational examples can be found in Edwards (1954, pp. 249–255) and McNemar (1962, pp. 102–104).

MORE THAN TWO SUBSYSTEMS WITH ONE SCORE PER PARTICIPANT AND MATCHED OR UNMATCHED PARTICIPANTS. The most common statistical methods developed for these comparisons are the *analyses of variance*. These analyses are used to test the significance of the differences among the means (central points) of the score distributions of the subsystems by using the variances of those distributions. Instead of *t* tests of significance, they yield *F*-ratios. The comparison makes possible a probability statement about the differences among subsystems. As long as the matching procedures presented in Chapter 8 are followed, the same statistical design can be used for both matched and unmatched samples. Matching procedures are designed to make the variances of the several distributions equal, and they are, as with other statistics, more efficient designs. There are *simple analyses of variance* which are used only to compare the differences among the subsystems. Examples of the computational procedures and the use of simple analyses of variance can be found in Lindquist (1953, pp. 44–66), Edwards (1960, pp. 117–135), and Snedecor (1956, pp. 237–239).

There are other more complex designs which yield more information. Frequently it is possible for the researcher to use a more complex design simply by planning more adequately for the statistical treatment of his data. One of the analyses most useful to the social innovative experimenter involves a comparison not only of the effects of the subsystems but also of their effects upon different classes of participants. Let us assume that the researcher wishes to compare the effects of three subsystems on three types of participants. He may, for example, have three different marginal groups—mentally ill, Job Corps members, and paraplegics—who are participating in equal proportions in three subsystems. By use of a multiple classification design, the researcher can find not only the effects of the subsystems but also whether the subsystems have a differential effect upon the three groups. A discussion of the computational procedures as well as the characteristics of the *multiple classification analyses of variance* can be found in Edwards (1960, pp. 136–157) and Snedecor (1956, pp. 291–300). The important point here for the experimenter is that the investment of more time in planning the design and the sampling procedures may yield important information not attainable by using more simple procedures.

Another useful type of analysis of variance is the *factorial design*. This is a design on which the subsystems and a second independent variable can be ordered so that they represent points along a continuum. Let us consider the researcher who wishes to compare three subsystems, each representing different degrees of freedom from control by societal authorities. The three subsystems might be those applicable to criminal rehabilitation, and therefore they could be arranged so that they represented little, some, and much autonomy from parole agents. At the same time, three criminal groups representing different degrees of institutionalization—short, middle, and long termers—might participate in all three subsystems. In such a case, the design would include three points (little, some, much) upon two dimensions (institutionalization and autonomy), the results of which could be analyzed in a factorial design.

The advantage of the factorial design is that it not only compares the effects of the subsystems and the effects upon the different participant groups, but also reveals any interaction effects. An interaction effect occurs when participants in the categories respond in a differential way to the subsystems. For example, the group with "little" institutionalization might show great benefit from the autonomous subsystem and little benefit from the autocratic subsystem, while the "much" institutionalized group might show the opposite of this. These interaction effects cannot be evaluated unless a design appropriate for this is developed. A discussion of factorial designs can be found in Edwards (1960, pp. 175–223) and Cochran and Cox (1957, pp. 148–181).

Other complex analysis of variance designs can be used, but they have only limited applicability in social innovative experiments. The factorial analysis of variance designs, for example, need not be restricted to two dimensions. It is possible to construct designs with several dimensions which yield increased information. But such very complex designs are typically too unwieldy for the practicalities of social innovative research. It is therefore usually the experimenter's choice to conduct two or three simpler experiments instead of one very complex experiment. When the complexities of a single design are so great, they may obscure some results or become so unwieldy that they are unfeasible to establish in the real-life setting.

An excellent example of this occurs in a *Latin Square design*, where all participants, in the ordinary design, would be required to participate in each subsystem for an equal number of days—a condition not only impractical but also not lifelike because most naturalistic social groups are open so that their members can come and go. As another example, certain *randomized block designs* require that participants spend equal time in each subsystem and it is then assumed that the individual's experience in one does not affect his experiences in the others (Edwards, 1960, p. 159). Certain assumptions in complex designs that have been primarily developed in other fields (agriculture, for example) are sometimes untenable in social innovative experiments. However, there are infrequent occasions when quite complex designs can be used. The interested reader is encouraged to pursue an extended discussion of them which may be found in Edwards (1960, pp. 158–174, 254–280) and Cochran and Cox (1957, pp. 95–145, 244–520).

TWO OR MORE SUBSYSTEMS WITH TWO SCORES PER PARTICIPANT (PRE AND POST MEASUREMENT) AND MATCHED OR UNMATCHED PARTICIPANTS. This is called the method of *covariance* and is a very useful method in social innovative research when two of the same measures are obtained on each participant. This occurs most often when measures are taken as participants enter the subsystem and when they leave. Covariance analyses are particularly relevant in experiments where it is difficult if not impossible to equate the participant in the experimental subsystems for initial scores on the desired assessment device. Consider, for example, the experimenter who wishes to compare the subsystems on behavioral change. When the participants enter the subsystems they are rated on a behavioral outcome scale and given a score. This measurement procedure is repeated when they leave the subsystem. Under these conditions, however, the participants in the subsystems could have significantly different scores upon entering the subsystems. By using a covariance analysis, the participants' scores can be adjusted for these initial score differences.

This method therefore is most often used to statistically equate participants upon the entry into the subsystems, so that any differences found between the subsystems at the end of the experiment can be attributable to the differential effects of the subsystems and not to differences in the initial level of performance of the participants. The usual analysis of covariance requires an equal number of participants in each subsystem, but Kempthorne has devised a method for treating subsystems with unequal numbers. Since this is a common occurrence in the naturalistic setting, it is a very valuable method. A thorough discussion of the linear hypothesis method of covariance analysis with an unequal number of participants in the subsystems may be found in Kempthorne (1952, pp. 28–67). Other discussions of covariance analyses with an equal number of participants in the subsystems may be found in Edwards (1960, pp. 281–300) and McNemar (1962, pp. 362–373).

TWO OR MORE SUBSYSTEMS WITH REPEATED SCORES ON EACH PARTICIPANT AND MATCHED OR UNMATCHED GROUPS. Whenever the appropriate assessment of a social innovative phenomenon requires several of the same measures on the same participants and the data are parametric, the statistic of choice is an *F*-ratio as found in what is termed a *repeated measurement design* or a *trend analysis of variance*. A discussion of analysis of variance when there are repeated measures on the same subject can be found in Edwards (1960, pp. 224–253) and a thorough discussion of trend analysis can be found in Lindquist (1953, pp. 340–351). There is one major difficulty in using the common repeated measurement and trend analysis designs for social innovative experiments. The requirement that the same participants continue to be measured during the course of the experiment cannot be met typically. Most natural social subsystems are open systems with changing membership. Accordingly, the longitudinal nature of such experiments makes the requirements of equal numbers of the same people for the entire course of the experiment usually unattainable. Nonetheless, when these requirements can be met, trend analyses are powerful comparative tools for the social innovative experimentalist.

The social innovative experimenter should use the most appropriate statistics available to compare the created subsystems. It is very likely that a mixture of all comparative methods will and should be utilized. Wherever graphs or narrative discussions give a more meaningful description and comparison, it is important that they be used. Furthermore, very often the data do not meet the assumptions for parametric statistics and hence nonparametric techniques are the most useful. Where appropriate, the more powerful parametric statistic is the statistic of choice. Where inappropriate, the researcher should not hesitate to use the newer and currently less well-developed nonparametric techniques. The paramount feature of the comparison must be that inferences from the results are clearly warranted and that the comparative evaluations are presented to the reader in a readily understandable manner.

Parametric and nonparametric techniques as applied to experimental social innovation have been presented briefly in the foregoing discussion. Table 10.1 is a summary of these methods. This cursory review of comparative methods would not be complete without emphasizing that the interested reader should pursure more detailed discussions of them in the many references provided. Certainly, many of the statistical classics should be in the social innovative researcher's library. It is always necessary that a statistician be a consultant to the research team, particularly during the planning phase of the social innovative experiment—a matter more fully considered in the discussion of the team approach (p. 72). It cannot be overemphasized that although it is the experimenter's ultimate responsibility to select the most appropriate comparative methods to evaluate his data, it is equally his responsibility to seek out the best consultation available. If this chapter on comparative methods does nothing more than make the researcher aware of the multitude of comparisons needed in social innovative experiments, and the resultant need for extensive experimental planning, it will have achieved its goal.

From the outset of the experiment, plans should be made to use computers for analyzing the voluminous data collected for the social innovative experiment. There are many comparative statistical techniques—particularly of the parametric variety—that have been programmed for computers. The Biomedical Computer Programs (Dixon, 1965) of the University of California at Los Angeles are one

Table 10.1. A Summary of Nonparametric and Parametric Statistical Tests Applicable to Social Innovative Experiments

Social Subsystem	Nonparametric Statistics Scale			Parametric Statistics Scale
	Nominal	Ordinal	Interval	Interval or Ratio
Two subsystems with matched participants		Sign Wilcoxon Signed Rank	Walsh	t
Two subsystems without matched participants	Fisher Chi-square	Median Mann-Whitney Kolmogorov-Smirnov Wald-Wolfowitz Wilcoxon Rank Sum		t
More than two subsystems with matched participants	Cochran Q	Friedman		One score per participant: Analyses of variance Simple type Multiple classification Factorial design Latin Square design Randomized block design
More than two subsystems without matched participants	Chi-square	Median Kruskal-Wallis		Two scores per participant: Analysis of covariance Repeated scores per participant: Analysis of variance Trend analysis

outstanding example. Most major universities have computer centers which the experimenter can use, provided the proper arrangements are made in advance as an integral part of the planning for an experiment. And the consultative advice of the statisticians and the computer programmers is an invaluable aid to the experimentalist.

The use of many different comparative methods in the longitudinal social innovative experiment, as well as the need for extensive planning (particularly with statisticians and computer experts), reveals that social innovative experiments require *statistical programs* rather than a statistic. But such programs cannot be complete until newer statistical methods are developed to meet the particular needs of the experimentalist doing research in social change. There is an urgent need for further development of nonparametric techniques—particularly where repeated measures on the participants are obtained—for use in evaluating social innovative experiments. Illustrative of the development of newer techniques is the work of Tryon (1958, 1959, 1965, 1966) and Tryon and Bailey (1966), especially in regard to the comprehensive program for combining relationship and comparative methods by expanding the use of cluster analysis. It will be useful to explore these correlative techniques and to expand their applicability to the data of social innovative experiments wherever the opportunity is afforded.

Chapter 11

Choosing Methods to Study the Social Relationships and Processes

There are typically a large number of measurements made during the course of any social innovative experiment. The investigator usually should try to find the relationships that may exist among them. He should also explore changes among these relationships that occur with the passage of time. Furthermore, he should determine whether or not the relationships among the many variables are different for the several experimental subsystems. The experimentalist usually should also attempt to explore the internal processes of the subsystems by finding the relationships among group processes such as performance, cohesiveness, leadership, reward, and morale. He therefore will need methods to determine these relationships and, when desired, to compare them for the several subsystems.

Correlations

The methods to determine these relationships are generically classified as the correlative methods. A correlation shows the degree of association between any two variables. The value of a correlation can vary from 1 to −1. A correlation of 1 exists when there is perfect positive agreement between any two distributions of scores. For clarity in illustrating a hypothetical 1 and −1 condition, the rank correlation (rho) can be used. Figure 11.1 shows the straight line formed by the points from two hypothetical sets of rank order scores for the same participants. The reader will note that the individuals involved have the same rank order on the two sets of scores. This is a perfect positive agreement which results in a rank correlation (rho) of 1. A correlation of −1, on the other hand, exists when the two distributions of scores show a perfect inverse relationship. Figure

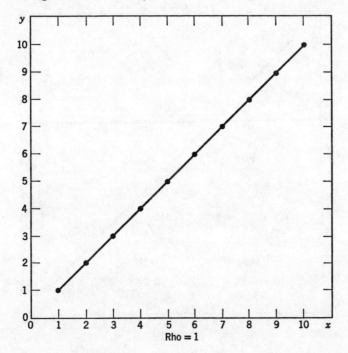

Figure 11.1. Regression line placed through the points (x,y) for a rank correlation of 1.

11.2 shows the regression line resulting from two distributions whose plotted points are exactly the opposite; namely, the highest score on one distribution goes with the lowest score on another. This graph illustrates the -1 rank correlation between the sets of scores on two variables.

The line drawn through the points in Figures 11.1 and 11.2 is commonly called the regression line. In the case where high scores on one distribution go with the high scores on the other, the slope of the regression line is positive and so is the value of the correlation; when an inverse relationship exists—when the high scores on one distribution go with the low scores on the other—a negative correlation and a negative slope of the regression line obtain.

It must also be clearly understood that correlations show relationships and do *not* reveal causation even in the rare instance where a correlation of 1 or -1 exists. It cannot even then be directly inferred that one set of scores causes the other or vice versa. The preceding hypo-

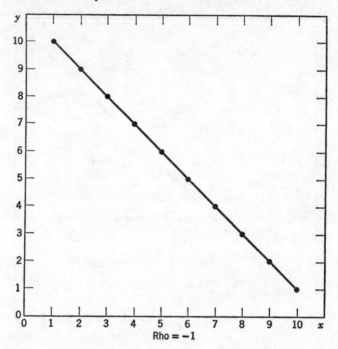

Figure 11.2. Regression line placed through the points (x,y) for a rank correlation of -1.

thetical graphs shown in Figures 11.1 and 11.2 are for the "pure" case and the experimenter usually will not have data in which there is perfect agreement. Rather, experimental data usually represent points that are at varying distances from the regression line. In these instances, the line of best fit (regression line) is placed through the points. Figure 11.3 presents a graph showing a plot of points when the correlation is positive, and Figure 11.4 shows the same thing when it is negative. In both instances, the graphs show that the regression line—the line of best fit—has points at varying distances from it. The regression line is the line of best fit—the line which reduces the sum of the squares of the distances between the points and the regression line to a minimum.

It is most important that the reader grasp the following points about correlations.

1. A correlation represents a line of best fit between the plot of the points of any two measures.

2. With the usual correlation, this is a straight line.

3. The basic data for computing a correlation are simply variables measurable on a continuous scale. Ordinal scales are therefore necessary and sufficient for computing a correlation.

4. Correlations do not reveal causation but the degrees of association between two variables.

5. The statistical symbol for a correlation is r.

These statements describe general theoretical notions for correlations. For purposes of understanding the various types of correlative techniques, the following brief descriptions are offered.

When both variables are truly dichotomous, the experimenter may compute a *phi coefficient*, r_ϕ.. The interested reader may find computational procedures and a discussion of it in Guilford (1956, pp. 311–315) and McNemar (1962, pp. 197–198). On the other hand, if the researcher has dichotomous data for which he assumes underlying continuous distributions, he should compute a *tetrachoric correlation*, r_t (Guilford, 1956, pp. 305–310; McNemar, 1962, pp. 193–197). Upon occasion, the researcher has only data that can be categorized in two,

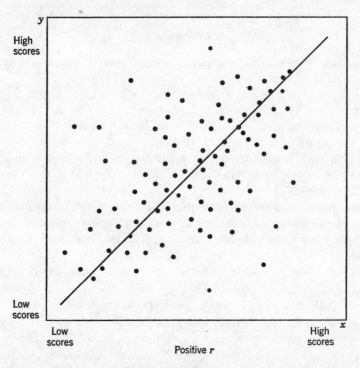

Figure 11.3. Regression line and plot of points (x,y) for a positive correlation.

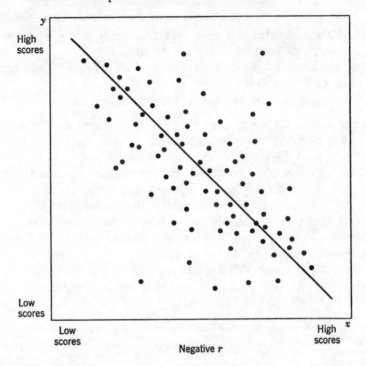

Figure 11.4. Regression line and plot of points (*x,y*) for a negative correlation.

three, or more categories such as high, middle, and low income groups. When this is the case, a *contingency coefficient, C,* may be computed. It is a measure of the degree of association but is not technically considered a correlation. A useful discussion of the contingency coefficient can be found in Guilford (1956, pp. 315–316) and McNemar (1962, pp. 198–202).

Sometimes the experimenter will find that one of his distributions is dichotomous while the other is continuous. The experimenter should compute a *point biserial correlation, r_{pb},* if he assumes the dichotomous variable to be truly discrete, and a *biserial correlation, r_b,* if he assumes that a continuous variable underlies the dichotomous data (Guilford, 1956, pp. 297–305; McNemar, 1962, pp. 189–193).

Frequently the social innovative experimentalist has rank order data. Examples of two rank order distributions which resulted in 1 and −1 correlations were given in Figures 11.1 and 11.2. When this is the case, a *rank correlation* (rho) can be computed (Edwards, 1954, pp. 193–197; McNemar, 1962, pp. 203–205). When there are several rank order distributions (a frequent occurrence if several raters rank the same data), a *Kendall coefficient of concordance, W,* is computed (p. 136). It shows the degree of agreement among all of the raters. The computational procedures and use of *W* are fully discussed in Siegel (1956, pp. 229–238).

The most commonly used measure of correlation, however, is the *Pearson product moment correlation, r.* This is frequently used when the data are measured on an interval or ratio scale. Thorough discussions with computational examples for the Pearson *r* can be found in Edwards (1954, pp. 142–170), McNemar (1962, pp. 112–135), and Guilford (1956, pp. 135–153).

While the preceding discussion has presented the correlational techniques by classifications of data, it would also be possible to classify them by their relationship to each other. Thus the Pearson product moment correlation, phi, and the point biserial correlation are all forms of *r*, whereas the tetrachoric correlation and the biserial correlation are estimates of phi and the point biserial correlation respectively. A helpful discussion of the similarities and differences among the various correlative techniques may be found in Guilford (1956, pp. 285–331).

There are other correlational methods that the experimentalist may need upon occasion. The two most important are the *partial correlation* and the *multiple correlation.* A partial correlation is computed when the experimentalist wishes to correlate two variables while eliminating the effect of a third. A discussion of the partial correlation is presented by McNemar (1962, pp. 164–167) and Guilford (1956, pp. 316–318). A multiple correlation is computed when the researcher wishes to correlate one variable with a group of other variables. A presentation of multiple correlation, its computation and uses, can be found in Guilford (1956, pp. 390–434).

There is also the rare occasion when a plot of two variables to be correlated reveals that their relationship is not linear. The plot forms a curved instead of a straight line. In such a case, it is appropriate to find the degree of association by determining the curved line that best fits the data. This is accomplished by computing the *correlation ratio, eta* (η). For information of its assumptions and computational procedures, the reader is referred to Guilford (1956, pp. 288–297).

Factor and Cluster Analyses

Although the social innovative experimenter occasionally has the need to independently compute a correlation, whether product moment, partial, or multiple, he is usually interested in multivariate analyses. These are methods by which the intercorrelations among a large number of measures can be determined. The data are programmed for computers and information comes to the researcher in printed form. These multivariate procedures are the social innovative researchers' most important methods to study relationships and processes because most experiments have many measures that are often repeated during the course of the experiment, and it is necessary to find their interrelationships. There are two commonly used methods of multivariate analyses, factor and cluster analysis. Both are based upon the computation of individual correlations just described.

Factor analysis had its roots in England where it was an extension of the early development of the Pearson product moment correlation coefficient. Much was contributed to its development by Spearman (1927), Burt (1941), Thomson (1940), Holzinger and Harman (1941), and Hotelling (1933). Factor analysis was later more fully developed by L. L. Thurstone. In 1947 he published a book, *Multiple Factor Analysis: A Development and Expansion of the Vectors of Mind,* which became a commonly used text. Cattell (1946) later presented methods for determining the factor structure among tests, persons, and occasions. The basic idea of factor analysis is that a vector can be placed through a subset of the interrelated variables and that this vector represents a dimension of measurement to which each variable is related. This dimension can therefore replace the separate variables so that the researcher can deal with a reduced number of variables without loss of generality. Of course, there can be few or many dimensions depending upon the configurations of the correlations. If a large number of score distributions are intercorrelated, it is possible that they would form several relatively independent clusters of measures. The relationship of each variable to any dimension is the *factor loading* on that dimension. The dimensions (factors) themselves may be interrelated or independent.

Many and varied themes have been played upon the basic ideas of factor analysis. Thurstone (1947), for example, believed that factor structure revealed the basic dimensions of the variables under investigation. Other factor analysts, however, believe that factor analysis shows that certain variables go together or are interrelated. Thus "factor structure" may be dependent upon one or many determinants such as the construction of the scales, the measurement situation, and basic dimensionality. An excellent and readable presentation of the development, logic, and methods of factor analysis can be found in Fruchter's book *Introduction to Factor Analysis* (1954).

Computer programs are available for the vast amount of work required in factor analysis. This is especially important for the experimenter who wishes to use these methods because the time required to compute a single factor analysis by hand is exceedingly great. The social innovative experimentalist will usually have to compute many. Computer programs for factor analysis are a part of the analytic techniques available in many university computer centers.

The thorough and complete development of the method of cluster analysis by Dr. Robert C. Tryon (1958, 1959, 1965, 1966) and his associates (Tryon and Bailey, 1966), along with the recently completed computer programs, gives the social innovative researcher his most useful multivariate method. Cluster analysis has the same premises as factor analysis concerning clusters of interrelated variables, and it is, in fact, a more global method because it also incorporates factor analysis as a special case. Tryon makes no assumption that the clusters represent dimensions or basic variables. Rather, he assumes from the outset that these interrelationships have to be explained from the knowledge of the experimenter about his subject matter.

This cluster method or, more accurately, series of methods, is usually the most appropriate technique in studying the relationships and processes of social subsystems. These methods combine factor and cluster analyses and, in addition, arrange them "in tandem" when required by the researcher. Thus the experimenter may make several analyses in sequence. The procedures can be arranged so that each new analysis in the sequence is derived from the preceding one. For example, the structure of one cluster analysis may be compared with the structure of a second cluster analysis in a single computer procedure. Two separate operations are involved here—the computation of the two cluster analyses and then the comparison of the cluster structures found. The computer can be programmed to perform the first operation (cluster analysis) and the second operation (comparing them) on the same computer run.

The use of cluster and factor analysis by computer program has recently been made very easy by the publication of a user's manual (Tryon and Bailey, 1965). Of equal importance to the social innovative researcher is a written description of the separate cluster programs presented in Tryon and Bailey (1966). The BC TRY cluster system provides many uses of practical and theoretical significance to social innovative research. The principal uses for the experimentalist are the following.

1. It may be used to reduce a large number of measurements on variables to a small number of clusters which have sometimes been termed dimensions. It is possible to have as many as 1000 separate measures.

2. Different cluster analyses can be *compared* through the use of an unusual correlative technique. This is especially important when studying processes because cluster analyses of data collected at different moments in time can be compared and developmental patterns revealed.

3. It is possible to compare individuals rather than scores on various social, behavioral, and perceptual variables.

4. It can be used for sampling purposes. Where there are a large number of variables or individuals, the BC TRY system provides a method for randomly selecting by computer individuals or variables that are unbiased samples of a particular population.

The cluster analysis results (the computer printout) provides the researcher with a great deal of information that is important to him. Most important to the social innovative researcher are the following.

1. Where the data are normal, it provides a set of means for each variable.

2. In such cases it also provides the standard deviation for each variable.

3. It provides intercorrelational matrices. This is important because the researcher can obtain the relationship of any variable with any other variable from this matrix. One should note here that the hand computation of a single correlation may take as much or more time than the machine computation of an entire cluster analysis.

4. It provides the clusters, that is, the correlation of each variable with every cluster in the analysis.

5. It provides a correlation matrix of the derived clusters.

6. It provides geometric drawings of the cluster. This is an important feature for those who more easily grasp geometric concepts.

7. In the case where more than one cluster analysis has been accomplished, it provides a comparative analysis of the cluster structure coming from the separate analyses.

8. After the clusters have been determined, each individual in the sample can be assigned on the "printout" a score on each of the derived clusters. This is an important time-saving device because the researcher is provided with new scores for each individual in the sample on each cluster. Such data can then be used for comparative purposes.

9. Cluster analysis has also been programmed for missing data. In naturalistic settings, individuals usually enter and leave the subsystems so quickly that missing data are a present and recurring problem.

Although there is no intention of providing the reader here with a detailed discussion of all facets of factor and cluster analysis which are so clearly presented by Tryon and Bailey (1966), it is important that he be aware of some of the applications of such analyses to social problems. To accomplish this, selected illustrations that yield information which is often important to the researcher are now presented.

Determining Dimensionality

The experimenter often wishes to discover the common dimensions of the many measures used in a given experiment. Illustratively, 120 different measures were administered during the course of the hospital study (Fairweather, 1964, pp. 273–282). These 120 variables were then cluster analyzed. Table 11.1 presents the cluster analysis. The reader will note that eight clusters were found.

Table 11.2 presents the relationship among these clusters. It shows that the eight dimensions are relatively independent.

These two tables clearly indicate to the researcher that many variables usually considered measures of improvement in treating mental illness are quite independent of each other. This is a significant empirical finding to mental health researchers and program planners who must determine which are acceptable criteria for improvement in treating the mentally ill. The use of such empirically derived information as an aid in defining or redefining the social change outcome criterion is fully discussed elsewhere (pp. 81–85).

Determining the Relationship Among Individuals

The interpersonal relationship structure among individuals is frequently an important aspect of the internal processes of a subsystem. The experimenter may wish to know, for example, whether the formal organization of the subsystems affects the participants' perception of others. Recent application of cluster analysis to this problem is also presented in the hospital study (Cressler, 1964, pp. 103–121). An eight-item picture sociometric was given to all individuals in the sample. These items were then scored in such a manner that each individual was given a score on the degree to which he preferred to associate with all others in his task group. Cluster analyses were performed on sociometric scores. The preference for members of the created task groups to which each individual was assigned is shown in Table 11.3. The size of the perceptual groups and an individual's affiliations with them can also be determined.

Table 11.1. The Eight Clusters

Cluster 1—Posthospital Adjustment
1. Follow-up
   a. Remains out of the hospital (social change outcome criterion)   .82
   b. Has socially supportive living situation   .71
   c. Is frequently employed   .45
   d. Is frequently employed in low status job   .43
   e. More frequently talks to other people   .41
2. Treatment prior to discharge
   a. Fewer days in experimental treatment program   .80
   b. Fewer weeks of hospitalization during lifetime   .47
3. Group processes measures
   a. Has fewer penalties imposed by task group   .40

Cluster 2—Social Interaction
1. Recreation hour behavior
   a. Frequently engages in social activity   .95
   b. Frequently engages in social interaction with other patients   .89
   c. Talks frequently   .81
   d. Frequently faces room   .41
2. Frequently chosen by others on the picture sociometric as a person one would
   a. Plan to go out with   .53
   b. Live on same street with   .49
   c. Like to work with   .49
   d. Like as a close friend   .49
   e. Seek out if help was needed   .48
   f. Stop to talk with   .46
   g. Say hello to   .45
   h. Recognize   .42
3. Group meeting behavior
   a. Makes many speeches   .45
   b. Spends time in speaking   .45
   c. Makes problem-oriented speeches   .45
   d. Frequently talks to group at large   .44
   e. Frequently talks to other patients   .42
4. Group processes measures
   a. Frequently seen as a helpful task group member by staff   .43
   b. Frequently seen as a helpful task group member by patients   .42

Cluster 3—Positive Attitudes about Treatment Program
1. Biographical evaluation of treatment program
   a. Frequently perceives program as leading to personal gain   .85
   b. Frequently would choose same ward   .84
   c. Frequently assesses treatment program as positive   .55
   d. Perceives the total treatment program as helpful   .45

Table 11.1. (*Continued*)

2. Staff and ward regulation attitude questionnaire
   a. Positively evaluates ward regulation .72
   b. Positively evaluates pass policy .62
   c. Positively evaluates ward doctor .53
   d. Positively evaluates staff nurse .53
   e. Positively evaluates money policy .53
   f. Positively evaluates aides .50

Cluster 4—Affective Involvement in Treatment Program
1. Biographical evaluation of treatment program
   a. Positive feelings during process of treatment program .79
   b. Negative feelings upon entry .74
   c. Gives general positive evaluation of treatment program .50
   d. Has strong affective involvement in treatment program .41

Cluster 5—Behavioral Nonconformity during Group Meeting
1. Group meeting behavior
   a. Frequently leaves group meeting early .81
   b. Frequently enters group meeting late .79
   c. Frequently whispers .42

Cluster 6—Social Preference
1. Frequently chooses others on picture sociometric as person one would
   a. Plan to go out with .87
   b. Like to work with .86
   c. Seek out if help was needed .84
   d. Live on same street with .82
   e. Stop to talk with .74
   f. Say hello to .73
   g. Recognize .69
   h. Like as a close friend .66

Cluster 7—Aspirations and Status
1. Job interview aspiration scale
   a. Perceives self as having high status job .90
   b. Perceives self as being willing to accept only high status jobs .83
   c. Expects high status job at discharge .67
   d. Expects to have high status job five years after discharge .56
   e. Expects to be advanced in job status .52
   f. Held high status job prior to hospitalization .41

Cluster 8—Tranquilizing Medication during Hospitalization
1. Greater total amount of medication received .94
2. Greater number of days medication received .81
3. Greater mean daily dosage .74
4. Greater number of dosage changes .57

Table 11.2. The Correlations Among the Eight Clusters

Clusters	1 Posthospital Adjustment	2 Social Interaction	3 Positive Attitudes about Treatment Program	4 Affective Involvement in Treatment Program	5 Behavioral Nonconformity in Large Group Meetings	6 Social Preference	7 Aspirations about Status	8 Tranquilizing Medication
1. Posthospital adjustment		.24	.20	.18	−.01	.02	.08	−.23
2. Social interaction	.24		.10	.15	.05	.17	.35	−.20
3. Positive attitudes about treatment program	.20	.10		.16	−.08	.22	−.01	−.03
4. Affective involvement in treatment program	.18	.15	.16		.12	.21	.05	−.02
5. Behavioral nonconformity in large group meetings	−.01	.05	−.08	.12		−.04	−.08	−.02
6. Social preference	.02	.17	.22	.21	−.04		.01	−.13
7. Aspirations about status	.08	.35	−.01	.05	−.08	.01		−.11
8. Tranquilizing medication	−.23	−.20	−.03	−.02	−.02	−.13	−.11	

Table 11.3. Comparison of the Task Groups on the Number and Percentage [a] of Patients in Each Cluster Group When Chosen by Others (Patient as a Social Object)

Cluster Group	Task Group							
	1		2		3		4	
	N	%	N	%	N	%	N	%
1	0	0	0	0	1	11	8	89
2	1	11	3	33	2	23	3	33
3	1	14	5	72	0	0	1	14
4	7	100	0	0	0	0	0	0
5	3	42	2	29	0	0	2	29
6	1	17	4	66	0	0	1	17
7	0	0	4	80	0	0	1	20
8	1	20	0	0	1	20	3	60
9	0	0	0	0	3	100	0	0

[a] The chance percent of patients is 25 in each task group.

Studying Dynamic Processes

In a recent study, Maynard (1966) constructed scales to measure 14 key group dynamic variables. Repeated measures were taken with four different groups every 90 days for six successive measurement periods—a total time of 450 days. The first measurement was taken when the groups were organized. The groups were open groups so that by the sixth time period all but three individuals present at the first measurement had departed from their respective groups. For purposes of the analysis, group and individual scores were assigned every individual in each group and six cluster analyses were then performed. Table 11.4 presents rank scores in cluster consistency for the six analyses. The table shows that at early stages of development, the groups were relatively undifferentiated in dimensionality. By the third time period, 180 days, group structure consisted of three variables which may be defined as leadership, morale, and performance. Table 11.4 also indicates that from 180 days on the social structure becomes so fixed that an almost wholly new sample did not change the social structure. Thus the point where the aggregate groups became a social subsystem occurred around 180 days. In addition, mean cluster scores were generated for each of the groups—

Table 11.4.   Rank Order Scores for Consistency [a] of Cluster Composition

Cluster Dimension	Time Periods in Days					
	0	90	180	270	360	450
Cohesiveness-morale	3	3	2	2	3	2
Performance-reward	5	6	4	1	3	3
Leadership-role clarity	5	2	2	2	3	3
Residual cluster	5	5	1	1	1	1
Rank Total	18	16	9	6	10	9

[a] Low scores represent most consistency.

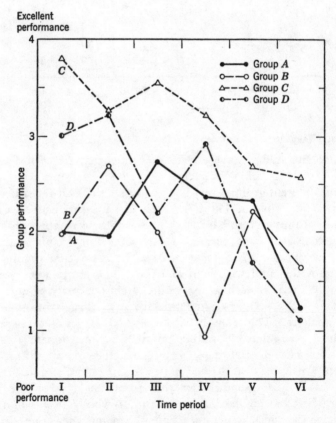

Figure 11.5.   Plot of the mean cluster performance scores for the four experimental groups.

four experimental groups—and each group was then independently plotted over the six time periods. A graph of their performance is shown in Figure 11.5. The contribution of cluster analysis in determining group structure and comparing it over time is one of its major contributions to experimental social innovation.

Comparing Subsystems on Dimensionality

The method just described is also suited to comparing two or more different subsystems or the same subsystem at different times. It provides a direct comparison between the dimensions discovered in one subsystem and those discovered in the others or of the dimensions of a subsystem at one time contrasted with the same subsystem at another. This method also yields an *index of similarity* for the dimensions of the clusters that are compared. The study just mentioned (Maynard, 1966) gives an example of such a comparative analysis. Table 11.4 shows the degree to which each cluster has a consistent membership of variables for the six time periods.

These applications of the methods of cluster and factor analysis as proposed by Tryon and his associates are, in essence, time-saving computer analyses of the relationships and processes of social subsystems. They are an indispensable part of the statistical techniques to be used by the social innovative experimentalist.

The Action and Evaluation Phases

Chapter 12

The Final Plan for the Experiment, the Data Collection, and the Analyses

Procedures to establish the administrative commitments necessary to carry out an experiment, to select the experimental problem, to define and describe the subsystems that are to be compared, to choose the areas of measurement and create devices to assess them, and to select the appropriate evaluative techniques have been presented in Chapters 3 through 11. All that remains of the planning phase now is the formal statement of the experimental hypotheses that are to be tested and the development of a final plan for scheduling all experimental processes.

Usually the experimental hypotheses are stated in terms of the comparative effectiveness of the subsystems' outcomes. Since the social innovative experimenter proposes only subsystems designed to improve the social position of their participants, the experimental hypotheses are always stated in a manner which predicts that the innovated subsystem or subsystems will be more beneficial to their participants than the usual social practice (control condition, p. 26). In the simplest case there are two subsystems. One is the usual social practice (control condition) and the other is an innovated experimental subsystem. Here the general experimental hypothesis is that the experimental subsystem will result in significantly more beneficial outcomes than the usual social practice. When several subsystems have an equal opportunity, in the judgment of the experimenter, to improve the social position of the participants, the experimenter may hypothesize that all new subsystems will produce significantly better outcomes than the usual social practice. On the other hand, when several different subsystems are involved, the experimenter may predict that each new subsystem can be rank ordered in terms of its potential beneficial effects. Thus he may predict that the first new subsystem will do better than the usual social practice, the second will do better than the first, and so on. In any case, it should be clearly evident that hypotheses are stated in such a manner that the innovative experimental subsystem or subsystems are always predicted to yield more beneficial outcomes than the control condition. This is true because experiments in social innovation are designed to accord their participants a more rewarding role in their society. Thus the social innovative experimenter cannot entertain the hypothesis that any new subsystem will result in no change or a worsening of the participants' social position (p. 32). All hypotheses are therefore one-sided (pp. 200–202).

The Experimental Plan

It is now necessary to make a plan for the entire experimental program. Such a plan specifies the manner in which the procedures listed in Table 2.2 are to be carried out and prepares a time schedule for their execution. It shows the times for the beginning and ending of the different phases of the research program—the planning, action, evaluation, and dissemination phases. The plan also contains a timetable for measurement and the introduction of new experimental procedures. An example of such a plan can be found in the community study referred to earlier (p. 34). It is presented in Table 12.1.

One of the research questions of the community experiment concerned the degree of professional leadership required for the operation of a community subsystem whose participants were discharged chronic mental patients. To explore the amount and type of professional supervision required, it was decided that leadership in the working-living situation would be changed three times. For the first eight months of operation, the supervisor would be a well-trained psychologist with several years' experience working with mental patients. At the end of the eight months he would be replaced by a less experienced psychologist who had not yet completed his training. Finally, at the end of sixteen months of operation he would be replaced by a lay leader who had no previous experience with mental illness. The three leadership periods in the action phase were scheduled in the research plan which is presented in Table 12.1. Longitudinal social innovative experiments ordinarily will require such introductions of *planned experimental change* at prearranged times during the course of the experiment.

The preceding example illustrates the necessity to fully describe

Table 12.1. General Plan for an Experiment Comparing Community and Hospital Treatment Subsystems

Program Phase	Time Scale	Research Activity
	minus 4 months	Trial of assessment devices under model field conditions
	minus 3 months	Modification and perfection of assessment devices Establish preliminary reliability of assessment devices
	minus 2 months	Establish location of both subsystems Preliminary testing of the samples
	minus 1 month	Draw initial samples for both subsystems Preliminary meetings for participants of both subsystems
	0 months	Initial testing for both subsystems First professional supervisor of community subsystem begins operations
	plus 6 months	First general testing of both subsystems First follow-up measures for both subsystems
	plus 7 months	Start training of second professional supervisor for community subsystem
	plus 8 months	Change to second professional supervisor of community subsystem
	plus 12 months	Second general testing of both subsystems Second follow-up measures for both subsystems First measures of community and hospital attitudes toward both subsystems
	plus 15 months	Start training of nonprofessional supervisor for community subsystem

Residual of Planning

Initiate subsystems

Action

185

Table 12.1   (*Continued*)

Program Phase	Time Scale	Research Activity
	plus 16 months	
		Change to nonprofessional supervisor of community subsystem
	plus 18 months	
Action		Third general testing of both subsystems
		Third follow-up measures for both subsystems
	plus 24 months	
		Fourth general testing of both subsystems
		Fourth follow-up measures for both subsystems
		Second measures of community and hospital attitudes to both subsystems
Close sub-systems	plus 28 months	
		Final measures of community attitudes which were impractical while subsystems were in operation
		Stop all data collection except for follow-up data
		Begin scoring, tabulation, and analysis of data gathered to date
Evaluation and dissemination	plus 30 months	
		Fifth follow-up measures for both subsystems
		Begin planning phase of next experiment
	plus 42 months	
		End write-up and publication of experiment
		Continue planning phase of next experiment

and elaborate upon each specific detail of the research procedure in the final research plan. It is also usually necessary to plan the size sample needed for the experiment prior to the onset of the action phase. It often happens that the use of naturally-occurring open human groups for social subsystems prevents establishing beforehand a date at which the sample size will be reached. Accordingly, the size of the sample is determined during the planning phase of the experiment and sampling is discontinued at the moment when the participant who represents the predetermined number enters the experimental subsystem.

The timing of all measurements and research innovations, as well as the beginning and end of the different phases, should carefully follow what has been determined in the final research plan. This is important because later comparisons between subsystems should not be unduly influenced by unplanned events. As a last important facet of the research plan, all of the researchers whose roles involve interaction with the participants should rehearse their required behaviors. Illustratively, those who are to administer the assessment devices should practice giving instructions, and raters should practice on samples of the experimental population. An excellent example of the corrective effect of trying out the instruments and practicing rating is presented by Goldman (1964, p. 49).

". . . However, the social behavior that we sought to measure was not all represented in the LAI, and so plans were made to alter the instrument. In the course of making practice observations, it also became apparent that, although the over-all technique was well suited to our needs, the fact still remained that many of the scoring techniques had been developed with a patient population apparently far more immobile and considerably less active than our own. To put it more succinctly, the observer all too often could not keep pace with our patients' movements and social activities. Thus recon-struction and modification of the LAI was in order and, consequently, a new scoring and procedural manual was written by the psychologist-observer . . . ."

It is clear that this practice aided in improving the instrument as well as preparing the rater for the action phase of the experiment.
Much of the trial period for practicing with assessment devices and role playing may be done in the ordinary social research laboratory or in other small-scale researches by carrying out pilot studies prior to the onset of the experiment proper. Such full-scale pilot studies are usually not feasible with social innovative experi-ments, because entire subsystems cannot be set up as models to be used for a few days or weeks and then abandoned. Therefore practicing the research roles, determining the reliability and practical-ity of using the instruments, and other pre-experimental tryouts usually must be done with the experimental population in situations that are not identical with the experimental subsystems that will later be created. Because the control condition in social innovative experiments is usually existing societal practice, it is advantageous to try out the experimental procedures in one of these settings. Since

there will be no opportunity to try the procedures in the new subsystems once they are created, it is very important that every experimental procedure be tried and perfected in the control situation prior to the action phase. All assessment devices should be tried, timing should be agreed upon, and roles should be rehearsed during the planning phase so that the experimental procedures go smoothly when the new subsystems are activated.

After planning is completed, the action phase may begin. This occurs when the new subsystems are activated and it ends when their operations are terminated. Almost all data are collected during the action phase. After the subsystems are closed down, the data analysis phase begins. This phase ends when the data are analyzed. The fourth and final phase then begins. This includes making inferences from the research results, publishing all pertinent information, and planning the next experiment. This final phase will be discussed more extensively in Chapter 13. The first three phases of the social innovative experiment are discussed in this chapter.

The creation of the social innovative design, the formulation of the research schedule, and rehearsal of research roles completes the first or planning phase of the experiment. After the social innovative plan has been created and role behaviors rehearsed, the experimental social subsystems can be activated.

The Action Phase: Data Collection

On a designated day the participants can be placed in the subsystems and the programs designed for each of the model social subsystems will begin. The roles for participants and staff alike can now be put into effect. This formally begins the action phase. It will usually be accompanied by the need for some revision in plans because unforeseen events will occur. As an example, on the initial day of activating the community research just mentioned, 15 chronic mental patients were moved from the hospital to a community dormitory. Here they were expected to operate a janitorial and gardening service. Many had performed such jobs in the hospital for a number of years and it was therefore expected that they would immediately begin work in this capacity in the community setting. It was soon apparent, however, that the hospital training they had received did not adequately prepare them for community work and, accordingly, a training program was devised to correct this deficiency. This is but one of the many changes that had to be made as the subsystem began to function, but the basic plan of operating a business and maintaining the members of the subsystem was not altered. Innovated subsystems can have new roles that cannot be tried prior to the experiment. In such a case it will be necessary that the specific behaviors required for such roles evolve during the first several weeks of the action phase. An example can be found in the evolution of the social worker's role in the small group program of the hospital study. It was recognized in the planning phase that a social worker's role would be needed to deal with relatives and the community. The precise manner in which this role could be integrated into the small group program could not be clearly understood before the subsystem was placed in operation. The role therefore evolved in the first few weeks of the action phase. Blochburger and Lewis (1964, pp. 259–261) give the following account.

". . . The social worker's role gradually evolved in the program as it progressed . . . . Not until about six weeks after the program's beginning did it become apparent that the social worker would have a unique and specialized function in the system. As the time neared when patients were ready to make leave plans after having completed the requirements of the program, the question arose as to how their plans should be evaluated . . . . An evaluation of the leave plans frequently involves interviews with family members; it seemed appropriate for the social worker to assume this function. Some plans required referral to other community agencies, such as employment offices, welfare agencies, and out-patient rehabilitation centers, many of which have a working relationship with the Social Work Service of the hospital. Also, some plans included the use of programs directly under Social Work Service administration, such as foster home care and follow-up supervision by social workers in the field office . . . . In retrospect, the evolution of the social worker as evaluator of group-approved plans came about rather naturally and smoothly. Once the roles were established, it was possible to refine the procedures and become engaged in a maximum effort to help the patients obtain the benefits that the system offered."

Adjustments often need to be made in the first days of the action phase so that the planned subsystem can fulfill its intended goals. It is probable that some adjustments will have to be made when any innovated programs are placed in action. It is important therefore that the research plan allow for some flexibility in the initial days of operation so that such needed changes can be accomplished. The changes that are needed and the procedures necessary to implement them should be recorded in detail as research data. The action phase is the time during which most data are collected. For this reason it is sometimes referred to as the data collection phase. During this phase of the experiment the operation of the subsystems is continued without change except for the adjustments needed at the beginning and those innovations that are part of the experimental conditions, such as the planned changes in leadership mentioned in Table 12.1.

Many types of interference which can occur during the course of the experiment could alter the subsystems' operation and would therefore destroy the experimental conditions so assiduously developed and established by the researchers. The investigators must be aware of such sources of interference and be prepared to invoke the administrative agreements which were made during the planning phase to prevent interference with the subsystems after the action phase has begun (pp. 51–62). Some sources of interference that may occur when subsystems have been activated are worthy of brief discussion.

First, a successful research may arouse the interest of the scientific and lay communities. Interested individuals may wish to visit the subsystems to see their operation at first hand. This is a particular problem when working with populations like the mentally ill, in whom the public is beginning to have a much greater interest. But permitting such visits may destroy the operation of the subsystems because it introduces new social variables that, ordinarily, are not planned for at the outset of the experiment. Frequent visits would, in fact, change the subsystems themselves. To prevent such intrusions the researcher may need to request support from his research institute to prevent visits that could in any way interfere with the experimental conditions. Preventing outside interference is sometimes difficult, particularly when the interested people are in some way associated with the funding or administration of the research program. Nonetheless, it is the responsibility of the researcher to try to prevent alterations in the experimental conditions. This is most important because future social subsystems will undoubtedly not be accompanied by the interest which new subsystems create. For maximum generalization, therefore, naturalistic conditions must be preserved if at all possible.

A second source of interference may be turnover among staff personnel. This is a recurring source of difficulty because of the longitudinal nature of social innovative research. For this reason it is important to establish procedures at the outset of the experiment for the training of new personnel who might be needed as replacements for those members who probably will leave. It is especially important that the effects of personnel changes are minimized during the action phase because role constancy is an essential experimental condition. Procedures for training new personnel should be included as an integral part of the planning phase. An example of training a new rater during the course of the action phase of the experiment is given by Goldman (1964, p. 53).

"The second observer was to become the sole rater during the last six weeks of the program, since commitments would take the original observer from the ward scenes."

". . . the second observer also (needed to) be equally familiar to the patients on both wards. Approximately ten days of instruction and practice were instituted in order to provide a fair test of reliability of the instrument and to insure a similarity in rater technique. Both judges independently rated 280 patients during 7 separate recreational periods . . . in no case did the average rater agreement fall below 90%."

It is also possible that certain research procedures will need to be altered during the course of the experiment. This often happens if any of the experimental techniques begin to interfere unduly with the naturalistic processes that are being investigated. In the community program, for example, weekly discussions with the participants were part of the initial research plan. These were structured discussions where the group was asked questions concerning their satisfaction with the organization and their roles. By the end of six months, all information about the developmental phase had been collected and it soon became apparent that the group discussions were interfering increasingly with the work and living situation of the participants. Accordingly, they were discontinued.

Another source of interference may be publicity. It often happens that new programs gain early publicity that either raises false hopes or prematurely records failure. In either case it has an effect upon the participants in the various subsystems. This effect may prevent direct future application of the experimental subsystem because such publicity will probably not be given to the replicates which are established as service programs. This is particularly true of new programs that excite interest, because once the novelty of the program has disappeared the interest of the curious wanes. From an experimental point of view, such publicity can be devastating because the results obtained may not be attributable to the social subsystems but rather to the attention paid the participants. Placebo effects are well documented in other research situations (Frank, 1961, pp. 65–74). Accordingly, it is exceedingly important to avoid this source of extraneous interference. Social innovative experiments are especially vulnerable to excessive publicity because the protection accorded researchers when they are carrying out laboratory studies is usually not accorded the social innovative experimentalist, particularly when his work is in the community. It is very important that the agreements about publicity reached with newspaper people and other interested persons prior to the onset of the experiment are honored.

Throughout the course of the action phase, sources of interference that require the experimenter to ask for the execution of the agreements made prior to the onset of the study will appear (pp. 51–62). Upon occasion, for example, it may be necessary to ask for maintenance of the agreement made about sampling. It is quite common that a sample is readily available at the outset of the study, but after several months of experimental action the initial sampling procedures are placed in jeopardy because the institutions involved have forgotten about them or other needs have arisen which interfere with existing sampling agreements. If this occurs, the experimentalist should advise the administrators who have agreed to the sampling procedures of this change and request a return to the original procedures. It cannot be overemphasized that it is the ultimate responsibility of the investigator to maintain the constancy of the social subsystems during the action phase.

It is not uncommon that new and interesting processes will occur during the course of the experiment which were unknown or unforeseen at its beginning. The researcher should design new instruments to measure these processes as they occur. Although adequate planning may reduce these unforeseen events to a minimum, in longitudinal experiments of several months' or years' duration, new processes that should be fully described will emerge. When these changes occur it is most important that new data collection procedures are arranged to measure them. The new procedures should require as little change as possible in the research plan. Also, occasionally one event occurs as a unique experience. In such a case, as much information as possible should be obtained about it. This might be called *information saturation* because special attention is given all aspects of any incident that occurs once and is not likely to be repeated. In the community project, for example, one of two lay supervisors who was hired in the action phase immediately formed a dislike for the research program. He subsequently quit his job. All information concerning his relationship with the group, his reasons for leaving, and the group's interaction with him were accumulated prior to the time he left so that the information could be studied later in great detail.

During the action phase, there are usually planned changes that are scheduled to occur at designated times. For instance, in the hospital study, the staffs were switched from one subsystem to the other at a prearranged time.

"To equate the number of days each of the two staffs spent in the two treatment programs, the staffs changed treatment programs half way through the experimental period, a procedure which later was entitled "the staff switch." Through this procedure, each staff spent an equivalent amount of time in the two experimental programs." (Fairweather, 1964, p. 33)

As another example, Table 12.1 shows that three different supervisors were introduced to the community subsystem at the planned times. In addition there are the continuous ratings, interviews, and testings which are scheduled for given dates, also shown in Table 12.1. All these scheduled activities must be executed at the appropriate times with the least interference possible in the processes of the subsystem.

There are, of course, many problems pertaining to the collection and storage of data which emerge during the action phase. As far as data collection is concerned, it is important to establish check sheets to make certain all data are obtained from each participant at every time of measurement. To minimize collection errors, a check sheet for each participant can be created and all incoming data can be recorded on the sheet as they arrive. Preventing errors is particularly important in longitudinal research where repeated measures are used because data that are not collected at the designated time cannot be retrieved. Another source of error is incomplete forms. To reduce the number of incompletions it is important that all responses to questionnaires, tests, and so on be reviewed while the respondent is still present so that he can complete whatever items he has missed. Furthermore, the administrator of the tests can reduce such deletions by being available to give additional instructions when necessary. This is exceedingly important with marginal populations, many of whom may be uneducated or emotionally disturbed. Finally, adequate storage space for the collected data needs to be provided. Here, it is most important that all information be clearly labeled and appropriately filed so that the data can be readily located when scoring is to be done.

It is also important that all researchers associated with the experiment coordinate their activities so that the preparation of measuring devices and the collection and labeling of the data can continue concomitant with the operation of the subsystems. To accomplish this, each researcher should be made responsible for particular aspects of the research so that all data collection continues without interruption. It is also important, when possible, that some of the data be scored during the action phase. Scoring manuals can be created for each instrument and used by the research staff to begin scoring the vast accumulation of data.

Eventually, it will be necessary to stop the operation of the subsystems when the action phase of the experiment has been completed. Planning for termination of the subsystems is part of the experimental plan. The future of the participants after termination of the action phase also needs to be considered as part of this plan. For example, the community program was continued as a private business by the discharged patients themselves upon completion of the action phase of that experiment. When the subsystem is located in the community and the action phase is completed, it is also necessary to cancel residential leases, make arrangements for the cessation of insurance coverage, dispose of the work tools, and so forth.

The experimenter thus must close down the entire operation. This is often difficult to do, particularly when the research has been successful with marginal people. Nonetheless, it is the experimenter's responsibility to do this because of the difference between experiments and service. Every experiment must have a beginning and an end; its information must then be evaluated in relation to the creation of new researches and the innovation of new subsystems. If the results are beneficial, it is the responsibility of a society's agents to utilize them in establishing new service programs. While the experimentalist must give society's representatives all of the information he has and, in fact, may even supply a member of the research team to aid in establishing such programs, it is the responsibility of society's members to put such service programs into effect on a day-to-day service basis. It is the experimenter's proper responsibility to innovate and evaluate new programs.

It is therefore most important that after the action phase the researcher sever his relationships with the social subsystems he has created so that he can pursue further innovative experiments that are hopefully more beneficial than the one just completed. However, even after the action phase has been completed, some data continue to be collected. Some follow-up information often needs to be obtained from the participants, who had been in the subsystems for several months or years, after the subsystems have ceased operation. This is particularly important when evaluating the permanence of the subsystems' outcomes upon the lives of the participants. In subsystems designed for such marginal people as the chronically mentally ill and long-term criminals, the experimenter is often interested in recidivism rates or other effects which may occur after the subsystems are no longer in operation.

The Evaluation Phase: Data Analyses

As soon as the subsystems' operations have been terminated, the scoring and analysis of the data begin. When possible and if staff permits, some of the scoring may already have been done during the data collection phase. However this may be, it is now necessary to complete scoring and prepare the data for computer analysis. Nowadays the data may be placed on standardized score sheets which, when inserted in the computer, punch the cards from which the analyses are made. If it is impossible to do this because of the nature of the data, computer keypunch sheets must be prepared. The data are then treated according to the plan established for data analysis in the planning phase.

However, certain decisions—the use of parametric or nonparametric comparative methods, for example—depend upon the empirical distributions of the data. Many of these distributions will be unknown at the time the data analyses were planned. Therefore alternative forms of analysis must have been set forth in the research plan— usually parametric and nonparametric alternatives—and now those methods appropriate to the collected data will be used in the analyses. The experimenter makes decisions about whether the data meet the assumptions for parametric statistics (p. 156) or whether missing- or nonmissing-data computer programs are to be used. Such decisions are typically made after the data are collected because the experimenter may not know the nature of the data prior to the experiment. In such a case, his choice of a particular method is made when the data are at hand so that he can choose the most appropriate method.

When the data have been analyzed by the appropriate comparative and relationship techniques described in Chapters 10 and 11, the researcher must determine from these analyses and his own experiences the inferences which can properly be made from this information. The final phase of the experimental plan can now be implemented.

The Dissemination Phase

Chapter 13

Inferences, Publications, and the Next Experiment

Inferences

After the analyses have been completed, the researcher makes inferences from them by integrating them with his own experiences. He makes inferences from all of the information accumulated during the course of an experiment. Thus tests of statistical significance obtained from the analyses of the data may be only one type of information from which the generalizations can originate. They are, however, the most unbiased source if they are properly applied. To understand this more completely it is necessary to recall that statistics are used to test the hypotheses set forth in the initial social innovative research plan (p. 50). Provided the statistical tests indicate a significant difference, they will allow the experimenter to reject the hypothesis that the several means, medians, or distributions of the subsystems' measurements—depending on the data and the nature of the tests—were derived from the same population. If the statistical hypothesis is rejected, that is, if the two or more statistics are not likely to have been derived from the same population, then the experimenter *infers* from them and all other experimental information what could most likely have brought about the differences in the statistics. Provided all experimental conditions have been met and there is no contrary information, he usually infers that the differences between the statistics represent the differential effects of the created subsystems.

The experimenter, however, must be aware that any differences in these statistics that he attributes to the subsystems constitute only an inference. That is, it is simply a probability statement. The experimenter tests the statistical hypothesis by use of probability tables that are typically found in statistical methods books. These tables allow the reseacher to find a level of statistical significance for the particular test employed, such as the *t* test, *F*-ratio, or chi-square. This level of significance may be defined as the probability that the two or more comparative statistics were derived from the same population. Thus, when the level of significance is arbitrarily set at .01, the experimenter may say that the obtained difference between the means, medians, or distributions would occur only rarely, that is, one time in 100 by chance alone. If the experimenter accepts this probability level as significant (an arbitrary decision) he may reject the hypothesis that the computed statistics were derived from the same statistical population.

In social innovative experiments, the researcher is always testing the hypothesis that the newly created subsystem or subsystems produces better results for the selected social problem than the control condition —the usual social method of handling the problem. This is a statistical one-sided hypothesis mentioned elsewhere (p. 150). Assuming that any measure used in the experiment will yield a higher score when the social position of the participants is enhanced, the experimenter is only interested in the statistical hypothesis that the innovative experimental subsystem or subsystems receive a higher mean score, median score, or distribution of scores than the usual social practice (control subsystem). This hypothesis is tested by a statistical test of significance.

Theoretically, each test of significance is drawn from a population of such tests. This population of tests typically forms a normal curve, and when the computed statistic falls in an arbitrarily selected area under this curve, the experimenter may reject the statistical hypothesis. The social innovative experimenter would thus reject the hypothesis that the mean score, median score, or distribution of scores of the innovated subsystem is equal to or less than such scores for the control subsystem.

One-sided hypotheses and their tests of significance as applied to social innovative experiments can be illustrated with the *t* test. In such a case, the experimenter will have two mean scores: one for the experimental subsystem and one for its control. He is interested in testing the hypothesis that the mean score for the experimental subsystem is equal to or less than the mean score for the control. Assuming that he accepts the .05 level of significance, a *t value* falling in this area in a theoretical distribution of *t values* may be used as sufficient evidence to reject the hypothesis that the mean score of the experimental subsystem is equal to or less than the mean score of the control subsystem. He can therefore infer from this rejection that the mean score for the experimental subsystem is significantly greater than the mean score for the control. Figure 13.1 shows that the *t value* must be of sufficient magnitude to fall in the shaded area under the curve. Thus it is only the one side of the distribution of tests of significance that the social innovative experimenter is interested in using. One-sided testing changes the common usage of most probability tables. The .01 level becomes the .02 level, the .02 becomes the .05, and so on. An excellent discussion of one- and two-tailed tests of significance has been presented by Jones (1952). Other discussions can be found in Edwards (1960, pp. 94–97) and McNemar (1962, pp. 61–69).

Suppose that the experimentalist is able to reject the statistical hypothesis that the obtained statistic for the experimental subsystem is equal to or less than the same statistic obtained for the control subsystem. Before making inferences about the effectiveness of the subsystems, he first must attempt to synthesize the results of the statistical tests of significance with other sources of information available to him. Statistical tests alone are not sufficient evidence for the experimenter interested in social change. Not only must he require a more stringent level of statistical significance than experimenters in other fields before proposing any changes, but he must also combine the data analysis with information gained through observation, discussion, and pursuit of the total problem. He thus adds to the evidence from the statistics the information that has arisen from his own experience.

As far as the tests of significance are concerned, it is most important that a stringent level of significance be adopted, because inferences made from such an experiment might be used by the agents of society to instigate social changes. The ethical experimentalist would not

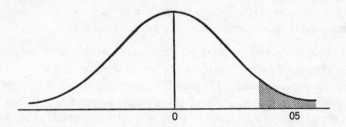

0   05

Figure 13.1. The social change experimentalist's one-tailed test of significance for the statistical hypothesis that the mean of the experimental subsystem $(m_{es}) \leqq$ the mean of the control (m_o) against the alternative $m_{es} > m_o$. If the computed t falls in the shaded area, the statistical hypothesis $m_{es} \leqq m_o$ can be rejected.

wish to support social change unless his results clearly suggest that such changes would appear to benefit significantly the population under investigation. Since the usual social practice with which the experimental subsystems are compared has been assiduously developed by society's agents over many years, it would be foolhardy to recommend a change in the manner society has developed to handle its problem unless a better solution has been manifestly demonstrated. This suggests that in statistical terms a .001 level for one-tailed tests should be established as the acceptable level for recommending changes. Although this is a conservative statistical position, it should be adopted because social changes are distasteful to many individuals and should not be recommended unless they are clearly warranted. The selection of a .001 level of statistical significance is, however, perfectly arbitrary. The acceptance of any level of significance as representing the point at which the hypothesis will be rejected is determined by the weight of many factors such as the data involved, the problem selected, the sample characteristics, and even the personality of the researcher.

Suppose, now, that the experimenter is able to infer from collating all his experimental information that one or several of the experimental subsystems produces a more beneficial outcome than the usual social practice. He is then faced with making a second inference that concerns the degree to which this beneficial solution can be a solution to the problem for a society. The degree to which the solution found in the subsystem can be generalized to solve the existing problem in the society depends upon three conditions:

1. How representative the subsystem's sample is of the problem population in a society.

2. How representative the subsystem's social context is of the social context in which the problem is typically found in a society.

3. How representative the social change outcome criterion is of a society's consensus about a solution to the problem.

The representativeness of these three components of generalization may be presented geometrically as the dimensions of a cube. In Figure 13.2 the numerical values of these dimensions represent the percentage of representativeness on each of these three dimensions. Thus, zero is no representativeness; .50 is 50% representativeness; and 1.00 is 100% or perfect representativeness. The volume of each of the three cubes, which is represented by the shaded area, shows the degree to which the experimental solution is a valid solution for a society, that is, the degree to which it solves the general social problem. Cube

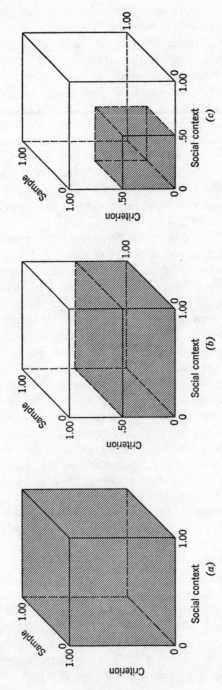

Figure 13.2. Shaded portions of the cubes represent the degree to which an experimental subsystem is a solution for a society's social problem. (*a*) When perfect (100%) representativeness exists on the three dimensions. (*b*) When perfect representativeness exists on two dimensions with 50% representativeness on the third. (*c*) When 50% representativeness exists on the three dimensions.

203

A shows that when the sample perfectly represents the problem population, when the social context within which the subsystem is implanted is perfectly representative of the social context of the problem in a society, and when the selected social change outcome criterion perfectly represents a consensual solution to the social problem, there is complete generalization from the experimental solution to the solution for a society. Cube B shows a dramatic drop of 50% generalizability when two dimensions are perfectly representative and one dimension is only 50% representative. Cube C shows a drop of 87.5% in generalization when each of the three dimensions are only 50% representative. These cubes, even though theoretical, dramatically illustrate the caution with which the experimenter should approach the problem of generalizing from the experimental situation to the society at large.

Figure 13.2 shows that one of the important facets in making inferences is the representativeness of the sample. In this respect, the important characteristics of the sample were defined while the sample was being obtained, and these sample attributes should now be contrasted with comparable national characteristics. For example, the researcher concerned with a sample of public school children between the ages of 6 and 12 would have ascertained many of the attributes of this population through the detailed historical questionnaire and other defining measures obtained during the planning phase of the experiment (pp. 113–116). The representativeness of this experimental sample can now be ascertained by checking the distributions of the defining variables with those of the national statistics, if available. When such national statistics are not available or are likely to be unreliable, the experimentalist should begin a compilation from his own sample so that generalization in future experiments can be made more accurately. In any event, the researcher should attempt to ascertain the representativeness of his sample by every means at his disposal. He should also clearly present the characteristics of his sample as well as comparative national data, where available, in the publication of his experiment, so that other experimentalists can determine the degree of similarity between the research sample and others that they may wish to use in the future.

There are other characteristics of the participants that the experimenter also needs to consider. Suppose that the children participating in such educational subsystems are volunteers. The generalizations then would necessarily be limited to children with the same attributes who are also volunteers. This is an increasingly important problem in social innovative experiments (pp. 117–118). At the very least, the same descriptive information about nonvolunteers should be obtained and their characteristics should be compared with those of the volunteers before generalizations are made.

Finally, before generalizing, failures in the subsystems as well as successes should be examined carefully. Any differences between failures and successes must be explored before the experimentalist can reasonably generalize from his results.

The degree of permissible generalization is also contingent upon the social context in which the experimental subsystems were implanted. In the educational example just mentioned, the experimentalist not only must consider the degree to which the sample is statistically similar to the general student population, but he must also be concerned about where the elementary schools are located. Let us assume that the sample of children comes from a lower-lower socioeconomic area as defined by a social class index such as the one developed by Tryon (Krech, Crutchfield, and Ballachey, 1962). The experimenter will have to limit his generalizations to similar socioeconomic and political areas.

Prior to generalization the researcher must also consider the degree to which the social change outcome criterion used in the experiment represents a consensual solution to a society's problem. The situational specificity of many of the measures typically used in social innovative experiments has been found in various studies (Fairweather, 1964, pp. 273–282; Forsyth and Fairweather, 1961). Such measures, including the social change outcome criterion, may not only be unrelated in the same situation but their relationships may change in different situations. It is therefore most important that the experimenter make his inferences only about the same or similar situations where similar criteria and samples are likely to be used. Because of the empirical nature of social innovative experiments, it is most important that generalizations be used as the basis for further experiments, so that new subsystems can be continuously established and compared.

Let us assume, in the grade school example just given, that the responsible agents of society are interested in academic achievement and define the social change outcome criterion as school grades. The experimentalist will collect many measures during the course of his experiment, one of which will be the social change outcome criterion— in this case, school grades. For example, he may use scores on academic achievement tests, or on intelligence tests, or various measures of social adjustment in addition to school grades. He must then find the correlations between these measures and the social criterion before generalizing about the effectiveness of the subsystems. Should the experimentalist find that achievement test scores were correlated only .30 with grades—the social change outcome criterion—he would point out this relatively low relationship in predicting school achievement to those responsible for admission policies or other educational procedures.

All these types of information must be considered before the experimenter can generalize. He must carefully consider the representativeness of the sample, the social context in which the research occurred, the degree to which the social change outcome criterion represents a society's consensus about problem solution, and the negative cases in formulating his research generalizations. To make such inferences, it is necessary to synthesize the results of all his experiences with the vast amount of data collected and the various statistical analyses. It is this general synthesis of all sources of information from which the inferences about the research results are made and from which new experiments can arise.

The probabilistic nature of inferences cannot be overstressed. The experimenter must always be aware that he is dealing with probabilities. Even though probabilities are set high—for example, one in 1000—it is still possible that the one-in-1000 chance of his drawing an incorrect inference has occurred. It is therefore important that the researcher not overgeneralize from his data. Because of this, information from programs initiated subsequent to the experiment itself, where the original experimental subsystems are established as service programs, should be documented and evaluated if possible. Every replication with similar findings increases the probability that the results of the initial experiment were accurate.

Each experiment generates new ideas that cannot be experimentally tested in the research itself. While these notions are often interesting and provocative, they become hypotheses for future researches and are not themselves established empirical facts. The researcher should clearly delineate the inferences that can properly be made on the basis of his research information from those general ideas he develops that may serve as hypotheses to be tested in future experiments. Generalizations from social innovative experiments not only result in the publication of scientific journal articles or books, but also may be used to change the lives of many individuals. Under these conditions, it is more desirable to be conservative about generalizations from any single experiment.

Some researches will not be successful. All parties in the research effort should clearly recognize this possibility of failure at the outset.

Information showing that certain subsystems probably do not benefit their participants is just as important as information demonstrating that some do. All information, whether negative or positive, can be useful in planning the next innovative experiment.

Finally, the experimenter must make recommendations to those agents of society who are interested in the research. He cannot evade this responsibility by simply revealing his statistical results. Accordingly, he must state whether or not a synthesis of all the experimental evidence shows that one or more of the subsystems benefits the participants and can serve as a solution to the social problem in a society. He must clearly state his inferences, cite the evidence for his conclusions, and *make recommendations about social change* to the interested agents of society.

Where a recommended subsystem is adopted by a society, selected members of the research team should aid interested administrators in establishing these new programs. Written descriptions, although stimulating and necessary, typically do not present the day-to-day operations of subsystems in such a manner that they can be adequately replicated. Furthermore, Figure 13.2 illustrates the importance of meticulously replicating each detail of a subsystem if the outcomes found in the specific experimental situation are to be generalized to other situations. Since members of research teams are the only persons completely familiar with all the details of innovated subsystems, it is important that at least one member of each team be trained to demonstrate each successful subsystem. These demonstrators should then be made available to those in positions of responsibility who are interested in placing the experimentally-validated subsystems in action. Individuals who demonstrate successful subsystems may be called *social action consultants*. Thus, in addition to publication, it is also the responsibility of the social innovative experimenter to provide an effective consulting service to society's members who wish to implement programs based upon his research results.

Publication

After inferences have been made from a synthesis of all the research data, it is necessary to publish the results of the study. It is the obligation of the research team to report in detail all aspects of the experiment. Each member of the research team should write about those aspects of the experiment that are most familiar to him. It is the research team leader's responsibility to carry out the agreements about publication made at the outset of the experiment (p. 67) and to be certain that they are followed as closely as possible. Although each researcher should write about those aspects of the experiment with which he has been most directly concerned, it should usually be the team leader's responsibility to edit all reports in order to reduce repetition and to make the final presentation as simple and understandable as possible. Here he must attempt to preserve each individual writer's style, at the same time integrating the separate writings into a meaningful whole.

It is possible that the writing phase of the project may result in some tension among research team members. This can occur because professional prestige is frequently accorded those who complete scientific writing. If any conflict does arise among members of the team, it is likely to take the form of some authors perceiving others as being in a more favorable position than they. Some authors may perceive their writings as unalterable. Accordingly, they may be unwilling to make changes, even when their writing appears poor or does not fit into the remainder of the presentation. For this reason, agreements are made about authorship *prior* to the experiment (p. 67). Therefore the editor's role and those of the various authors should be clearly set forth and agreed upon before the experiment is carried out. If possible, such contracts should be in writing and signed by the various members of the research team so that they can be referred to at a later date if needed. These agreements should include topical area of writing, location of author's names, editorial prerogatives, and the like.

In all aspects of publication, it is the editor's responsibility to try to meet each author's needs to the extent possible in such team endeavors. The editor must, however, have the final voice in determining the form of the manuscript because in such a team effort one uncooperative author can write a chapter or section so out of harmony in style and content with the remainder of the publication that it can seriously detract from the publication of an important longitudinal research. While the editor—who is usually the research team leader —must attempt to preserve each individual's style and assigned area of writing, it is also necessary for him to be aware of the total document and, accordingly, he must make the final decisions that concern the publication's overall organization.

The results of the social innovative experiment typically should be presented in one publication rather than in a series of shorter articles. This is necessary because interested readers should be able to explore all facets of the experiment in one manuscript. It is also important that initial drafts of the manuscript be read by individuals who are capable of editing them from their point of view. This procedure helps clarify communication by checking with others the degree to which the authors are clearly presenting the research program. However, the recommendations that come from others should be accepted or rejected by the editor or author solely on their merits in terms of increasing the communication of the experimental findings.

Such experiments can usually be published in book form. It is important for the researcher to explore all avenues of book publication and to select a publisher who can best present the publication to the audience that the experimenter and his team wishes to reach. It is a primary responsibility of the social innovative experimentalist to publish so that the results are available to all interested persons. The final document should present a clear description of the sample, with the participants described in terms of their defining characteristics; a clear and lucid description of the subsystems including all roles; a description of the internal processes and the external processes; comparisons of the subsystems on the social change and other outcome criteria; a presentation of relationship and process analyses; and, finally, a description of all phases of the research. As an example, the reader might refer to Fairweather (1964).

It is also important, particularly when the populations are marginal people, such as the mentally ill and criminals, that the participants' names be deleted from the manuscript. Anonymity should be a feature of any research. This is of special importance with marginal group members, many of whom might be personally embarrassed by revelation of their names, despite the fact that they are willing participants in created social subsystems. This procedure merely emphasizes respect for the wishes of the participants.

The Next Experiment

During the preparation of the manuscript and while synthesizing the results of the experiment, the researcher may begin to plan his next experiment. Since social innovative experiments are mainly empirical in nature, such researches will usually proceed in step-wise fashion— each being built upon the results of the immediately preceding one. The first studies are, of course, more broadly conceived than those that occur later. For example, the community project (p. 34) established that recidivism rates may be reduced, employment increased, and self-perceptions enhanced when a particular type of community living-working situation is provided for previously hospitalized mental patients. The next experiment might create different community subsystems for comparative purposes, because the value of at least one subsystem located in the community for these chronically hospitalized participants has already been established. Succeeding experiments with other community subsystems might well be organized around different social tasks and group compositions. It is inherent in the experimental process to proceed from gross to finer comparisons. Each succeeding experiment thus contributes new and more refined knowledge to solution of the social problem under consideration. As the final step in a current experiment, the experimental processes involved in the planning of a new experiment can now begin. The most beneficial social subsystem in the preceding experiment will now become the control condition for a new experiment and the methods for experimental social innovation will be started in a new cycle from planning through publication of results.

Section III
An Institution for
Social Innovation

Chapter 14

The Prospective Center for Experiments and Training

The need for experimental social innovation and the methodology by which it can be accomplished have been presented in earlier chapters. Throughout these chapters there has been frequent reference to the need for a central place where social innovative researchers can plan new experiments, analyze data, discuss research results with others, create demonstration teams, and train new experimentalists. Few, if any, places now exist to meet these requirements, so that centers for training in social innovative experiments and how to conduct them need to be established. This chapter represents a prospectus regarding their location, values, accouterments, and procedures.

Of course, such centers would only have value to a society if they were able to contribute to the solution of its social problems. They may be incorporated into society at this time only if society's representatives are receptive and some experimenters themselves are interested. Although both social innovative experimentalists and society's representatives are interested in the solution to social problems, there may be at this time some areas of mutual distrust. The experimentalist may fear domination of his research efforts by legislators and bureaucrats. Specifically, he may fear that his work, rather than innovating and comparing *new* subsystems, would merely become another arm of government with his role defined as the justification of preconceived political judgments rather than the attempt to provide innovative solutions to pressing social problems. On the other hand, some of society's representatives may not like certain research proposals because the proposed innovations may be perceived as undermining their own interests and beliefs. They may fear the emergence of a "scientific group" which may not be very politically realistic and which may use such centers to place in operation undesirable social changes. Furthermore, such people might ask themselves whether or not the proposed centers would give rise to a technocracy that might gain power and become a competitive political force. If these possible sources of mutual distrust should exist and could not be resolved, it is doubtful that any useful centers could be established.

Such potential misgivings of both experimentalists and society's representatives about the establishment of these centers might be correct. But they need not be. First, it must be assumed that many individuals and groups in a society are interested in solutions to social problems. The crux of the issue, however, is whether or not they are willing to agree on the logical proposition that, at least for certain social problems, there is no known solution, and, consequently, that one must be found. If this proposition is tenable, establishment of such centers would be a feasible first step toward resolution of such problems. For example, the social innovative experimenter would be in general agreement with the feeling of some legislators, as presented by Blum and Funkhouser (1965), namely, that social scientists have not been interested enough in providing practical solutions to social problems, particularly those that could be put to general use. For this reason, the general applicability of any innovated subsystem is one of the experimenter's criteria for the selection of alternative solutions to social problems (p. 39). Indeed, the whole philosophy of social innovative experiments rests upon the assumption that no empirical *comparative* evidence exists about proffered solutions for social problems, regardless of who might have initiated such proposals.

Even more important, whatever the philosophical arguments may be, it is possible that the fears on both sides could be minimized by making appropriate contractual agreements. In Chapter 6, it was clearly stated that the social change outcome criterion accepted by the experimenter is the one that the agents of society would accept as a solution to the social problem under consideration. Accordingly, any experiment that does not concern itself with this consensual criterion would not be financed. On the other hand, the researcher only engages in experiments voluntarily. Thus a *contractual* agreement between society and the social innovative experimenter provides a practical instrument that can be used to resolve many potential misgivings about such experiments. Contracts between the proposed centers and society's representatives are the very foundation for carrying out such experiments, for they require a "meeting of the minds." Consequently, social innovative experiments must meet both the needs of society and the needs of the experimenter. For its part, society can withhold money from those experiments it does not wish to pursue;

and, by the same token, the experimentalist has the freedom not to contract if he so chooses.

Furthermore, if such centers were appropriately organized, experimental social innovation would be integrated into the very fabric of society because both society's representatives and the center's experimentalists would be committed to the solution of the identical problems. This is yet another reason why the social change outcome criterion must be determined by the representatives of society; they are ultimately responsible for problem solutions. Moreover, any change in the criterion must come from the representatives of society (pp. 81–85). Therefore, one of the paramount values of centers for experimental social innovation would be their adherence to democratic ideals. Such experiments would provide information for the agents of society in areas where there is insufficient knowledge. They would not replace or interfere with democratic processes. Rather, their information would provide a cornerstone for enlightened decision-making by supplying actual evidence about possible solutions to social problems. It is also important to recall here that social innovative experiments would be conducted by establishing *small models* in a natural community setting. Thus their execution would not interfere with ongoing social processes while the experimenters are seeking information upon which recommended social change might be based.

There is another important way in which mutual fears of societal representatives and social scientists can be resolved. It concerns the location of such training centers and the institutions with which they might become affiliated. There appear to be at least four types of social institutions where such centers could be located. Each type has advantages and disadvantages.

The first type of institution is the university. This location for such a center would require that the university extend itself into the community—a matter about which there has been much reluctance in the past. Furthermore, the multidisciplinary nature of the training center's subject matter and research approach might not fit well in any single university department. Accordingly, the center would have to be established independent of the various departments so that it would not become embroiled in intradepartmental or interdepartmental administrative problems. If such problems were avoided, the center would be free to devote the majority of its time to carrying out its research and training mission. The advantages of establishing such institutes in universities are numerous. The university could provide a scholarly atmosphere most necessary for scientists, as well as make contracts with all granting agencies. The educational norms of the institution would permit the establishment of the necessary training programs. The disadvantages are mainly attributable to some of the folkways of the university—disengaging itself from action approaches to social problems, possible chauvinism of various academic disciplines, and the difficulty any large institution has in establishing a new academic branch with somewhat different values from those traditional in that setting.

A second possible location is the industrial institution. An industrial organization could provide the proposed center with an administrative apparatus for making all agreements, as well as being able to provide space, computers, and other research necessities. The disadvantages might be in developing the needed scholarly social atmosphere and in modifying appropriately the industrial goal of creating a product for short-term profit. This is all the more important in locating centers concerned with marginal persons, because many such people would not be able to survive without some outside monetary aid and hence would not be self-supporting. This could generate a conflict in corporations with production values because humanitarian approaches are not always compatible with the profit motive.

Another institution that could accept and develop these centers would be a government agency. It could provide all the necessities except one—the freedom for experimental social innovation to be carried out without restriction by an agency's mission or policies. This freedom is typically assured by means of a contract. The main advantage of a research center for social innovation as a part of a governing structure would be that it could help in the establishment of social change as a tradition of the society. It could provide a new and experimental basis for the action of governments to meet changing social conditions. Therefore it would be an alternative to the present typical system of social change, which is guesswork in reaction to crises. If the government were to establish its own centers, it is also possible that experimental social researchers might be inhibited in creating innovative solutions to social problems. It is far more likely that the center would become an arm or branch of the government, rather than an independent research organization which carries out its own experiments and recommends solutions to the governmental agencies based upon research findings.

Finally, such centers could be established by private foundations. They could provide, it would appear, all the accouterments needed by social innovative experimenters. An added advantage of such centers being established under foundation sponsorship would be that new experimental social change-oriented traditions could be established more easily because the centers would be newly created and would not be regulated by the norms of an already-existing large institution. Also, this situation would provide the greatest freedom for contractual negotiations about possible experiments. Contracts for experiments in social innovation could be made with all governmental agencies, other private foundations, and individual donors. One disadvantage might be the difficulty such a foundation may have in making arrangements for training programs with suitably-located universities.

These are some of the advantages and disadvantages of locating such research and training centers in four of society's existing institutions. Such centers would have an inherent value to society. For example, institutes for experiments in social innovation could play a major role in breaking down the barrier of man's reluctance to gain knowledge about his own behavior and social systems. If such centers were established and began fulfilling their function as information centers for legislators, educators, industrial representatives, and other agents of society their social value would, it appears, become so great that fear of exploring society's forces would dissipate, and be replaced by increasing requests for the services that they would render. This acceptance, gradual though it would be, should in turn increase the range of possible problems that a society would allow the researchers to explore. Nonetheless, it appears that initially such centers will face all of the resistance incidental to the establishment of new social organizations typical of any change in a society.

Let us assume for the moment that such centers have been created and are located in a place providing the necessary social climate for their research and training endeavors. First, the philosophy that such a proposed center should have and the services it would provide should be explored. The center will, of course, be a subsystem with its own values and norms. Its primary value would be its orientation toward the solution of social problems. Because of this focus on all aspects of social changes, it inevitably would become multidisciplinary in its approach to problems. This would occur because the solution to social problems includes the incorporation of as many pertinent variables as possible in the designs for inquiry into such solutions, regardless of the academic discipline involved.

Another norm for conduct of the training center would be at least initially created. This is the belief in the necessity for an empirical solution to complex social problems. Since twentieth-century America has no "proving ground" for its own ideas about social change, such a center establishes one. At the same time, it provides the social atmosphere which supports the empirical scientist who is not an adherent of any scientific belief system except the one that states social problems can be scientifically investigated. This norm of empirical comparative evaluation of alternative approaches to critical social problems would be reinforced by some experiments that demonstrated success in bettering the lives of the members of a society. One research would follow another, so that eventually new problems would be anticipated and reforms could be instituted *before* social crises arise. To those who say that such experiments would take too long, it is important to be aware that while the first experiments would indeed take a long time, successive approximations to problem solution, along with the day-to-day observations required, would yield innovative programs with demonstrated success at a quickening pace. This is all the more possible if the new centers were to fulfill their educational function of training new experimenters who themselves would conduct experiments and train other researchers.

The center must have a scholarly atmosphere of freedom of inquiry necessary for the pursuit of problem solutions. It would create a research atmosphere for the training of new experimentalists while also emphasizing the necessity of a commitment to humanitarian values. The center would further accentuate a scholarly social atmosphere by providing a place where researchers could go after the action phase of an experiment was completed to finish analyses of their data, and to disseminate the new information obtained. It would be in the center that researchers could discuss their results with other persons, and here the cross-fertilization of ideas and the development of new methods would occur. Discussions could be held with legislators, experimenters, interested citizens, and others.

After the dissemination phase is completed, it would also be important that new research be initiated so that the center does not develop solely norms of inaction limited to verbal discussion. If this occurs, the norm of repeated experiments under naturalistic conditions would disappear and the center would become just another educational institution separated from the society whose problems it was created to explore. It is also for this reason that each social innovative experiment should have a beginning and an end. The end of an experiment is the signal for the commencement of a new one, and this continuous process would help establish a dynamic norm of social change with which such centers should be vitally concerned. If research programs do not have an end the possibility of change is diminished, for each experiment might become continuous and change into a service operation which develops its own bureaucracy whose goal is to perpetuate the experimental subsystems that have been created for comparison. Therefore the norm of the institute must be continuous experimentation with innovated programs. Staff size would be small to prevent the development of an inflexible organization.

Another practice that would prevent institutional stagnation would be the continuous study of the center itself. These studies would result in recommendations designed to effect needed changes in the center and thus establish change as one of its primary norms. If a social center for experimental social innovation is truly to be a mechanism for rational social change, it must avoid forces that prevent change. It must, in fact, be rewarded for trying something new.

Since the center would be a meeting ground for the discussion of alternative solutions to social problems as well as for revealing the results of experiments designed to test these alternatives, it would provide a continuous forum directly concerned with solutions to pressing and anticipated social problems. As experiments proceed from gross explorations to more precise approximations of problem solution through this continuous research effort, the flow of information from the center to the community would become constant. Thus a communication system between the community and the center would be established. Such frequent and open communication should eventually lead to the identification of significant social problems prior to the development of a social crisis. *The center thus would itself be a mechanism for social change.* It would help create those changes that are necessary for social survival while preserving those that are necessary for the stability of society. It is important to recall here that experimental social innovative designs require current social practices as the baseline comparison social subsystem for any such experiment.

It is this necessity for any new experiment to show a significantly greater benefit than existing practices which provides for gradualness in recommended changes. Hence gradual and continuing change can occur without social upheaval through the shared responsibility of community leaders and researchers continuously striving for problem solution and communicating through the facilities of the center. The research and communication processes of the center would offer a way *to make effective the solution of social problems by reforms before the emergence of crises.* This is exceedingly important because after a crisis has emerged gradual reforms are often inadequate, so that radical, untested, and unevaluated solutions occur. Such solutions are frequently very disruptive to a society.

It would be the social innovative experimenter's responsibility to play the role of educator for representatives of society where technical research matters are concerned. He would explain the meaning of his statistics and other more scientific matters so they would be clearly understood by society's representatives. Using the lack of relationships among improvement criteria in mental illness, for example, the experimentalist would discuss the relative independence of these variables so that society's representatives are definitely aware that they would probably get different answers about the value of treatment programs for the mentally ill, depending on whether their patients are evaluated in terms of employment, status, feelings of self-enhancement, or other criteria (Fairweather, 1964, pp. 273–282). The experimenter could not avoid this educational responsibility since no realistic choice of a social change outcome criterion can be made by society's representatives unless they are aware of the magnitude and nature of such technical relationships.

If they were developed to their full potential, such centers could provide one basis for settling social conflicts. Advocates of one subsystem and advocates of another, provided the subsystem had a reasonable and beneficial value for society, could be subjected to actual test through the research activity of the center. Discussions of the results and the evidence presented could serve as the basis for more rational solutions to such social problems. It is even possible that such an approach might have meaning for the solution of broader international problems, where different approaches to international problems could be subjected to comparison through these innovative experiments.

The center for experimental social innovation would have, at any one time, several researches being conducted on important social problems in selected institutions and community locations. For example, one research team might be exploring living and working situations for ex-convicts, another working with the mentally ill, a third with school subsystems, and a fourth with the socially disadvantaged. Researchers in the center would represent many different experimental approaches and, accordingly, information about newly created research procedures and empirical results with different populations would be mutually explored. Similarities and differences among populations and methods would lead to a sharing of information and the cross-fertilization of ideas among workers with such varied marginal populations.

The exchange of ideas among researchers interested in different social problems would be exceedingly important as a social norm of such centers. This exchange would be generally contrary to the current trend of academic specialization which results in the isolation of research findings for particular problems so that communalities among them are rarely perceived. Although the blind, paraplegics, chronically mentally ill, drug addicts, and ex-convicts, to name a few, are all marginal people, it has been common practice for researches done with these different populations to be so independent that exchange of information concerning research results is negligible if, indeed, there is any at all. These rigid boundaries are reinforced by the *separate but equal* status of disciplines in the educational institution and the independent agencies of the Federal, state, and local governments responsible for solving such problems. This situation exists despite current research results indicating that heterogeneous groups of individuals representing all marginal groups—mentally ill, socially disadvantaged, the blind, and the like—could probably participate together in living and working situations (Sanders, MacDonald, Maynard, 1964; Maynard, 1964). Experimental programs combining these various populations in search of more generalizable solutions are currently difficult, if not impossible, to achieve, because any given granting agency can only finance researches with one of these populations. For example, the National Institute of Mental Health usually provides funds for the mentally ill; the American Foundation for the Blind is concerned with the research funds for the blind; research funds for the socially disadvantaged come from the Office of Economic Opportunity, and so forth.

This arbitrary division of marginal man into these separate categories rigidly defined by administrative dictum prevents researchers and administrators in these related fields from sharing ideas and stimulating each other's research efforts. This is true despite the similarity of the problems facing the affected individuals. A center for experimental social innovation would place under one roof all problems of marginal man and would therefore increase the communication among individuals interested in these problems. It might even bring about a questioning of the classification system which creates these arbitrary divisions of marginal man—a social problem of immense proportions itself.

The centers could also help establish administrative procedures for implementing community and institutional research. In Chapter 4, the need for contractual agreements with legal, medical, educational, industrial, union, and other community institutions prior to the onset of experimental social innovation was discussed. Currently, it is necessary for such administrative procedures to be contracted for by each researcher as an independent matter (pp. 51–62). The centers could provide administrative procedures for contractual arrangements to be made by them rather than by the individual researcher. If this were the case, broad general agreements with the aforementioned social institutions, and others where necessary, could readily be accomplished. This procedure would drastically reduce both the number of individual agreements now necessary and the investment of the researcher's time and effort in this nonresearch activity.

The center would also have as a primary task the development of new experimental methods for its research. Although the encompassing methods developed by Tryon and his associates (Tryon and Bailey, 1966), for example, are an excellent point of departure, new methods are already needed and the demand will be greater and continuous. For example, there is a great need at the moment for new nonparametric techniques to statistically compare repeated measures on subsystems with unequal numbers of participants. Other methods will be needed as new problems arise. Thus the development of experimental methods would have to be a continuing process because they would be aimed at solutions to dynamically changing social problems.

What of the staffing patterns for such institutes? Who would be employed by them and what would their statuses be? First, a core staff including a director and office staff would be needed initially to organize and administer the center. The director, himself a social innovative experimentalist, would be familiar with the necessary staffing patterns and organizational characteristics from his own experiences. Organization of the center would develop gradually. The staff would initially all have participated in some social innovative experiments. Where this is not possible, individuals from the various disciplines interested and motivated toward the solution of social problems could comprise the staff. However, the director would have to establish some formal training procedures in order to fully acquaint the new members with social innovative experimental procedures. Once organized, the staff of the center would train other experimentalists—some could remain as staff members of the initial center and others could establish new centers. Teams of researchers, as described in Chapter 5, could then be formed and each new team could be financed by a grant or grants received from agencies interested in a particular social problem. Here every effort should be made to apply to all concerned granting agencies so that coordinated activities would occur. As new teams are developed with new experimental programs designed for different social problems, the number of consultants needed to advise the members of the center about legal, medical, political, statistical, economic, and other matters would increase. Eventually, a roster of consultants who could be continuously used by the staff would be created. In addition to the research staff and consultants, the center would provide at least one individual who could demonstrate to others each subsystem found to be most beneficial. This person would assist interested agency personnel in establishing on a service basis those programs already found to be beneficial through social innovative research (pp. 31–33).

There are two features about the employment of experimentalists for social innovation that are of extreme importance in establishing positions for the centers. All research positions should be full time and, when possible, established on a career basis because of the length of time required for longitudinal studies and because of the gradual accumulation of knowledge by experimentalists. It might require several years of research, for example, before a researcher is sufficiently familiar with the variables associated with a particular social problem for him to create a meaningful subsystem as an alternative solution for the problem.

The requirement of immediate solution to difficult social problems as embodied in short-term studies is not useful in the arena of social innovative experiments. Rather, it is the long-term commitment of repeated attempts at problem solution that eventually produces results. Relatively permanent employment for social innovative researchers is therefore an essential condition for meaningful contributions. Another aspect of employment is equally important—salary and status. For experimental efforts in social innovation to attract capable researchers and students, the salaries and statuses granted them should be equivalent to that of any other institute or center. For example, their income and other benefits should be the equivalent of those for personnel of the current man-in-space effort. Are not the solutions to social problems as important to man's survival as his knowledge of outer space? Such salary and status in this culture would provide a social climate which indicates that society defines social innovative experiments as equal in importance to other physical and social science research.

It is also important that some positions of the center be set aside for professors of various academic disciplines and for other interested individuals who wish to participate in social innovative experiments while on leave from their current positions. Such positions would allow interested academicians to be fully aware of ongoing experiments and new methods. They could also participate in them. On the other hand, all positions—whether visiting or staff—should be full-time because commitment to the solution of social problems is an all-encompassing pursuit. Furthermore, a full-time commitment might prevent the development of chauvinism for specific disciplines by emphasizing the goal of the center, namely, solving social problems rather than developing expertness in a single subject matter.

The center would, of course, need equipment and space for its staff and students. It would be desirable that space comparable to other institutes be given the research center, not only to meet the work needs of its employees but also to give physical evidence that experimental social innovation is important. By far the most indispensable equipment for the center is machine equipment for data processing. The center needs access to automated scoring machines, card-punching equipment, tapes, and, most of all, high-speed computers. This is exceedingly important because the voluminous amount of data collected often requires rapid analyses so that the next experimental phase can begin. Most data collected can be designed so that they are machine scored and analyzed. The entire process of scoring, card punching, and preparing tapes for the analysis of the data can now be accomplished mechanically (pp. 161–163). The use of machines for these purposes greatly reduces the amount of time required to evaluate the experimental data and, accordingly, increases the number of researches that can be completed during any given time period.

Computers are also necessary for data collection—a field that is almost totally undeveloped in naturalistic social experiments. Here, on-line computers could be used so that information is immediately processed and analyzed while dynamic processes are continuing. For example, while groups are performing their work, information concerning their leadership and communication could be recorded and analyzed. It might then be used to effect needed changes in group structure while the work was progressing. Or, again, information about various small cities in a socially deprived area—Appalachia, for example—could be analyzed by computers to arrive at the potential type of industry that might be useful to a particular city. These examples may stimulate the reader himself to think about the many fascinating possible uses for computers in real-life research situations, if they were used with the same orientation to problem solution that exists in space science. Even now the astronauts use them in their small living quarters. Surely such imaginative procedures have their counterpart in terrestrial living situations where the data would be at least as important.

The center also has a crucial training function. Nowadays, recruiting students is made cumbersome by the discipline-bound nature of most graduate training programs. As an initial procedure until adequate staff and curricula are developed, therefore, students of the center would take courses in various academic departments. However, it would be the eventual goal of the center to offer most of its own courses. This is exceedingly important regardless of the center's location because it would be necessary that the center develop norms that stress social problem solution and social responsibility. These norms need to be established as part of the training program so that they can be adopted by the student. Furthermore, since social innovative experiments are longitudinal in time, they would require long-range commitments by students. It would be important that early in his training the student become aware of this commitment so that he may attempt another course of action should these requirements seem inappropriate for him.

To emphasize the nature of this commitment, the center should provide the student with immediate research experience. Upon occasion it is necessary for the social innovative experimentalist to live and work under field social conditions in order to obtain his data. Illustratively, in the community project described earlier (p. 34), experimenters drove trucks in order to be in the situation where desired behavioral data could be obtained. They also learned the work methods, bookkeeping, and other procedures of janitorial and gardening services in order to establish appropriate training and work programs. This gross departure from the traditional role of the "professional" person can be quite unacceptable to some individuals. Therefore the student should have a trial period during which he can discover whether or not his stated interest continues while working under field conditions. During the trial period it would not only be important that the student positively evaluate this role, but it would be equally important that the staff perceive him as a mature individual capable of assuming it.

In this regard, the staff should make detailed evaluations of each individual expressing an interest in a career as an experimentalist since the responsibility to society of such researchers cannot be overstressed. It is important to note here that adequate selection and training procedures in dedication to the solution of social problems would be as important a part of the training as the content of the subject matter and the research methods themselves. Indeed, it is perhaps more important, for experimental social innovation is not value-free and, consequently, individual researchers must be devoted to the humanitarian principles of their society. Furthermore, the delay in reward brought about by longitudinal studies requires that experimenters gain their personal satisfaction as much from humanitarian pursuits as from frequent professional publication. Because of the long-term commitment and responsibility required of the experimentalist, it would be a recommended procedure that an agreement about termination between the trainee and the staff be understood when the student enters the program. It would be important here that either staff or trainee could terminate the student's activities in the center when it appears to either party that further participation is not in the interest of the student or the center or both.

The training program for prospective researchers would be a combination of academic studies and research experience. Doctoral dissertations, far from being only exercises, would be real-life experiments with meaningful social problems. Since the social values of the center would require that any individual—staff, student, or visitor—be concerned with and involved in the solution to social problems, any research done—whether dissertation or not—would have to be longitudinal, naturalistic, and meaningful. Many different social problems would be under investigation by different research teams at any one time. A graduate student could therefore take the problem of his choice and become involved in it. His initial role probably would be as a member of a research team for, as described in Chapter 5, the approach to research on social problems is necessarily a team approach. It would be important therefore that the student learn to be a team member at the outset, for there would be no place in social innovative experiments for the uncooperative individual. Training would be received in all aspects of research—formulating hypotheses, obtaining administrative commitments, organizing the research team, analyzing the data, computer programming, and publication. Thus the student would participate in experiments from their beginning to their end. The student, in addition to course work, would receive training about research by executing it in the real-life situation.

It is most important to repeat that social innovative experiments would include training for research in ongoing service programs. Therefore the usual arbitrary divisions among training, research, and service so frequently set forth in administrative budgets, such as those of the Veterans Administration, would not be applicable here. Training, research, and service would occur at the same time and would be inseparable. There would be *one* budget that would be used to accomplish all three functions at the same time.

The eventual goal of training would be to combine the various disciplines into a unitary whole which focuses upon solutions to social problems. A multidisciplinary orientation would be developed by attempting to solve social problems since they involve all disciplines by their very nature. The experimentalist would develop through his graduate training a perception of a multidisciplinary world quite incompatible with the restrictions inherent in a single academic discipline. Thus a multidisciplinary research role would be created. This is quite a different concept from that of an interdisciplinary team comprised of several representatives, each coming from a different academic discipline. In the latter case the whole perspective on the problem is never quite achieved, for the individual rarely transcends the values of the discipline in which he has been trained. Over time, the research and training center would establish its own theoretical systems from which hypotheses would then be generated. These theoretical models would combine the variables from the different disciplines into a meaningful formula which would be perceived as a whole by the social innovative experimentalist. Thus disciplinary chauvinism would hopefully tend to disappear. It seems necessary therefore to propose training a new generation of researchers—social innovative experimentalists.

From what sectors of modern society could such a new generation of researchers be recruited? Within the context of contemporary American society, a number of possibilities exist. As might be expected, the bulk of such training recruits are likely to be found in the relatively advantaged middle-class segment of the society, among those students whose values and attitudes about humanitarian pursuits and social responsibility predispose them to consider such a multidisciplinary career. But the very diversity of subcultures in this society suggests that other potential sectors of recruitment would be absolutely essential if significant and relevant experimental social innovation is to be carried forward. At the present time, urban centers all over the nation are experiencing difficulties in perceiving the needs, interests, and values of socially and economically disadvantaged groups. A clear perception of these problems and needs requires application of the insight and understanding which only members of these subcultures themselves possess through a lifetime of experience. Thus this new generation of researchers will also have to be recruited from such ethnic and regional American subcultures as the Puerto Rican, Indian, Negro, Mexican, Oriental, Appalachian, and Piedmonter, as well as from the Caucasian middle-class stratum of American social life.

Similar considerations would apply to the recruitment of trainees from cultures other than those to be found within the orbit of contemporary American society. The center could be of even broader value to a society by training experimentalists from different countries in its experimental methods. It would seem important here that the countries' own experimenters be trained, rather than relying on the host country to provide research personnel. It is highly probable that the situational specificity of various cultures, indeed, the degree of specificity of the problems within those cultures, would take so long for an outsider to understand that new social subsystems aimed at solving social problems could not be established in one culture by individuals from another. Foreign students trained at the centers could then return to their countries and carry out experiments there. This would require a commitment to problem solution by the representatives of the culture and the researcher. Because of the similarities of the methods for experimental social innovation that would be useful in every country, another basis for cooperation among nations, namely, a common language and goals, might result.

Be that as it may, the initial goal of the center for experiments and training would be the comparative evaluation of alternative subsystems for the solution of pressing social problems in twentieth-century America. Establishment of such centers could provide this society with a new social subsystem that itself would continuously evaluate social processes and allow needed social change to occur in a rational, planned, and systematic manner. Eventually, it could lead to a system of reform which is truly effective, because changes could occur before a crisis arose and not in hurried response to it. No society, as far as is now known, has yet established experimental procedures whose goal is to recommend changes in its social organization designed to benefit its members. Perhaps this is because no society has yet fully accepted the premise that a meaningful life for its members is limited only by a man's lack of creativity and the shackles of his institutions. This society could.

References

Alcoholics Anonymous. *Alcoholics Anonymous: the story of how thousands of men and women have recovered from alcoholism.* (Rev.) New York: Alcoholics Anonymous, 1955.

Altman, I. *See* McGrath and Altman, 1966.

American Psychological Association. *Ethical standards of psychologists.* Washington D.C.: American Psychological Association, 1953.

American Psychological Association, Board of Professional Affairs. Special issue: Testing and public policy. *Amer. Psychologist,* 1965, **20** (11), whole issue.

Anastasi, Anne, *Psychological testing.* (2nd Ed.) New York: Macmillan, 1961.

Bailey, D. E. *See* Tryon and Bailey, 1965.

Bailey, D. E. *See* Tryon and Bailey, 1966.

Ballachey, E. *See* Ferguson, McReynolds, and Ballachey, 1953.

Ballachey, E. L. *See* Krech, Crutchfield, and Ballachey, 1962.

Benjamin, L. *See* Katz and Benjamin, 1960.

Berelson, B. *Content analysis in communication research.* New York: The Free Press of Glencoe, 1952.

Bierstedt, R. Sociology and humane learning. *Amer. Sociological Rev.,* 1960, **25** (1), 3–9.

Blochberger, C. W. and Lewis, Jane S. The social worker's role. *In* G. W. Fairweather (Ed.), *Social psychology in treating mental illness: an experimental approach.* New York: John Wiley & Sons, 1964, 258–270.

Block, J. *The Q-sort method in personality assessment and psychiatric research.* Springfield, Ill.: Charles C. Thomas, 1961.

Blum, R. H. and Funkhouser, M. L. A lobby for people? *Amer. Psychol.,* 1965, **20** (3), 208–210.

Borgatta, E. *See* Meyer and Borgatta, 1959.

Bredemeier, H. C. and Toby, J. *Social problems in America: casualties and costs in an acquisitive society.* New York: John Wiley & Sons, 1960.

Broadhurst, Ruth. *See* Moss, Freund, and Broadhurst, 1959.

Brunswik, E. Organismic achievement and environmental probability. *Psychol. Rev.,* 1943, **50**, 255–272.

Brunswik, E. *Perception and the representative design of psychological experiments.* Berkeley, Calif.: University of Calif. Press, 1956.

Bureau of the Census. *A chapter in population sampling.* Washington, D.C.: U.S. Govt. Printing Office, 1947.

Burt, C. *The factors of the mind: an introduction to factor analysis in psychology.* New York: Macmillan, 1941.

California, State of, Dept. of Corrections. *California prisoners, 1961, 1962 and 1963.* Sacramento, Calif.: Dept. of Corrections, Research Div., 1965.

229

California, State of, Dept. of Mental Hygiene. *Cohort follow-up program reports,* Nos. 3 & 4. Sacramento, Calif.: Dept. of Mental Hygiene, 1963.

Campbell, D. T. *See* Webb, Campbell, Schwartz, and Sechrest, 1966.

Caplow, T. and McGee, R. J. *The academic marketplace.* New York: Basic Books, 1958.

Cattell, R. B. *Description and measurement of personality.* Yonkers, N.Y.: World Book Co., 1946.

Caudill, W. A. *The psychiatric hospital as a small society.* Cambridge, Mass.: Harvard Univ. Press, 1958.

Chein, I., Gerard, D. L., Lee, R. S., and Rosenfeld, Eva. *The road to H.* New York: Basic Books, 1963.

Cochran, W. G. *Sampling techniques.* New York: John Wiley & Sons, 1963.

Cochran, W. G. and Cox, Gertrude M. *Experimental designs.* (2nd ed.) New York: John Wiley & Sons, 1957.

Cohen, M. *See* Katz and Cohen, 1962.

Conant, J. B. *The American high school today.* New York: McGraw-Hill Book Co., 1959.

Cox, Gertrude M. *See* Cochran and Cox, 1957.

Cressler, D. L. Amount and intensity of interpersonal choice. *In* G. W. Fairweather (Ed.), *Social psychology in treating mental illness: an experimental approach.* New York: John Wiley & Sons, 1964, 103–121.

Cressler, D. L. *See* Fairweather, Sanders, Maynard and Cressler, in preparation, 1966.

Cronbach, L. J. *Essentials of psychological testing.* (2nd ed.) New York: Harper & Row, 1960.

Crutchfield, R. S. *See* Krech, Crutchfield, and Ballachey, 1962.

Cumming, J. The inadequacy syndrome. *Psychiat. Quart.,* 1963, **37,** 723–733.

Deutscher, I. Words and deeds: social science and social policy. *Social Problems,* 1966, 13 (3), 235–254.

Dixon, W. J. and Massey, F. J., Jr. *Introduction to statistical analysis.* (2nd ed.) New York: McGraw-Hill Book Co., 1957.

Dixon, W. J. (Ed.) *BMD Biomedical computer programs.* (Rev.) Los Angeles, Calif.: Health Sciences Computing Facility, University of California, 1965.

Edwards, A. L. *Experimental design in psychological research.* (Rev.) New York: Holt, Rinehart and Winston, 1960.

Edwards, A. L. *Statistical methods for the behavioral sciences.* New York: Holt, Rinehart and Winston, 1954.

Elliott, Mabel A. and Merrill, F. E. *Social disorganization.* New York: Harper & Row, 1961.

Etzioni, A. *Complex organizations: a sociological reader.* New York: Holt, Rinehart and Winston, 1961.

Etzioni, A. and Etzioni, Eva. *Social change.* New York: Basic Books, 1964.

Etzioni, Eva. *See* Etzioni and Etzioni, 1964.

Fairweather, G. W. (Ed.) *Social psychology in treating mental illness: an experimental approach.* New York: John Wiley & Sons, 1964.

Fairweather, G. W., Moran, L. J., and Morton, R. B. Efficiency of attitudes, fantasies, and life history data in predicting observed behavior. *J. consult. Psychol.,* 1956, **20,** 58.

Fairweather, G. W., Sanders, D. H., Maynard, H., and Cressler, D. L. *Treating mental illness in the community: an experiment in social innovation.* In preparation, 1966.

Fairweather, G. W. and Simon, R. A further follow-up comparison of psychotherapeutic programs. *J. consult. Psychol.,* 1963, 27, 186.

Fairweather, G. W., Simon, R., Gebhard, Mildred E., Weingarten, E., Holland, J. L., Sanders, R., Stone, G. B., and Reahl, G. E. Relative effectiveness of psychotherapeutic programs: a multicriteria comparison of four programs for three different patient groups. *Psychol. Monogr.,* 1960, 74, No. 5 (Whole No. 492).

Fairweather, G. W. *See* Forsyth and Fairweather, 1961.

Fairweather, G. W. *See* Moran, Fairweather, and Morton, 1956.

Ferguson, J., McReynolds, P., and Ballachey, E. Hospital Adjustment Scale. Stanford, Calif.: Stanford University Press, 1953.

Flanagan, J. C. *Performance record for the personal and social development program.* Chicago: Sci. Res. Assoc., 1956.

Forsyth, R. P. and Fairweather, G. W. Psychotherapeutic and other hospital treatment criteria: the dilemma. *J. abnorm. soc. Psychol.,* 1961, 62, 598–604.

Frank, J. D. *Persuasion and healing.* Baltimore, Md.: Johns Hopkins Press, 1961.

Freund, H. G. *See* Moss, Freund, and Broadhurst, 1959.

Fruchter, B. *Introduction to factor analysis.* Princeton, N.J.: D. Van Nostrand Co., Inc., 1954.

Funkhouser, M. L. *See* Blum and Funkhouser, 1965.

Galbraith, J. K. *The affluent society.* Boston, Mass.: Houghton Mifflin Co., 1958.

Gebhard, Mildred E. *See* Fairweather, Simon, Gebhard, Weingarten, Holland, Sanders, Stone, and Reahl, 1960.

Gerard, D. L. *See* Chein, Gerard, Lee, and Rosenfeld, 1963.

Ghiselli, E. E. *Theory of psychological measurement.* New York: McGraw-Hill Book Co., 1964.

Goffman, E. *Asylums* (Essays on the social situation of mental patients and other inmates). Chicago: Aldine Pub. Co., 1962.

Goldman, A. R. The recreational hour: an evaluation of behavior in an unstructured situation. *In* G. W. Fairweather (Ed.), *Social psychology in treating mental illness: an experimental approach.* New York: John Wiley & Sons, 1964, 45–76.

Gouldner, A. W. Anti-minotaur: the myth of a value-free sociology. *Social Problems,* 1962, 9 (3), 199–213.

Guilford, J. P. *Fundamental statistics in psychology and education.* New York: McGraw-Hill Book Co., 1956.

Guilford, J. P. *Psychometric methods.* (2nd ed.) New York: McGraw-Hill Book Co., 1954.

Hammond, K. R. Representative versus systematic design in clinical psychology. *Psychol. Bull.,* 1954, 51, 150–159.

Hammond, K. R. Subject and object sampling—a note. *Psychol. Bull.,* 1948, 45, 530–533.

Harman, H. H. *See* Holzinger and Harman, 1941.

Harrington, M. *The other America: poverty in the United States.* New York: Macmillan, 1962.

Heyns, R. W. and Lippitt, R. Systematic observational techniques. *In* G. Lindzey (Ed.), *Handbook of social psychology.* Vol. I. Reading, Mass.: Addison-Wesley Publishing Co., 1954, 370–404.

Hiller, E. T. *Social relations and structures.* New York: Harper & Row, 1947.

Holland, J. L. *The psychology of vocational choice.* Waltham, Mass.: Blaisdell Pub. Co., 1966.

Holland, J. L. *Vocational Preference Inventory, Manual.* (6th Rev.) Iowa City, Ia.: Educational Research Associates, 1965.

Holland, J. L. and Richards, J. M., Jr. Academic and nonacademic accomplishment: correlated or uncorrelated? *J. of Educ. Psychol.,* 1965, 56, 165–174.

Holland, J. L. *See* Fairweather, Simon, Gebhard, Weingarten, Holland, Sanders, Stone, and Reahl, 1960.

Hollingshead, A. B. and Redlich, F. C. *Social class and mental illness: a community study.* New York: John Wiley & Sons, 1958.

Holzinger, K. J. and Harman, H. H. *Factor analysis: a synthesis of factorial methods.* Chicago: University of Chicago Press, 1941.

Hotelling, H. *Analysis of a complex of statistical variables into principal components.* Baltimore: Warwick and York, 1933.

Hughes, C., Tremblay, M., Rapoport, R., and Leighton, A. H. *People of Cove and Woodlot.* Vol. II. New York: Basic Books, 1960.

Humphrey, H. H. The behavioral sciences and survival (An address to the American Orthopsychiatric Association in March 1963 by Vice President Humphrey when he was then a Senator from Minnesota). *Amer. Psychol.,* 1963, 18 (6), 290–294.

Hunter, M., Schooler, C., and Spohn, H. E. The measurement of characteristic patterns of ward behavior in chronic schizophrenics. *J. consult. Psychol.,* 1962, 26, 69–73.

Hyman, H. H. *Interviewing in social research.* Chicago: University of Chicago Press, 1954.

Jones, L. V. Tests of hypotheses: one-sided vs. two-sided alternatives. *Psychol. Bull.,* 1952, 49 (1), 43–46.

Jones, M. *The therapeutic community: a new treatment method in psychiatry.* New York: Basic Books, 1953.

Katz, I. Review of evidence relative to the effects of desegregation on the intellectual performance of Negroes. *Amer. Psychol.,* 1964, 19 (6), 381–399.

Katz, I. and Benjamin L. Effects of white authoritarianism in biracial work groups. *J. abnorm. soc. Psychol.,* 1960, 61, 448–456.

Katz, I. and Cohen, M. The effects of training Negroes upon cooperative problem solving in biracial teams. *J. abnorm. soc. Psychol.,* 1962, 64, 319–325.

Kempthorne, O. *Design and analysis of experiments.* New York: John Wiley & Sons, 1952.

Koch, S. Psychological science versus the science-humanism antinomy: intimations of a significant science of man. *Amer. Psychol.,* 1961, 16, 629–639.

Krech, D., Crutchfield, R. S., and Ballachey, E. L. *Individual in society.* New York: McGraw-Hill Book Co., 1962.

Kuznets, G. *See* Tryon, Tryon, and Kuznets, 1941a.

Kuznets, G. *See* Tryon, Tryon, and Kuznets, 1941b.

Landis, P. H. *Social problems in nation and world.* Philadelphia, Pa.: J. B. Lippincott Co., 1959.

Lazarsfeld, P. F. and Thielens, W., Jr. *The academic mind: social scientists in a time of crisis.* New York: The Free Press of Glencoe, 1958.

Lee, R. S. *See* Chein, Gerard, Lee, and Rosenfeld, 1963.

Lehmann, E. L. *Testing statistical hypotheses.* New York: John Wiley & Sons, 1959.

Leighton, A. H. *See* Hughes, Tremblay, Rapoport, and Leighton, 1960.

Lewin, K. *Principles of topological psychology.* New York: McGraw-Hill Book Co., 1936.

Lewin, K., Lippitt, R., and White, R. Patterns of aggressive behavior in experimentally created "social climate." *J. soc. Psychol.*, 1939, **X**, 271–299.

Lewis, Jane S. *See* Blochberger and Lewis, 1964.

Lindquist, E. F. *Design and analysis of experiments in psychology and education.* Boston, Mass.: Houghton Mifflin Co., 1953.

Lippitt, R. Field theory and experiment in social psychology: autocratic and democratic group atmospheres. *Amer. J. Soc.*, 1939, **45**, 26–49.

Lippitt, R. *See* Heyns and Lippitt, 1954.

Lippitt, R. *See* Lewin, Lippitt, and White, 1939.

Luce, R. D. and Raiffa, H. *Games and decisions.* New York: John Wiley & Sons, 1957.

Maccoby, Eleanor E. and Maccoby, N. The interview: a tool of social science. *In* G. Lindzey (Ed.), *Handbook of social psychology.* Vol. I. Reading, Mass.: Addison-Wesley Pub. Co., 1954, 449–487.

Maccoby, N. *See* Maccoby and Maccoby, 1954.

MacDonald, W. S. Patients' attitudes toward mental illness, status, staff, ward regulations, and the future. *In* G. W. Fairweather (Ed.), *Social psychology in treating mental illness: an experimental approach.* New York: John Wiley & Sons, 1964, 133–149.

MacDonald, W. S. The large-group meeting hour: an evaluation of behavior in a structural situation. *In* G. W. Fairweather (Ed.), *Social psychology in treating mental illness: an experimental approach.* New York: John Wiley & Sons, 1964, 77–102.

MacDonald, W. S. *See* Sanders, MacDonald, and Maynard, 1964.

McGee, R. J. *See* Caplow and McGee, 1958.

McGrath, J. E. and Altman, I. *Small group research.* New York: Holt, Rinehart and Winston, 1966.

McNemar, Q. *Psychological statistics.* (3rd ed.) New York: John Wiley and Sons, 1962.

McReynolds, P. *See* Ferguson, McReynolds, and Ballachey, 1953.

Madge, J. *The tools of social science.* London, England: Longmans, Green, and Co., 1953.

Mannheim, K. *Ideology and Utopia.* New York: Harcourt, Brace & World, 1936.

Massey, F. J. *See* Dixon and Massey, 1957.

Maynard, H. Functional dimensions of small groups in a mental hospital treatment program. Unpublished doctoral dissertation. University of Oregon, 1966.

Maynard, H. The effect of group composition on task performance. Unpublished masters thesis. University of Oregon, 1964.

Maynard, H. *See* Fairweather, Sanders, Maynard, and Cressler, in preparation, 1966.

Maynard, H. *See* Sanders, MacDonald, and Maynard, 1964.

Merrill, F. E. *See* Elliott and Merrill, 1961.

Merton, R. K. *Social theory and social structure*. New York: The Free Press of Glencoe, 1949.

Merton, R. K. and Nisbet, R. A. (Eds.) *Contemporary social problems*. New York: Harcourt, Brace & World, 1961.

Meyer, H. J. and Borgatta, E. *An experiment in mental patient rehabilitation*. New York: Russell Sage Foundation, 1959.

Miller, D. C. *Handbook of research design and social measurement*. New York: David McKay Co., 1964.

Moran, L. J., Fairweather, G. W., and Morton, R. B. Some determinants of successful and unsuccessful adaptation to hospital treatment of tuberculosis. *J. consult. Psychol.*, 1956, 20, 125–131.

Moran, L. J. *See* Fairweather, Moran, and Morton, 1956.

Moroney, M. J. *Facts from figures*. (3rd Rev.) Baltimore, Md.: Penguin Books, 1956.

Morton, R. B. *See* Fairweather, Moran, and Morton, 1956.

Morton, R. B. *See* Moran, Fairweather, and Morton, 1956.

Moses, L. E. Nonparametric statistics for psychological research. *Psychol. Bull.*, 1952, 49, 122–143.

Moss, C. S., Freund, H. G., and Broadhurst, Ruth. Need for a multidisciplinary approach to clinical research: footnote to a drug study. *Psychol. Rep.*, 1959, 5, 699–700.

Myrdal, G. *An American dilemma*. New York: Harper & Row, 1944.

Nisbet, R. A. *See* Merton and Nisbet, 1961.

Olshansky, S. The transitional sheltered workshop: a survey. *J. soc. Issues*, 1960, 16, 33–39.

Oppenheimer, J. R. *See* U.S. Atomic Energy Commission, 1954.

Park, R. E. Human migration and the marginal man. *Amer. J. Sociol.*, 1928, XXXIII, 881–893.

Prest, A. R. and Turvey, R. Cost-benefit analysis: a survey. *Economic Journal*, 1965, 75, 683–735.

Rabb, E. and Selznick, Gertrude J. *Major social problems*. (2nd ed.) New York: Harper & Row, 1964.

Raiffa, H. *See* Luce and Raiffa, 1957.

Rankin, Elizabeth A. *See* Tipler and Rankin, 1964.

Rapoport, R. *See* Hughes, Tremblay, Rapoport, and Leighton, 1960.

Raven, B. H. *A bibliography of publications relating to the small group*. (2nd ed.) Los Angeles, Calif.: University of Calif., 1961. [Tech. Rep. 1, Contract Nonr 253 (54).]

Reahl, G. E. *See* Fairweather, Simon, Gebhard, Weingarten, Holland, Sanders, Stone, and Reahl, 1960.

Redlich, F. C. *See* Hollingshead and Redlich, 1958.

Richards, J. M., Jr. *See* Holland and Richards, 1965.

Riley, M. W., Riley, J. W., Jr., and Toby, J. *Sociological studies in scale analysis*. New Brunswick, N.J.: Rutgers University Press, 1954.

Riley, J. W., Jr. *See* Riley, Riley, and Toby, 1954.

Rose, A. M. The social responsibility of the social scientist. *Social Problems,* 1953, 1 (1), 85–90.

Rosenfeld, Eva. *See* Chein, Gerard, Lee, and Rosenfeld, 1963.

Sanders, D. H., MacDonald, W. S., and Maynard, H. The effect of group composition on task performance and role differentiation. *In* G. W. Fairweather (Ed.), *Social psychology in treating mental illness: an experimental approach.* New York: John Wiley & Sons, 1964, 196–209.

Sanders, D. H. *See* Fairweather, Sanders, Maynard, and Cressler, in preparation, 1966.

Sanders, R. *See* Fairweather, Simon, Gebhard, Weingarten, Holland, Sanders, Stone, and Reahl, 1960.

Sanford, N. Will psychologists study human problems? *Amer. Psychol.,* 1965, 20, 192–202.

Schenck, H., Jr. Myth-image of the scientist. *The Nation,* Sept. 14, 1963, 140–142.

Schooler, C. *See* Hunter, Schooler, and Spohn, 1962.

Schwartz, M. S. *See* Stanton and Schwartz, 1954.

Schwartz, R. D. *See* Webb, Campbell, Schwartz, and Sechrest, 1966.

Sechrest, L. *See* Webb, Campbell, Schwartz, and Sechrest, 1966.

Selznick, Gertrude J. *See* Rabb and Selznick, 1964.

Sherif, Carolyn W. *Attitude and attitude change: the social judgment-involvement approach.* Philadelphia: Saunders, 1965.

Sherif, Carolyn W. *See* Sherif and Sherif, 1956.

Sherif, Carolyn W. *See* Sherif and Sherif, 1964.

Sherif, M. and Sherif, Carolyn W. *An outline of social psychology.* (Rev. ed.) New York: Harper & Row, 1956.

Sherif, M. and Sherif, Carolyn W. *Reference groups.* New York: Harper & Row, 1964.

Siegel, S. *Nonparametric statistics for the behavioral sciences.* New York: McGraw-Hill Book Co., 1956.

Simon, R. *See* Fairweather and Simon, 1963.

Simon, R. *See* Fairweather, Simon, Gebhard, Weingarten, Holland, Sanders, Stone, and Reahl, 1960.

Smith, R. J. The impact of an innovative treatment program on the structure and culture of a large state mental hospital. *In Social Rehabilitation of the Chronic Mental Patient,* Secton III. Philadelphia State Hospital, 3rd Interim Report, National Institute of Mental Health, March 1961.

Snedecor, G. W. *Statistical methods.* (5th ed.) Ames, Iowa: Iowa State University Press, 1956.

Spearman, C. *The abilities of man.* London: Macmillan, 1927.

Spohn, H. E. *See* Hunter, Schooler, and Spohn, 1962.

Stalnaker, J. M. Psychological tests and public responsibility. *Amer. Psychol.,* 1965, 20 (2), 131–135.

Stanton, A. H. and Schwartz, M. S. *The mental hospital.* New York: Basic Books, 1954.

Stephenson, W. *The study of behavior: Q-technique and its methodology.* Chicago: University of Chicago Press, 1953.

Stevens, S. S. Mathematics, measurement, and psychophysics. *In* S. S. Stevens (Ed.), *Handbook of experimental psychology.* New York: John Wiley & Sons, 1951.

Stone, G. B. *See* Fairweather, Simon, Gebhard, Weingarten, Holland, Sanders, Stone, and Reahl, 1960.

Stonequist, E. V. *The marginal man.* New York: Charles Scribner's Sons, 1937.

Thielens, W., Jr. *See* Lazarsfeld and Thielens, 1958.

Thomas, W. I. *Source book for social origins.* Boston, Mass.: Richard G. Badger, 1909.

Thomson, G. W. *An analysis of performance test scores of a representative group of Scottish children.* London: University of London Press, 1940.

Thurstone, L. L. *Multiple-factor analysis: a development and expansion of the vectors of mind.* Chicago: University of Chicago Press, 1947.

Tipler, Doris L. and Rankin, Elizabeth A. The nurse's role. *In* G. W. Fairweather (Ed.), *Social psychology in treating mental illness: an experimental approach.* New York: John Wiley & Sons, 1964, 245–257.

Toby, J. *See* Bredemeier and Toby, 1960.

Toby, J. *See* Riley, Riley, and Toby, 1954.

Tolman, E. C. Psychology versus immediate experiance. *Philosophy of Science,* 1935, **2**, 356–380. Also appears as Chapter 10 in E. C. Tolman, *Collected papers in psychology.* Berkeley, Calif.: University of Calif. Press, 1951.

Torgerson, W. S. *Theory and methods of scaling.* New York: John Wiley & Sons, 1958.

Tremblay, M. *See* Hughes, Tremblay, Rapoport, and Leighton, 1960.

Tryon, Caroline M. *See* Tryon, Tryon, and Kuznets, 1941a.

Tryon, Caroline M. *See* Tryon, Tryon, and Kuznets, 1941b.

Tryon, R. C. Cumulative communality cluster analysis. *Educ. psychol. Measmt.,* 1958, **18**, 3–35.

Tryon, R. C. Domain sampling formulation of cluster and factor analysis. *Psychometrika,* 1959, **24**, 113–135.

Tryon, R. C. Psychology in flux: the academic-professional bipolarity. *Amer. Psychol.,* 1963, **18**, 134–143.

Tryon, R. C. Unrestricted cluster and factor analysis with applications to the MMPI and Holzinger-Harman problems. *Multivar. Behav. Res.,* 1966, **2**, 229–244.

Tryon, R. C. and Bailey, D. E. *User's manual of the BC TRY system of cluster and factor analysis (tape version for IBM 709, 7090, 7094 programs in Fortran II).* Berkeley, Calif.: University of Calif. Press, 1965.

Tryon, R. C. and Bailey, D. E. The BC TRY computer system of cluster and factor analysis. *Multivar. Behav. Res.,* 1966, **1**, 95–111.

Tryon, R. C., Tryon, Caroline M., and Kuznets, G. Studies in individual differences in maze ability. IX. Ratings of hiding, avoidance, escape, and vocalization responses. *J. comp. Psychol.,* 1941a, **32**, 407–435.

Tryon, R. C., Tryon, Caroline M., and Kuznets, G. Studies in individual differences in maze ability. X. Ratings and other measures of initial emotional responses of rats to novel inanimate objects. *J. comp. Psychol.,* 1941b, **32**, 447–473.

Turvey, R. *See* Prest and Turvey, 1965.

Tyhurst, J. S. The role of transition states—including disasters—in mental illness. *In Symposium on Preventive and Social Psychiatry,* April 15–17, 1957. Washington, D.C.: Walter Reed Army Institute of Research, 149–169.

U.S. Atomic Energy Commission. *In the matter of J. Robert Oppenheimer.* Transcript of hearing before Personnel Security Board, Washington, D.C., April 12, 1954 through May 6, 1954. Washington, D.C.: U.S. Govt. Printing Office, 1954.

Vitale, J. H. The impact of the study upon the hospital: opinions of administrative and staff personnel. *In* G. W. Fairweather (Ed.), *Social psychology in treating mental illness: an experimental approach.* New York: John Wiley & Sons, 1964, 213–244.

Warner, W. L. *Social class in America.* New York: Harper & Row, 1960.

Webb, E. J., Campbell, D. T., Schwartz, R. D. and Sechrest, L. *Unobtrusive measures: nonreactive research in the social sciences.* Chicago, Ill.: Rand-McNally, 1966.

Weingarten, E. *See* Fairweather, Simon, Gebhard, Weingarten, Holland, Sanders, Stone, and Reahl, 1960.

White, R. *See* Lewin, Lippitt, and White, 1939.

Whyte, W. F. *Street corner society. The social structure of an Italian slum.* (2nd ed.) Chicago: University of Chicago Press, 1955.

Wilcoxon, F. and Wilcox, Roberta A. *Some rapid approximate statistical procedures.* (Rev. ed.) Pearl River, N.Y.: Lederle Laboratories, American Cyanamid Co., 1964.

Wohl, S. A. Follow-up community adjustment. *In* G. W. Fairweather (Ed.), *Social psychology in treating mental illness: an experimental approach.* New York: John Wiley & Sons, 1964, 160–168.

Yablonsky, L. *The tunnel back.* New York: Macmillan, 1964.

Yates, F. *Sampling methods for censuses and surveys.* London: Charles Griffin and Co., Ltd., 1949.

Znaniecki, F. *The social role of the man of knowledge.* New York: Columbia University Press, 1940.

Index